Natalie King, Sam Holyman & Claire

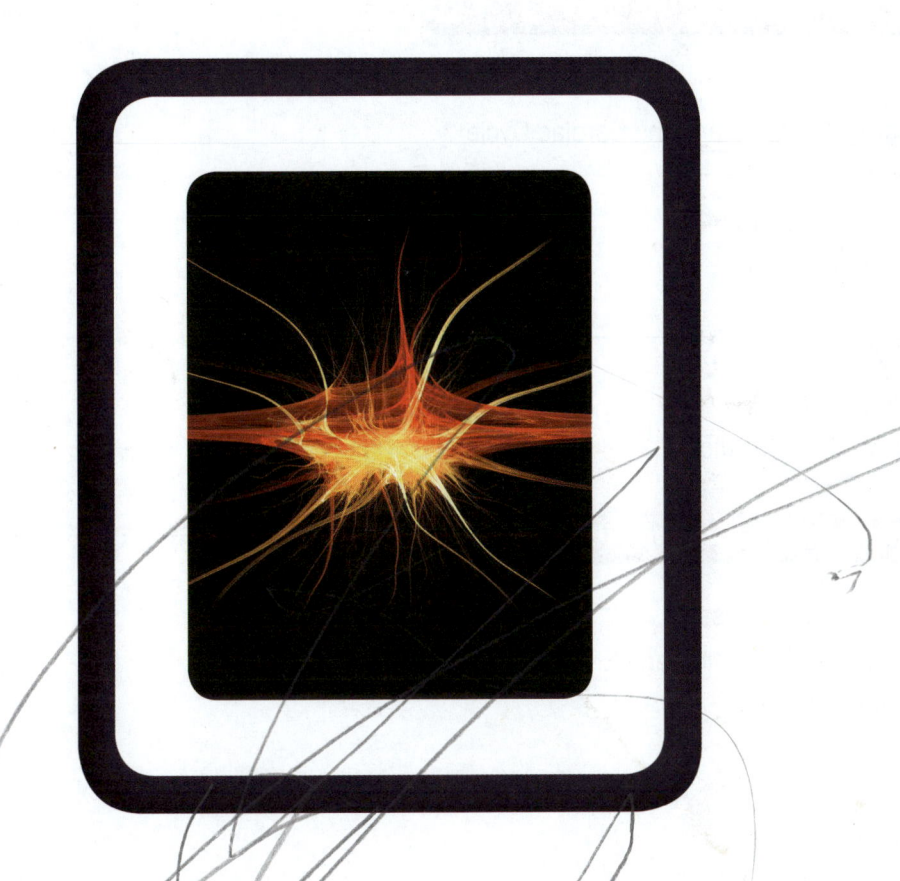

ESSENTIALS

OCR GCSE

Extended Science B

Contents

Revised

4 Fundamental Scientific Processes
6 Fundamental Chemical Concepts

B5: The Living Body

10 Skeletons ✓
12 Circulatory Systems and the Cardiac Cycle ✓
15 Running Repairs
17 Respiratory Systems
20 Digestion
21 Waste Disposal
23 Life Goes On
25 Growth and Repair
28 Exam Practice Questions

C5: How Much? (Quantitative Analysis)

30 Moles and Molar Mass
32 Percentage Composition and Empirical Formula
33 Quantitative Analysis
35 Titrations
37 Gas Volumes
39 Equilibria
42 Strong and Weak Acids
43 Ionic Equations and Precipitation
44 Exam Practice Questions

P5: Space for Reflection

46 Satellites, Gravity and Circular Motion
48 Vectors and Equations of Motion ✓
50 Projectile Motion
51 Action and Reaction
54 Satellite Communication
56 Nature of Waves
58 Refraction of Waves
61 Optics
62 Exam Practice Questions

Contents

Revised

B6: Beyond the Microscope

- 64 Understanding Microbes
- 66 Harmful Microorganisms
- 68 Useful Microorganisms
- 70 Biofuels
- 72 Life in Soil
- 75 Microscopic Life in Water
- 78 Enzymes in Action
- 80 Gene Technology
- 82 Exam Practice Questions

C6: Chemistry Out There

- 84 Electrolysis
- 86 Energy Transfers - Fuel Cells
- 87 Redox Reactions
- 88 Alcohols
- 90 Depletion of the Ozone Layer
- 91 Hardness of Water
- 93 Natural Fats and Oils
- 94 Detergents
- 96 Exam Practice Questions

P6: Electricity for Gadgets

- 98 Resisting
- 100 Sharing
- 102 It's Logical
- 104 Even More Logical
- 106 Motoring
- 108 Generating
- 110 Transforming
- 112 Charging
- 114 Exam Practice Questions

- 116 Answers
- 119 Glossary
- 125 Periodic Table
- 126 Equations Sheet
- 127 Index

Fundamental Scientific Processes

Scientists carry out **experiments** and collect **evidence** in order to explain how and why things happen. Scientific knowledge and understanding can lead to the **development of new technologies** which have a huge impact on **society** and the **environment**.

Scientific evidence is often based on data that has been collected through **observations** and **measurements**. To allow scientists to reach conclusions, evidence must be **repeatable, reproducible** and **valid**.

Models

Models are used to explain scientific ideas and the universe around us. Models can be used to describe:
- a complex idea like how heat moves through a metal
- a system like the Earth's structure.

Models make a system or idea easier to understand by only including the most important parts. They can be used to explain real world observations or to make predictions. But, because models don't contain all the variables, they do sometimes make incorrect predictions.

Models and scientific ideas may change as new observations are made and new data are collected. Data and observations may be collected from a series of experiments. For example, the accepted model of the structure of the atom has been modified as new evidence has been collected from many experiments.

Hypotheses

Scientific explanations are called hypotheses. Hypotheses are used to explain observations. A hypothesis can be tested by planning experiments and collecting data and evidence. For example, if you pull a metal wire you may observe that it stretches. This can be explained by the scientific idea that the atoms in the metal are in layers and can slide over each other. A hypothesis can be modified as new data is collected, and may even be disproved.

Data

Data can be displayed in **tables, pie charts** or **line graphs**. In your exam you may be asked to:
- choose the most appropriate method for displaying data
- identify trends
- use the data mathematically, including using statistical methods, calculating the **mean** and calculating gradients of graphs.

Pie Chart

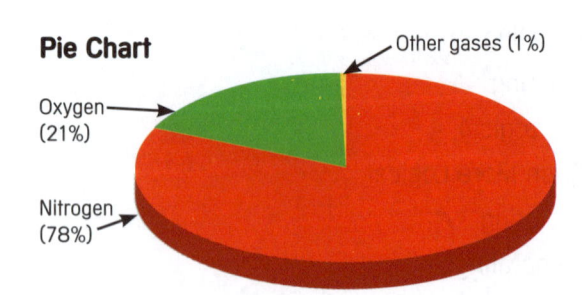

- Other gases (1%)
- Oxygen (21%)
- Nitrogen (78%)

Line Graph

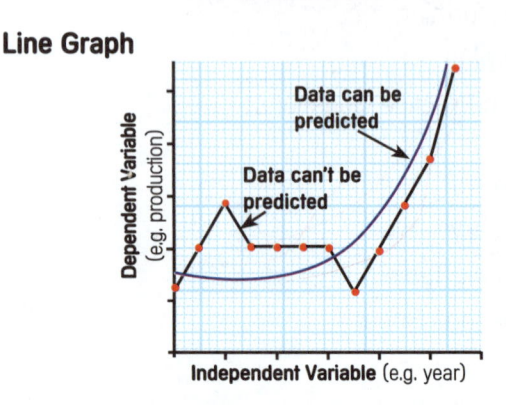

Dependent Variable (e.g. production) vs Independent Variable (e.g. year)
- Data can be predicted
- Data can't be predicted

Table

Pressure (Atmospheres)	Yield (%) Temperature (°C)			
	250	350	450	550
200	73	50	28	13
400	77	65	45	26

Key Words: Model • Variable • Data • Hypothesis

Fundamental Scientific Processes

Data (Cont.)

Sometimes the same data can lead to different conclusions. For example, data shows that the world's average temperatures have been rising significantly over the last 200 years. Some scientists think this is due to increased combustion of fossil fuels, whilst other scientists think it's a natural change seen before in Earth's history.

Scientific and Technological Development

Every scientific or technological development could have effects that we do not know about. This can give rise to **issues**. An issue is an important question that is in dispute and needs to be settled. Issues could be:

- **Social** – they impact on the human population of a community, city, country, or the world.
- **Environmental** – they impact on the planet, its natural ecosystems and resources.
- **Economic** – money and related factors like employment and the distribution of resources.
- **Cultural** – what is morally right and wrong; a value judgement must be made.

Peer review is a process of self-regulation involving experts in a particular field who **critically examine** the work undertaken. Peer review methods are designed to maintain standards and provide **credibility** for the work that has been carried out. The methods used vary depending on the type of work and also on the overall purpose behind the review process.

Evaluating Information

Conclusions can then be made based on the scientific evidence that has been collected and should try to explain the results and observations.

Evaluations look at the whole investigation. It is important to be able to evaluate information relating to social-scientific issues. When evaluating information:

- make a list of **pluses** (pros)
- make a list of **minuses** (cons)
- consider how each point might **impact on society**.

You also need to consider whether the source of information is reliable and credible and consider opinions, bias and weight of evidence.

Opinions are personal viewpoints. Opinions backed up by valid and reliable evidence carry far more weight than those based on non-scientific ideas. Opinions of experts can also carry more weight than opinions of non-experts. Information is **biased** if it favours one particular viewpoint without providing a balanced account. Biased information might include incomplete evidence or try to influence how you interpret the evidence.

Fundamental Chemical Concepts

You need to have a good understanding of the concepts (ideas) on these four pages, so make sure you revise this section before each exam.

Atoms

All substances are made up of **atoms**. Atoms have:
- a **positively** charged **nucleus** made of **protons** and **neutrons** (except hydrogen)
- **negatively** charged **electrons** that orbit the nucleus.

Atomic Particle	Relative Charge
Proton	+1
Neutron	0
Electron	−1

An atom contains the same number of electrons (negatively charged particles) and protons (positively charged particles), so each atom is electrically neutral. This means that it has no overall charge.

A Fluorine Atom

Key: ● Proton ● Neutron ✕ Electron

Elements and Compounds

An **element** is a substance made up of just one type of atom. Each element is represented by a different chemical symbol, for example:
- Fe represents iron
- Na represents sodium.

These symbols are all arranged in the **periodic table**.

Compounds are substances formed from the atoms of more than one element, which have been joined together by a chemical bond:
- **Covalent** bonds – two atoms **share** a pair of **electrons**. (The atoms in molecules are held together by covalent bonds.)
- **Ionic** bonds – atoms **lose electrons** to become **positive ions** or **gain electrons** to become **negative ions**. The electrostatic attraction between oppositely charged ions is an **ionic bond**.

A Covalent Bond between Hydrogen and Carbon in Methane

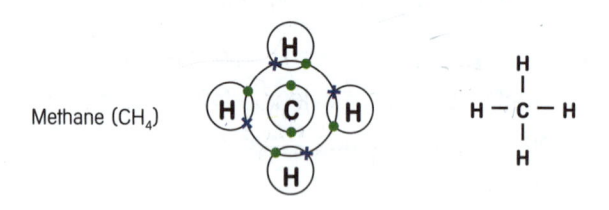

Methane (CH_4)

An Ionic Bond between Sodium and Chlorine in Sodium Chloride

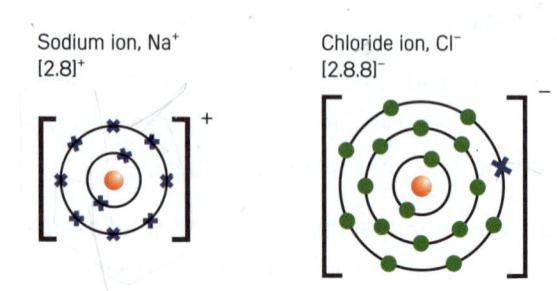

Sodium ion, Na^+ $[2.8]^+$

Chloride ion, Cl^- $[2.8.8]^-$

Key Words Atom • Nucleus • Proton • Neutron • Electron • Element • Compound • Covalent • Ionic

Fundamental Chemical Concepts

Formulae

Chemical symbols are used with numbers to write **formulae** that represent compounds. Formulae are used to show:
- the different elements in a compound
- the number of atoms of each element in the formula.

Sulfuric Acid

$2H_2SO_4$

Two sulfuric acid molecules → Two hydrogens, One sulfur, Four oxygens

If there are brackets around part of the formula, everything inside the brackets is multiplied by the number outside.

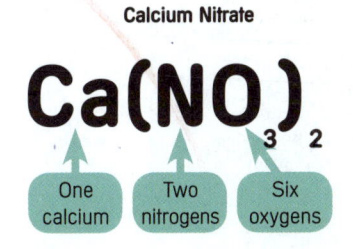

Calcium Nitrate

$Ca(NO_3)_2$

One calcium, Two nitrogens, Six oxygens

$(NO_3)_2$ means $2 \times NO_3$, i.e. $NO_3 + NO_3$.

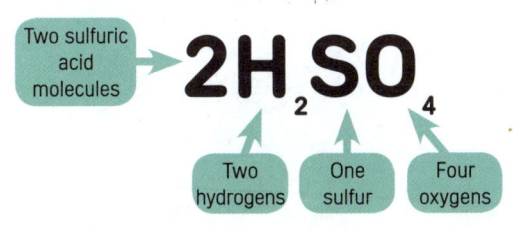

Displayed Formulae

A **displayed formula** shows you the arrangement of atoms in a compound.

A displayed formula shows:
- the different types of atom in the molecule, (e.g. carbon, hydrogen)
- the number of each different type of atom
- the bonds between the atoms.

Ethanol, C_2H_5OH — Covalent bond

Ethene, C_2H_4

Equations

In a chemical reaction the substances that you start with are called **reactants**. During the reaction, the atoms in the reactants are rearranged to form new substances called **products**.

We use equations to show what has happened during a chemical reaction. The reactants are on the left of the equation and the products are on the right.

No atoms are lost or gained during a chemical reaction so the equation must be balanced: there must always be the same number and type of atoms on both sides of the equation.

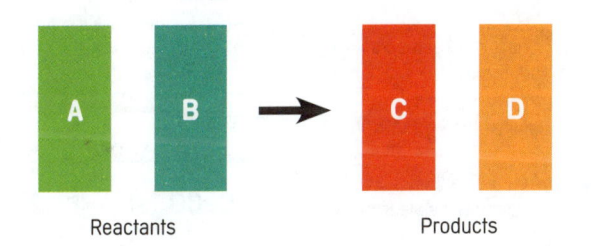

A + B → C + D

Reactants → Products

Key Words   Reactant • Product

Fundamental Chemical Concepts

Writing Balanced Equations

Example 1

1. Write a word equation.
2. Substitute in symbols and formulae.
3. Balance the equation.
   - First, you need to add another MgO to the product side to balance the Os.
   - You now need to add another Mg on the reactant side to balance the Mgs.
   - There are two magnesium atoms and two oxygen atoms on each side – it's balanced.
4. Write a balanced symbol equation.

Reactants	→	Products
magnesium + oxygen	→	magnesium oxide
Mg + O$_2$	→	MgO
Mg + O O	→	Mg O
Mg + O O	→	Mg O Mg O
Mg Mg + O O	→	Mg O Mg O
2Mg(s) + O$_2$(g)	→	2MgO(s)

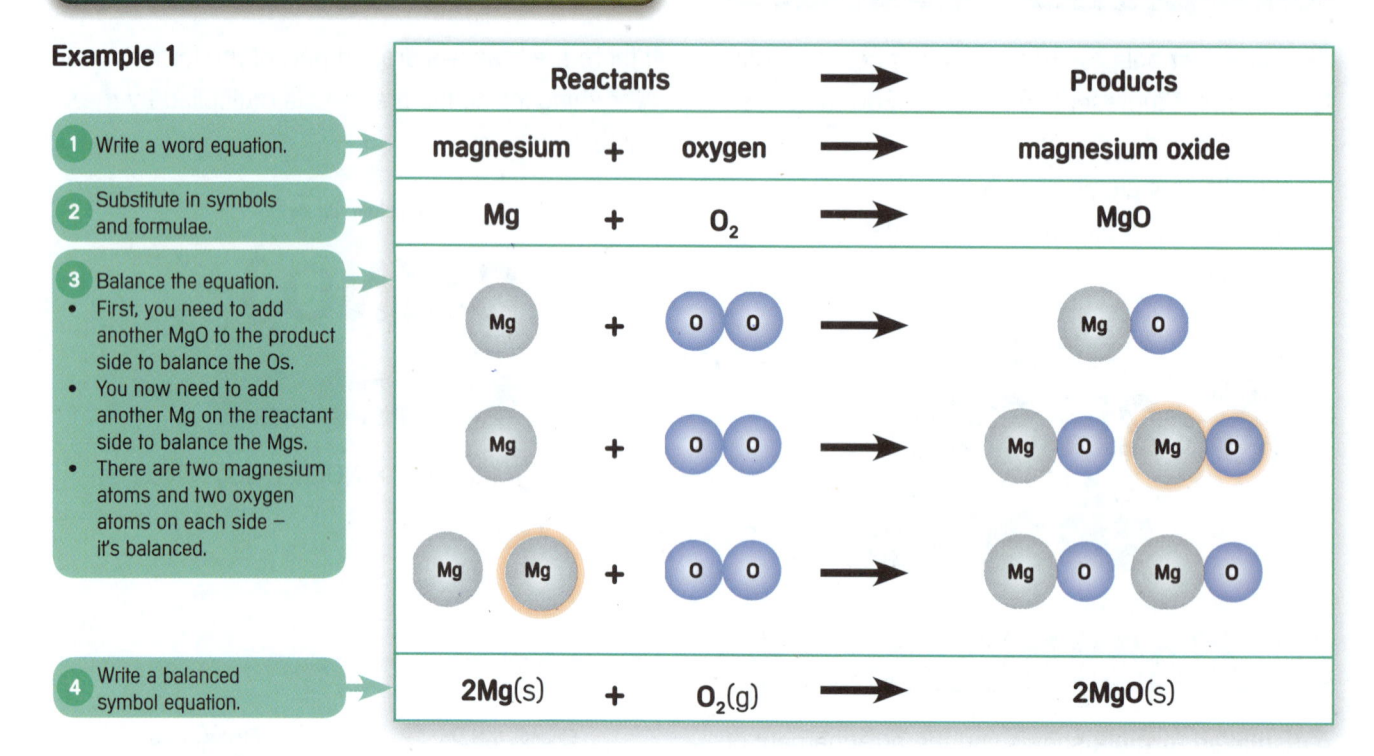

When you write equations, you may be asked to include the **state symbols**: (aq) for aqueous solutions (dissolved in water), (g) for gases, (l) for liquids and (s) for solids.

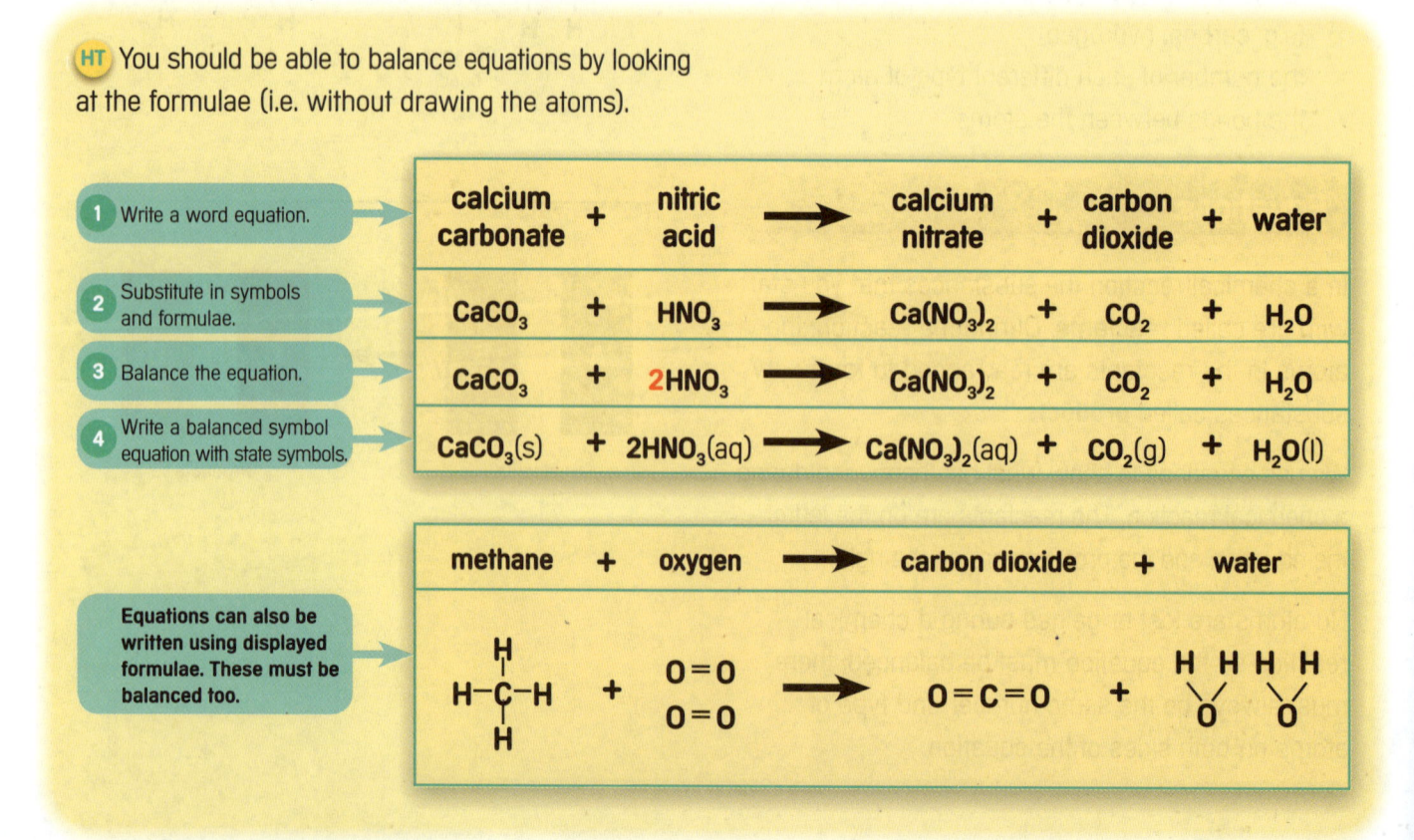

HT You should be able to balance equations by looking at the formulae (i.e. without drawing the atoms).

1. Write a word equation.
2. Substitute in symbols and formulae.
3. Balance the equation.
4. Write a balanced symbol equation with state symbols.

calcium carbonate + nitric acid	→	calcium nitrate + carbon dioxide + water
CaCO$_3$ + HNO$_3$	→	Ca(NO$_3$)$_2$ + CO$_2$ + H$_2$O
CaCO$_3$ + 2HNO$_3$	→	Ca(NO$_3$)$_2$ + CO$_2$ + H$_2$O
CaCO$_3$(s) + 2HNO$_3$(aq)	→	Ca(NO$_3$)$_2$(aq) + CO$_2$(g) + H$_2$O(l)

Equations can also be written using displayed formulae. These must be balanced too.

methane + oxygen	→	carbon dioxide + water
H–C–H (with H top and bottom) + O=O, O=O	→	O=C=O + H H (over O), H H (over O)

8

Fundamental Chemical Concepts

Compounds and their Formulae

Acids

Ethanoic acid	CH_3COOH
Hydrochloric acid	HCl
HT Nitric acid	HNO_3
HT Sulfuric acid	H_2SO_4

Carbonates

Calcium carbonate	$CaCO_3$
Copper(II) carbonate	$CuCO_3$
HT Magnesium carbonate	$MgCO_3$
HT Sodium carbonate	Na_2CO_3
HT Zinc carbonate	$ZnCO_3$

Chlorides

Ammonium chloride	NH_4Cl
HT Calcium chloride	$CaCl_2$
HT Magnesium chloride	$MgCl_2$
Potassium chloride	KCl
Silver chloride	$AgCl$
Sodium chloride	$NaCl$

Oxides

Aluminium oxide	Al_2O_3
Copper(II) oxide	CuO
Iron(II) oxide	FeO
HT Magnesium oxide	MgO
HT Manganese oxide	MnO_2
HT Sulfur dioxide	SO_2
HT Zinc oxide	ZnO

Hydroxides

Copper(II) hydroxide	$Cu(OH)_2$
Iron(II) hydroxide	$Fe(OH)_2$
HT Potassium hydroxide	KOH
HT Sodium hydroxide	$NaOH$

Sulfates

HT Ammonium sulfate	$(NH_4)_2SO_4$
HT Magnesium sulfate	$MgSO_4$
HT Potassium sulfate	K_2SO_4
HT Sodium sulfate	Na_2SO_4
HT Zinc sulfate	$ZnSO_4$

Others

Ammonia	NH_3
Calcium hydrogencarbonate	$Ca(HCO_3)_2$
Carbon dioxide	CO_2
Carbon monoxide	CO
Chlorine	Cl_2
Ethane	C_2H_6
HT Ethanol	C_2H_5OH
HT Glucose	$C_6H_{12}O_6$
Hydrogen	H_2
Methane	CH_4
Oxygen	O_2
HT Silver nitrate	$AgNO_3$
Water	H_2O

Quick Test

1. What are the negative particles in an atom called?
2. Where are the protons and neutrons found in an atom?
3. What is an ion?
4. What three things can displayed formulae tell you?

B5 Skeletons

Types of Skeleton

Animals can have an internal **skeleton**, an external skeleton or no skeleton.

Internal skeletons:
- provide a framework and shape for the body
- grow with the body
- are easy to attach **muscles** to
- have **joints** to allow flexibility.

Some animals including humans have an internal skeleton made mainly from **bone** and **cartilage**, which are **living tissues**. Humans' outer ears, noses and ends of long bones are made of cartilage.

Some animals, such as sharks, have internal skeletons made only of cartilage.

Insects have **external skeletons** (**exoskeletons**) made from **chitin**. Some organisms, like worms and jellyfish, have soft bodies without hard skeletons.

The advantages of an internal skeleton are that the bones grow with the body, it's easy to attach muscles, and it provides better flexibility.

Long Bones

Long bones have a **hollow shaft**. They weigh less and are stronger than solid bones. The head of the bone is covered in hard, slippery cartilage to lubricate movement against other bones. The shaft contains bone marrow and blood vessels.

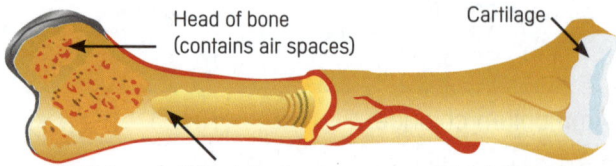

Head of bone (contains air spaces)

Cartilage

Hollow shaft (contains bone marrow and blood vessels)

HT Growing Bones

All the bones in an embryo are made from soft, flexible cartilage. During growth, the cartilage is replaced by calcium and phosphorus salts, which make the bone hard. This is called **ossification**.

Children have cartilage in their bones because they're still growing. Adults only have cartilage at the ends of their bones. Whether a person is still growing or not can be determined by the amount of cartilage present.

Broken Bones

Despite being strong, bones can easily be broken by a sharp knock. X-rays are used to detect fractures in bones. Bones can break or fracture in different ways:
- A **simple fracture** is when the bone breaks cleanly.
- A **greenstick fracture** is when the bone doesn't break completely.
- A **compound fracture** is when the broken bone breaks through muscle and skin.

As people get older, they are more likely to suffer from **osteoporosis**, a condition in which bones are weakened and break more easily.

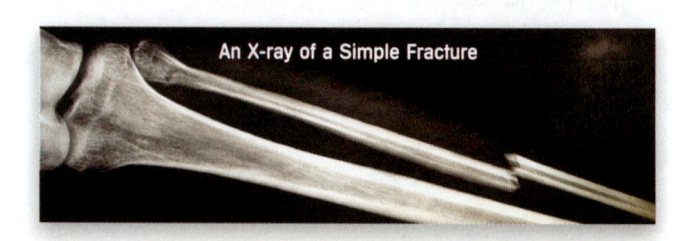

An X-ray of a Simple Fracture

HT It can be dangerous to move someone with a suspected fracture, especially if their spine might be injured, as moving them could make it worse.

Cartilage and bone can get infected if they're damaged. But they can re-grow and repair themselves.

Key Words: Skeleton • Cartilage • Chitin • Ossification

Skeletons B5

Joints

A **joint** is where two or more bones meet. **Ligaments** join bones to other bones.

Muscles contract to make the bones move. **Tendons** attach muscles to bones.

Bony plates are fused together in the **skull**. They're called **fixed joints**.

There are different types of **synovial joint** which allow different types of movement:
- **Hinge joints** (e.g. the elbow, the knee) bend in only one direction.
- **Ball and socket joints** (e.g. the shoulder, the hip) allow rotation.

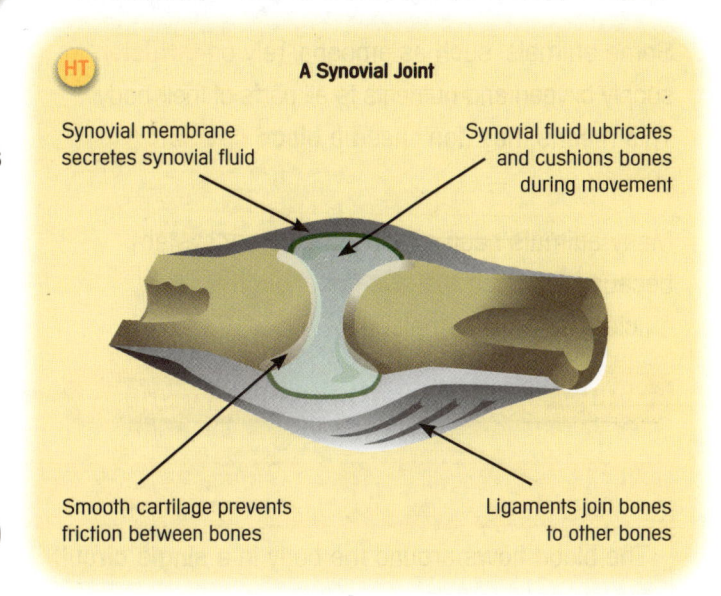

HT A Synovial Joint

- Synovial membrane secretes synovial fluid
- Synovial fluid lubricates and cushions bones during movement
- Smooth cartilage prevents friction between bones
- Ligaments join bones to other bones

Moving the Arm

In the arm the **biceps** and the **triceps** are the main muscles. They're **antagonistic muscles**: when one **contracts**, the other **relaxes**.

1. To bend the arm, the biceps contracts, pulling the radius bone. The triceps relaxes.
2. To straighten the arm, the triceps contracts, pulling the ulna bone. The biceps relaxes.

HT The elbow joint acts as a **pivot**. The biceps muscle is attached close to the elbow so it only contracts a short distance.

The radius bone acts as a lever so the hand moves much further.

A larger distance is moved by the hand than the muscles. A larger force is exerted by the muscles than is exerted by the hand.

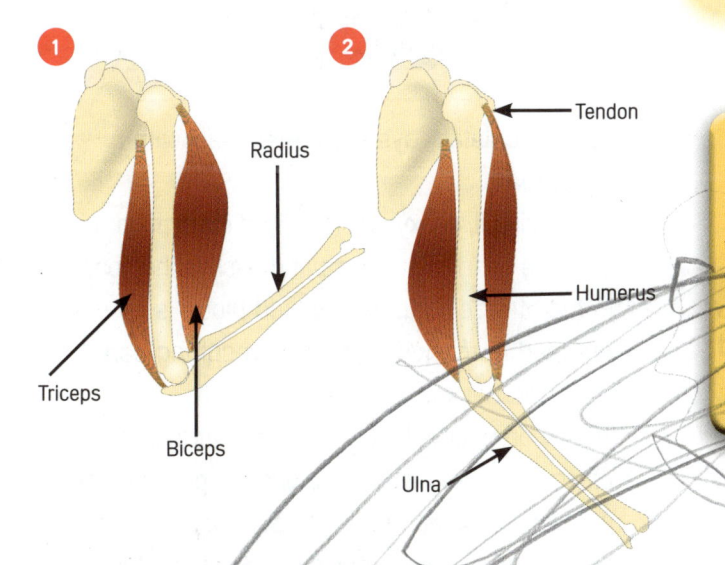

Labels: 1 – Triceps, Biceps, Radius; 2 – Tendon, Humerus, Ulna

Quick Test
1. Name two types of joint.
2. What is meant by antagonistic muscles?
3. **HT** What does the synovial membrane do?
4. **HT** Why is it dangerous to move a person with a suspected fracture?

Key Words Ligament • Synovial joint • Antagonistic muscles

B5 Circulatory Systems and the Cardiac Cycle

Circulatory Systems

Some animals, such as amoeba, rely on **diffusion** to supply oxygen and nutrients to all parts of their body. This means they don't need a **blood circulatory system**.

Many animals need a blood circulatory system because diffusion alone is not enough for the efficient transfer of materials.

Other animals, such as insects, have an **open circulatory system**. Insect blood isn't contained in blood vessels; it fills up the body cavity.

Some animals, for example, humans, have a **closed circulatory system**. In closed circulatory systems, blood is pumped through vessels called arteries, veins and capillaries.

Single and Double Circulatory Systems

Single Circulatory System

The blood flows around the body in a **single circuit**, for example, in fish.

Heart → Gills → Body → Heart

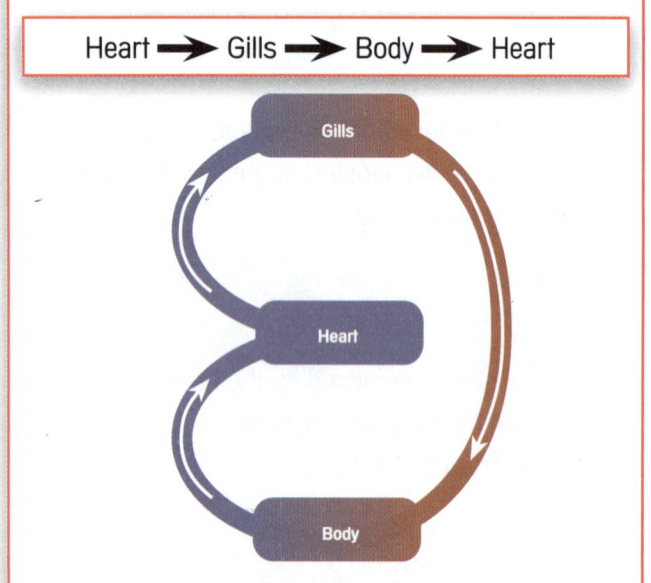

(HT) A single circulatory system has a heart with **two chambers**.

Deoxygenated blood is pumped to the gills, then the **oxygenated blood** is pumped to the body.

There is enough pressure to get the blood around the body. Pressure is lower and materials are transported more slowly around the body.

Double Circulatory System

The blood flows through the heart in **two circuits**, for example, in humans.

Heart ⇌ Lungs   Heart ⇌ Body

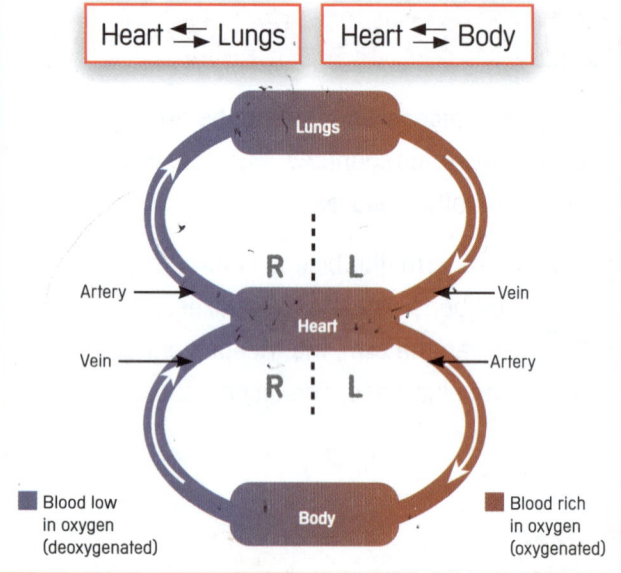

A double circulatory system has a heart with **four chambers**:

- In one circuit, deoxygenated blood is pumped from the heart to the lungs and back to the heart.
- In the other circuit, oxygenated blood is pumped from the heart to the respiring body cells and back to the heart.
- The blood returns to the heart for a further pump otherwise there wouldn't be enough pressure for the blood to go around the body. Blood is under higher pressure in a double circulatory system, so materials are transported more quickly.

Key Words: Diffusion • Circulatory system

Circulatory Systems and the Cardiac Cycle B5

The Heart

The **heart** consists of powerful muscles that contract and relax to pump blood around the body. It needs a constant supply of glucose and oxygen to release energy through respiration. The heart never gets tired or needs rest so it has high energy requirements:

- The **coronary artery** supplies the heart itself with glucose and oxygen.
- The **pulmonary vein** carries oxygenated blood from the lungs to the heart.
- The **aorta** carries oxygenated blood from the heart to the rest of the body.
- The **vena cava** carries deoxygenated blood from the parts of the body back to the heart.
- The **pulmonary artery** carries deoxygenated blood from the heart to the lungs.

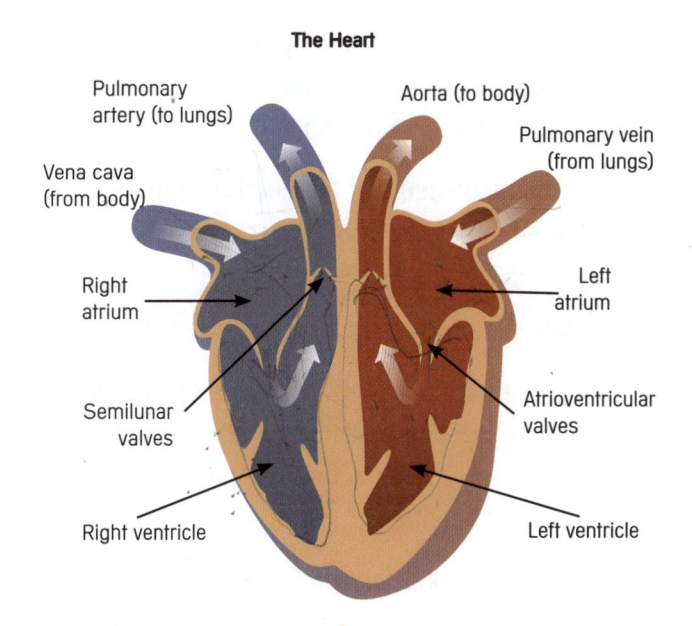

The Heart

Pulmonary artery (to lungs), Aorta (to body), Vena cava (from body), Pulmonary vein (from lungs), Right atrium, Left atrium, Semilunar valves, Atrioventricular valves, Right ventricle, Left ventricle

HT The Cardiac Cycle

The cardiac cycle is the sequence of events that occurs when the heart beats. During each heart beat:

1. The heart relaxes and blood enters both **atria** from **veins**. The atrioventricular valves are open.
2. The atria contract to push blood into the **ventricles**.
3. The ventricles contract, pushing blood into the arteries. The semilunar valves open to allow this whilst the atrioventricular valves close.

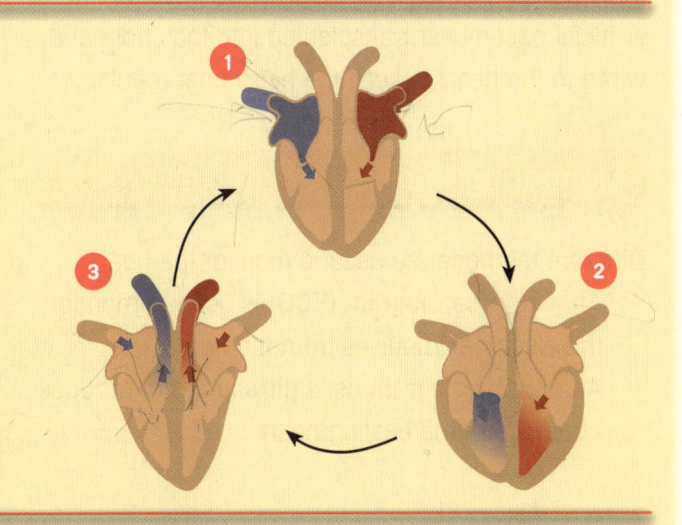

Understanding Circulation

Galen was a Greek doctor who treated gladiators in Rome around 200AD. He believed that blood flowed like a tide between the liver and the heart.

In 1628, **William Harvey**, a British doctor, found that:
- the heart pumped the blood around the body through **blood vessels**
- arteries carried blood under high pressure away from the heart
- veins had **valves** to prevent backflow.

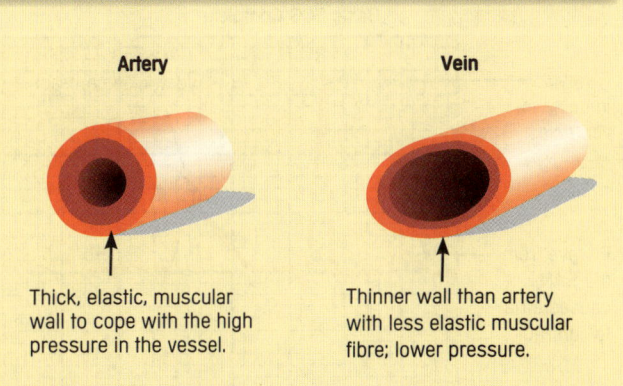

Artery — Thick, elastic, muscular wall to cope with the high pressure in the vessel.

Vein — Thinner wall than artery with less elastic muscular fibre; lower pressure.

Key Words: Oxygenated • Deoxygenated

13

B5 Circulatory Systems and the Cardiac Cycle

Pulse Rate

You can take your **pulse rate** by placing two fingers on your neck, wrist, ear or temple and counting the number of pulses in one minute.

The pulse is a measure of the heart beat (muscle contraction) to put the blood under pressure.

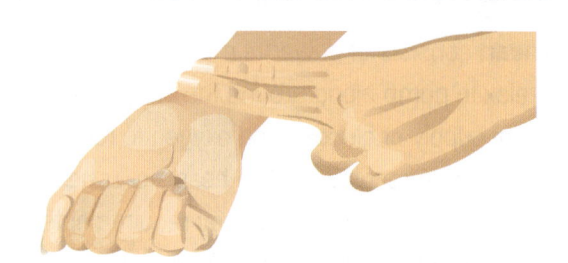

Controlling the Heart Beat

The heart beat is controlled by groups of cells called the **pacemaker**. These cells produce small electrical impulses, which spread across the heart muscle, stimulating it to contract.

During exercise, muscles demand more energy so the heart rate speeds up to supply **oxygen** and **glucose** to respiring muscles more efficiently.

If the pacemaker fails, it's common to have an artificial pacemaker transplanted into the chest and wired to the heart to keep the heart beat regular.

HT The **sinoatrial node** (**SAN**) produces impulses that spread across the atria to make them contract.

The **atrioventricular node** (**AVN**) relays impulses that spread over the ventricles to make them contract.

Nerves connecting the heart to the brain can increase or decrease the pace of the SAN in order to regulate the heart beat.

Hormones, like adrenaline, also alter the heart rate.

Monitoring the Heart

Different methods are used to monitor the heart:
- An **electrocardiogram** (**ECG**) is used to monitor the electrical impulses from the heart.
- An **echocardiogram** uses **ultrasound** to produce an image of the beating heart.

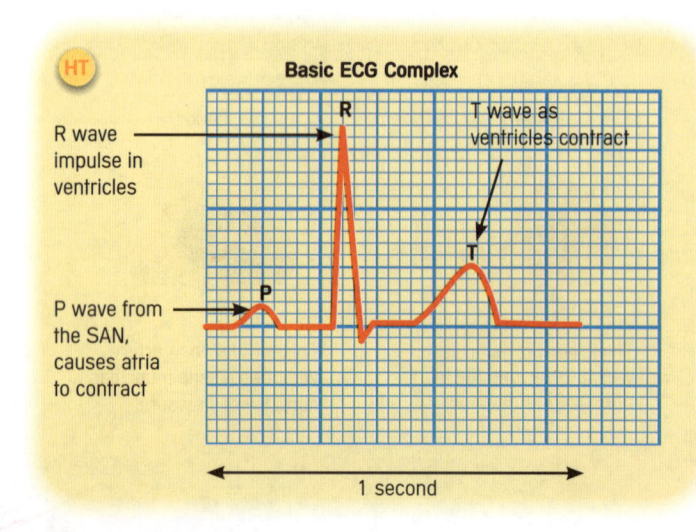

An ECG Electrocardiogram

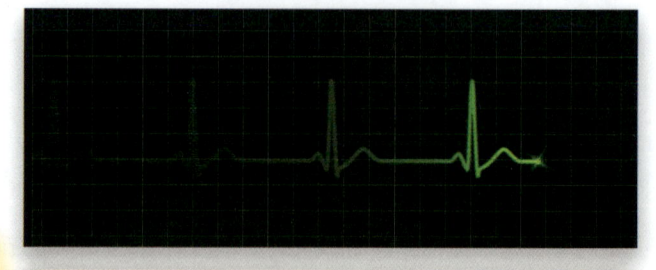

Basic ECG Complex
- R wave impulse in ventricles
- P wave from the SAN, causes atria to contract
- T wave as ventricles contract
- 1 second

Quick Test

1. Name an organism without a circulatory system.
2. What sort of circulatory system do humans have – open or closed?
3. What is meant by a double circulatory system?
4. **HT** How do pacemaker cells coordinate heart muscle contractions?

Key Words: Pacemaker • Electrocardiogram • Echocardiogram

Running Repairs B5

Heart Conditions and Diseases

Irregular heart beat occurs if the pacemaker becomes faulty. An artificial pacemaker can be implanted to restore the regular heart beat.

The cuspid and semilunar **valves can become weak or damaged**, allowing blood to flow backwards and reducing **blood pressure**. Artificial valves can be used to replace them.

The **coronary arteries** that supply the heart with oxygen and glucose can become blocked by fat and **cholesterol**, reducing blood flow to heart muscle and causing a coronary **heart attack** and **coronary heart disease**. **Bypass surgery** uses blood vessels from the leg to replace the blocked arteries.

'Heart-assist devices' are used to help the heart muscles while they recover after a heart attack, as well as heart transplants.

Some people are born with a hole in the heart. This means blood can move from the right side to the left, so oxygenated and deoxygenated blood can mix, resulting in less oxygen in the blood. Surgery can close the hole.

> **HT** A **hole in the heart** is normal in a foetus as they receive oxygen from the mother via the placenta so they don't need a double circulatory system.
>
> At birth, the hole should close. If it doesn't, deoxygenated blood is able to mix with oxygenated blood so the efficiency of transporting oxygen to tissues is reduced.
>
> The hole can be closed using surgery, but it usually closes soon after birth so the baby can have an efficient double system with no mixing of bloods.

Replacement Heart Vs Repaired Heart

Artificial valves or a pacemaker may fix a damaged heart. A severely damaged heart can be replaced by a donor heart.

> **HT** Many factors need to be considered when deciding whether a patient needs a heart **transplant**, pacemaker, or replacement valves fitted.
>
> There are advantages and disadvantages to repairing or replacing the heart.
>
> The advantages of pacemakers and heart valves are:
> - There is less risk of rejection.
> - They involve a much less traumatic operation.
> - Pacemakers and valves can be mechanical, so a human donor isn't needed.
> - Shorter waiting time than for a donor heart.
> - The patient must take anticoagulants for the rest of their life.
>
> But the disadvantage is:
> - They may need replacing.
>
> The advantages of heart transplants are:
> - The transplanted organ will last for the lifetime of the patient so it will not need to be replaced.
> - The patient will feel better immediately and can lead a full life.
>
> But the disadvantages are:
> - It is a major, expensive operation.
> - The replacement heart must come from a dead donor.
> - There is a long waiting time for a suitable donor (must be right age, size, etc.).
> - The patient will need to take immunosuppressants for the rest of their life.

Key Words Artery • Cholesterol

B5 Running Repairs

Blood Clotting

Blood **clots** are nature's way of preventing you from bleeding to death when injured. Blood normally clots at cuts, but sometimes it clots abnormally inside blood vessels.

When you have a cut platelets in the blood gather at the site, forming a clot. This clot prevents further blood loss but it can't do the job forever. A substance called **fibrin** starts to build over the wound. The combination of platelets, fibrin and plasma combine to make a **scab**.

When blood clots abnormally inside blood vessels, **anticoagulant** drugs such as warfarin, heparin and aspirin can be used to reduce clotting.

Haemophilia is an inherited disease where the blood fails to clot due to a faulty clotting protein. Sufferers can bleed to death.

Blood Groups

There are four different **blood groups**: A, B, AB and O. These groups are determined by the A and B markers on the surface of red blood cells.

Rhesus is another marker. There is **Rhesus positive** and **Rhesus negative**.

Each group can be divided into positive and negative.

Blood Donation and Transfusion

Blood **transfusions** save millions of lives. The **National Blood Transfusion Service** collects blood from volunteer blood donors. Donors go to a centre where their blood **haemoglobin** levels are checked. Then, about 500 cm^3 of blood is taken from a **vein** in their arm. The blood is screened for diseases and if it's safe it's then stored in sealed packages ready to be transfused into a patient who needs it.

The donor's blood group has to be matched to the recipient's. If it isn't, the donated blood will clump inside the recipient and cause problems.

Many people give blood because they may at one time have had a blood transfusion and know how vital it is. Other people just want to help save lives. It's a quick and simple procedure and it may be the difference between life and death for someone.

Matching Blood Types for Transfusions

Red blood cells have markers called **agglutinins** on their surface, which make them clump if they contact the corresponding antigen.
- A person with blood group A has A-agglutinins.
- A person with blood group B has B-agglutinins.

Unsuccessful blood transfusions can cause agglutination (blood clumping).

Blood Group	Agglutinins on Red Blood Cell Surface	Antibodies Circulating in Blood	Can Accept Blood From…
A	A	Anti-B	A or O
B	B	Anti-A	B or O
AB	A and B	None	Any
O	None	Anti-A and anti-B	O

Key Words: Clot • Anticoagulant • Haemoglobin • Vein • Agglutinins

Respiratory Systems B5

Structures for Gas Exchange

Living organisms must carry out **gas exchange** to get oxygen so they can release energy from food by **aerobic respiration**. Some organisms, such as amoeba and earthworms, are small enough to obtain oxygen by **diffusion** through their moist permeable skin. But bigger, more complex organisms need specialised structures like lungs or gills to obtain oxygen.

Gas Exchange in Fish

Fish have **gills** to obtain oxygen from water. Gills can only function in water so fish can't live out of water. The fish gulps water through its mouth and pushes it out of its gills.

The tadpole stage of an **amphibian** has gills, so it must live and grow in water.

But adult amphibians, such as frogs, use lungs to breathe air so they can live on land. Amphibians need moist habitats as they absorb oxygen through the skin.

> **HT** Fish use gills to exchange gases:
> - The oxygen is absorbed by the many fine filaments in the gills.
> - The oxygen is transported away from the gill filaments by the blood supply.
>
> Fish can't breathe air because it isn't dense enough to push between the gill filaments. Amphibians can easily lose water through their permeable skin. Both organisms' methods of gas exchange restricts them to their habitat.

Gas Exchange in Humans

The human **thorax** (chest cavity) contains:
- the **trachea** – a flexible tube, surrounded by rings of cartilage to stop it collapsing
- **bronchi** – branches of the trachea
- **bronchioles** – branches of a bronchus
- **lungs** – to inhale and exhale air for gas exchange
- **alveoli** (**air sacs**) – site of gas exchange
- **intercostal muscles** – to raise and lower the ribs
- **pleural membranes** – to protect and lubricate the surface of the lung
- the **diaphragm** – a muscular 'sheet' between the thorax and abdomen.

Oxygen enters the blood in the lungs and leaves the blood in body tissues.

Carbon dioxide enters the blood in body tissues and leaves via the lungs.

The surface area affects the exchange of gases. A large surface area for absorption results in more oxygen being absorbed. Lungs have a huge surface area.

The Lungs
(Trachea (windpipe), Lung, Pleural membrane, Bronchiole, Bronchus (bronchi), Alveolus (alveoli), Diaphragm, Rib, Intercostal muscle)

Key Words — Aerobic respiration • Diffusion • Trachea • Bronchi • Bronchioles • Alveoli

B5 Respiratory Systems

Breathing

During **breathing** (**ventilation**), the volume and pressure of the chest cavity are changed by:
- the intercostal muscles
- the diaphragm.

When the intercostal muscles contract, the ribcage moves upwards and outwards. The diaphragm also contracts and flattens. This increases the volume of the chest cavity. The pressure inside the lungs falls, so air rushes in. This is **inspiration**.

When the intercostal muscles relax, the ribcage moves downwards and inwards. The diaphragm also relaxes and moves upwards. This decreases the volume of the chest cavity. The pressure inside the lungs rises, so air is pushed out. This is **expiration**.

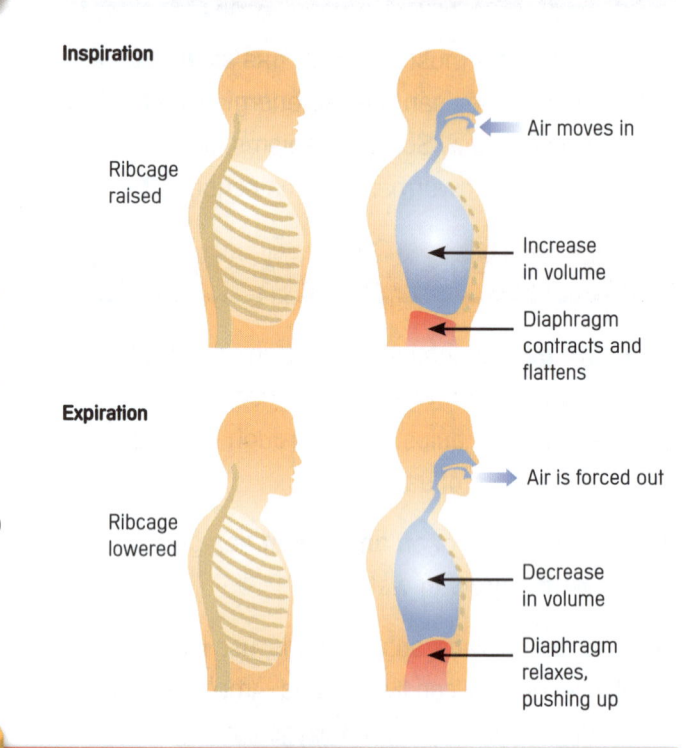

Inspiration
- Ribcage raised
- Air moves in
- Increase in volume
- Diaphragm contracts and flattens

Expiration
- Ribcage lowered
- Air is forced out
- Decrease in volume
- Diaphragm relaxes, pushing up

Measuring Lung Capacity

Measurements can be taken to calculate lung capacity:
- **Tidal air** is the volume of air breathed in or out in a normal breath.
- **Vital capacity** air is the maximum volume of air that can be used for gas exchange in the lungs – a maximum breath in followed by a maximum breath out.
- **Residual air** is the volume of air that stays in the lungs when we breathe out.

The Alveoli

Carbon dioxide diffuses from the blood into the alveoli, and oxygen diffuses from the alveoli into the blood. This is called **gas exchange**.

HT Gas exchange surfaces are well adapted. The alveoli are adapted for gas exchange by having:
- a massive surface area
- a moist, thin, permeable surface
- an excellent blood supply.

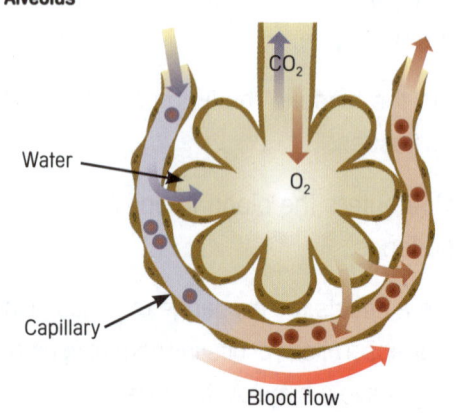

An Alveolus
- CO_2
- Water
- O_2
- Capillary
- Blood flow

Key Words: Ventilation • Inspiration • Expiration • Tidal air • Vital capacity • Residual air

Respiratory Systems B5

Protection against Disease

The **respiratory system** has defences to protect itself from disease. The **trachea** and **bronchi**:
- produce **mucus** to trap dust and microorganisms
- are lined with millions of **cilia** (ciliated cells) which move the mucus (with dust and microorganisms) from the lungs into the throat, where it's swallowed.

A Breathing Tube in the Lungs

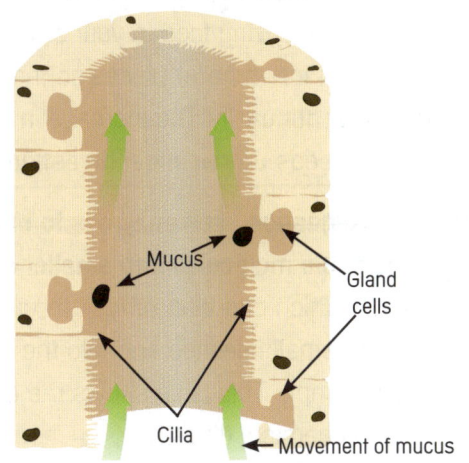

Respiratory Diseases

There are many respiratory (lung) diseases:
- **Asbestosis** is an industrial disease caused by inhaling asbestos fibres. These fibres get trapped in air sacs, reducing gas exchange. It causes excessive coughing, breathlessness and death.
- **Asthma** causes coughing, wheezing, a feeling of tightness in the chest and difficulty breathing. It can be treated using an inhaler containing medicine to relax the bronchiole muscles.
- **Bronchitis** is the inflammation of the bronchi.
- **Cystic fibrosis** is genetically inherited. Too much overly sticky mucus is produced in the lungs, making breathing difficult.
- **Lung cancer** is often caused by lifestyle choices such as smoking. The tar in cigarette smoke causes cells in the lungs to mutate and grow uncontrollably, reducing surface area in the lungs.
- **Pneumonia** is usually caused by a virus or bacterial infection. It causes inflammation in the lungs where fluid builds up.

HT During an asthma attack the lining of the bronchioles becomes inflamed. Fluid and mucus builds up in the airways and the muscles around the bronchioles contract, constricting the airways.

The respiratory system is prone to diseases because the lungs are a 'dead end'.

A Girl with Cystic Fibrosis Using an Inhaler

Quick Test
1. Name four heart conditions.
2. Name the genetic condition where blood does not clot.
3. Name a lung disease which has an industrial cause.
4. Name the blood groups.

Key Words — Respiratory system • Asbestosis • Asthma

B5 Digestion

The Human Digestive System

Physical digestion includes chewing food in your mouth, and squeezing food in your stomach to break it down into smaller pieces so that it can pass through your gut easily. The increase in surface area also speeds up **chemical digestion**.

Chemical digestion uses **enzymes** **to break down large insoluble molecules into smaller** soluble molecules, which can then **diffuse** through the walls of the small intestine and into the blood plasma or lymph. This table shows the enzymes involved in chemical digestion:

Location	Specific Enzyme	What it Breaks Down
Mouth	• Carbohydrase	• Carbohydrates (e.g. starch into sugars)
Stomach	• Protease	• Proteins into amino acids
Small Intestine	• Carbohydrase • Protease • Lipase	• Carbohydrates into sugars • Proteins into amino acids • Fats into fatty acids and glycerol

Hydrochloric acid is released by cells in the wall of the stomach. It creates the correct pH that helps the enzyme protease to work effectively. The small soluble products of digestion are absorbed into the blood in the small intestine by diffusion.

HT The stomach acid provides the optimum pH for the protease enzyme to work, breaking down protein. Other digestive enzymes in the mouth and small intestine have higher optimum pHs.

Your body produces bile to **emulsify** fat droplets, which are hard to digest. The bile breaks down large droplets into smaller droplets to increase their surface area, which enables lipase enzymes to work much faster. Bile comes from the gall bladder to aid digestion.

Starch breaks down in two stages:

Starch (large polymer) —Carbohydrase→ Maltose (double sugar) —Carbohydrase→ Glucose (single sugar)

Mouth – has salivary glands which make saliva

Oesophagus (gullet) – peristalsis occurs here

Liver and gall bladder – produces bile

Pancreas – makes digestive enzymes and insulin

Stomach – digestion of proteins

Large Intestine – absorption of water into blood

Small Intestine – digestion and absorption of food into blood

Absorption in the Small Intestine

Once the large food molecules are broken down into small, soluble molecules they must be absorbed into the bloodstream through the small intestine. The food molecules pass from the small intestine into the blood through the process of diffusion. There is a high concentration of food molecules inside the small intestine but a lower concentration in the blood. The movement of molecules is from a high to a low concentration.

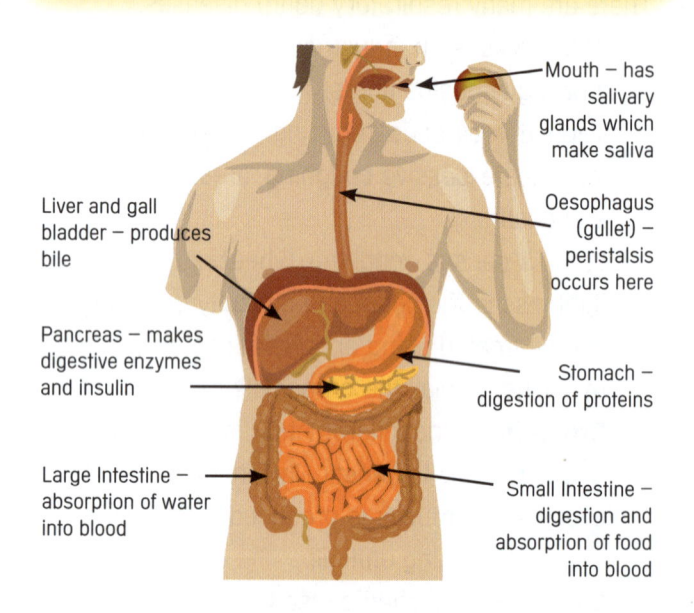

Food enters the blood in the small intestine and leaves in the body tissues.

HT The inside of the small intestine is well adapted for the efficient absorption of food:
- It is long, and has a thin lining.
- It has a large surface area provided by villi and microvilli (finger-like projections).
- It has a permeable surface and rich blood supply.

Key Words: Digestion • Enzyme • Diffusion • Emulsify

Waste Disposal B5

Waste Products

Getting rid of solid waste through the anus – mainly undigested food – is called **egestion**.

Getting rid of waste products made by body processes, for example carbon dioxide, urea and sweat, is called **excretion**.

- **Carbon dioxide** is produced by **respiration** and removed by the lungs when you breathe. It is toxic to the body at high levels so must be removed.
- **Urea** is produced from excess **amino acids** broken down in the liver. It's removed by the kidneys.
- **Sweat** is excreted through the skin. The water then evaporates to cool down the skin.

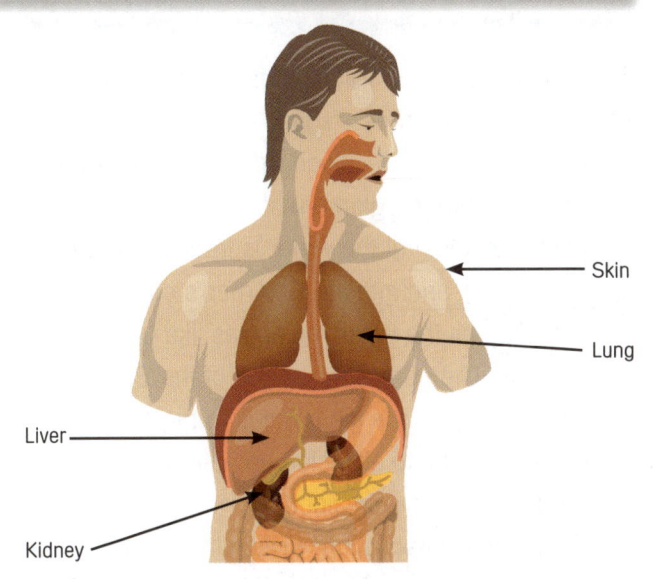

The main organs of excretion are the lungs, kidneys and skin.

Excretion

The volume of **urine** produced is affected by heat and exercise (how much you **drink** and **sweat**):

- If you drink a lot of water, you'll produce a lot of pale, **dilute urine**.
- If you don't drink enough water, or water is lost as sweat during exercise, you'll produce a small amount of **concentrated urine**.

This ensures your body's water content is kept **balanced**.

> **HT** If the brain detects high levels of carbon dioxide in the blood, the breathing rate is increased to remove the excess carbon dioxide.

The Kidneys

It's essential that the right amount of water is maintained in the blood. If there isn't enough water in the blood, you become dehydrated and the blood is thick and difficult to pump. If there's too much water in the blood, your blood pressure could go dangerously high. The amount of water in the blood is controlled by the kidneys.

The kidneys clean the blood. They excrete urea, water and salts. The kidneys contain millions of tiny **tubules** which are very close to the blood capillaries.

The kidneys filter blood at high pressure to separate the small molecules from the blood. They then reabsorb the useful substances, such as sugar and water.

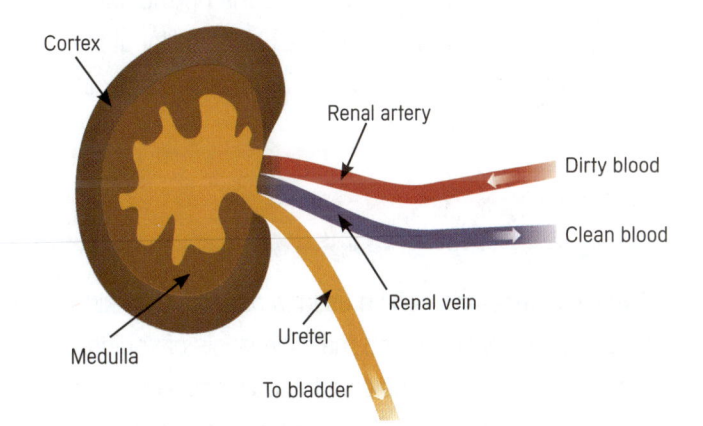

Protein foods are broken down into amino acids. Part of the breakdown results in the production of a poison, urea in the liver. The kidneys remove all of the urea from the blood.

Key Words: Egestion • Excretion • Respiration • Amino acids

B5 Waste Disposal

Kidney Tubules and the Nephron

The kidneys contain millions of tiny filtering units called **nephrons**. Three stages take place here:

1. **Ultrafiltration** – the blood from the renal artery is forced into the glomerulus under high pressure. Most of the water is forced out of the glomerulus and into the Bowman's capsule, including all the small molecules like urea and glucose. The horseshoe shape of the Bowman's capsule allows the glomerulus (a big ball of blood vessels) to sit inside and allows high pressure to be maintained.

2. **Selective reabsorption** – Useful substances like glucose are reabsorbed into the blood, which runs very close by. The coiled up tubule is long and folded to allow time for the useful substances to pass back into the blood.

3. **Salt and water regulation** – The hairpin bend of the Loop of Henlé is where the water is reabsorbed into the blood. It extends from the cortex to the medulla, allowing plenty of time for reabsorption of water and ions. Complex movements of ions and water across the loop result in the production of concentrated urine.

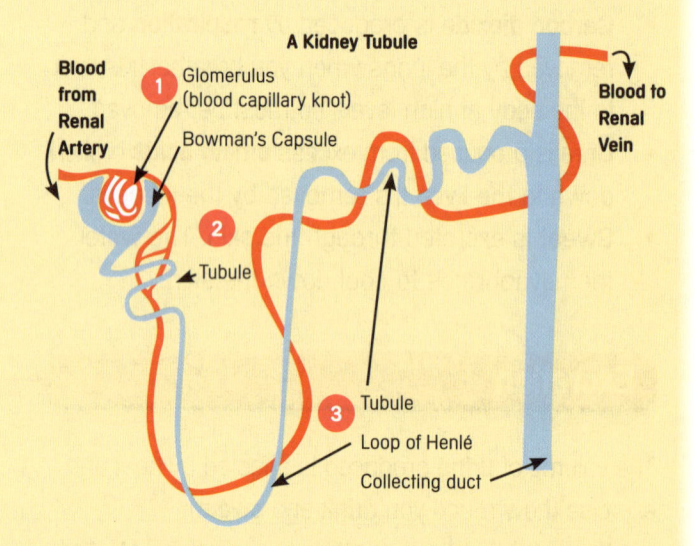

A Kidney Tubule

Controlling Water Content of Blood

The amount of water reabsorbed by the kidneys, and so the concentration of urine, is controlled by the **anti-diuretic hormone** (**ADH**). ADH is produced by the pituitary gland. ADH directly affects the permeability of the renal tubules. It increases the permeability of the kidney tubules so more water is reabsorbed back into the blood. This control mechanism is an example of **negative feedback**.

When water content of the body is low, ADH is released. This makes the tubules more permeable and more water is reabsorbed.

Dialysis

A **dialysis machine** can be used in patients with kidney failure to remove **urea** and maintain levels of sodium, water and glucose in the blood. Blood is taken from a vein and run into a dialysis machine. It comes into close contact with a partially permeable membrane, which separates the blood from the dialysis fluid. The waste diffuses from the blood into the dialysis fluid. The sodium and glucose are replaced in the blood.

Each dialysis session takes about three hours and must be carried out two or three times a week.

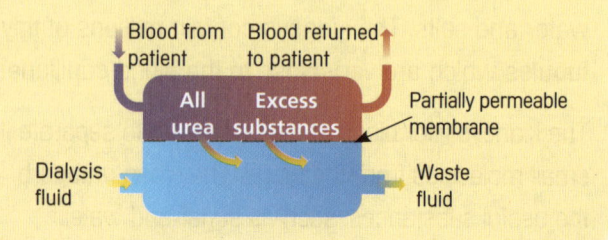

Key Words — Ultrafiltration • Anti-diuretic hormone

Life Goes On B5

Sexual Reproduction

The diagrams show the key parts of the male and female reproductive systems.

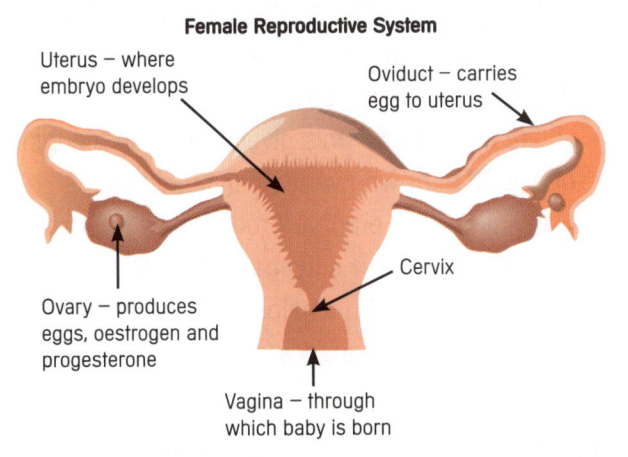

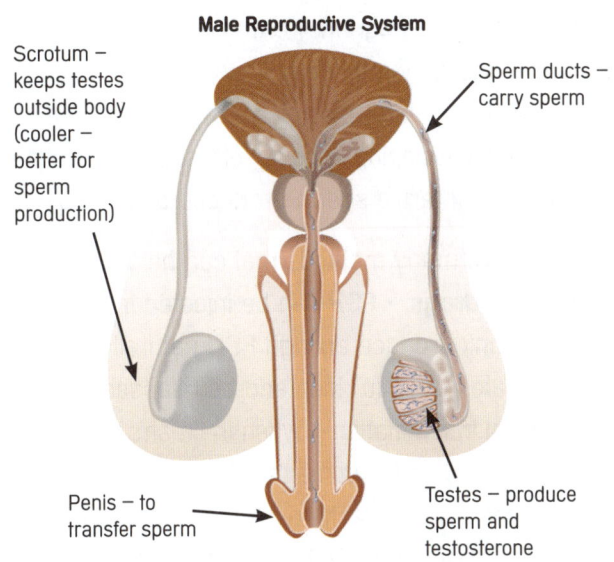

Female Reproductive System
- Uterus – where embryo develops
- Oviduct – carries egg to uterus
- Cervix
- Ovary – produces eggs, oestrogen and progesterone
- Vagina – through which baby is born

Male Reproductive System
- Scrotum – keeps testes outside body (cooler – better for sperm production)
- Sperm ducts – carry sperm
- Penis – to transfer sperm
- Testes – produce sperm and testosterone

These diagrams are not to scale.

The Menstrual Cycle

During the **menstrual cycle**, the uterus lining has different thicknesses. There are four stages:

1. The uterus lining breaks down (this is a period).
2. The uterus wall is repaired and gradually thickens.
3. An egg is released from one of the ovaries (**ovulation**).
4. The uterus lining stays thick in preparation for a **fertilised** egg. If no fertilised egg is detected, the cycle starts again.

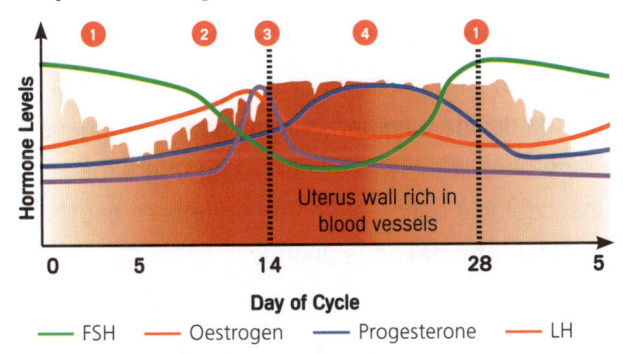

Uterus wall rich in blood vessels

Day of Cycle
— FSH — Oestrogen — Progesterone — LH

FSH (follicle-stimulating hormone) is a **hormone** that stimulates the egg to ripen in the ovary. The ovary releases **oestrogen**, a hormone that stimulates the uterus lining to thicken, and stimulates the release of **LH** (luteinising hormone). LH is the hormone that controls **ovulation** about halfway through the menstrual cycle. After ovulation, **progesterone** is produced by the ovary to preserve the uterus lining. FSH and LH are released by the pituitary gland in the brain.

As oestrogen and progesterone levels fall towards the end of the cycle, **menstruation** occurs (i.e. the uterus lining breaks down).

HT Negative Feedback

The FSH stimulates the ovaries to secrete oestrogen. The oestrogen has a negative feedback effect, reducing FSH release.

Fertility in Humans

Fertility in humans can be controlled by the artificial use of sex hormones. Contraceptive pills and fertility drugs do this.

HT Hormonal contraceptives work by mimicking pregnancy and inhibiting FSH release.

Key Words: Menstrual cycle • FSH • LH

B5 Life Goes On

Infertility Treatments

Fertilisation and pregnancy aren't guaranteed for everyone. Infertility may be caused by:
- blocked fallopian tubes or sperm ducts
- eggs not developing or being released from ovaries
- insufficient fertile sperm produced by testes.

But there are many methods that can help:
- **Fertility drugs** – **FSH** can be injected in women who don't produce enough FSH naturally. FSH stimulates eggs to ripen and be released.
- **Artificial insemination** – when the man's sperm count is low or the woman's oviducts are blocked, sperm is placed directly in the **uterus** and oviducts.
- *In vitro fertilisation* (**IVF**) – sperm and eggs are mixed together outside the body. The **embryos** that grow are transplanted into the uterus.
- **Egg donation** – if the woman doesn't produce fertile eggs, they can be donated by another woman, fertilised by IVF and transplanted. (Sperm can also be donated.)
- **Ovary transplant** – this gives a woman a supply of eggs if her own ovaries don't function.
- **Surrogacy** – an embryo produced by IVF can be implanted into a **surrogate mother** who carries the baby. This helps women who can't have a normal pregnancy or can't carry a baby to full-term.

When infertility treatments are successful, the result of a healthy baby for an infertile couple is wonderful.

Problems with Fertility Treatments

In **egg**/**sperm donation**, the embryo carries genes from only one parent and genes from a donor. **Surrogacy** can lead to emotional attachment, meaning the surrogate mother may find it hard to give the baby to its biological parents. **IVF** is expensive and doesn't have a high success rate. Twins or triplets are more likely to be produced as more than one embryo is implanted.

There is also the issue of what to do with leftover embryos that are no longer needed. Many people don't agree with disposing of human embryos. Some couples choose to give their unwanted embryos to another couple. Some may donate them to research, which raises more ethical and moral questions.

Foetal Screening

Ultrasound scans can reveal multiple pregnancies, developmental problems, or a baby's sex, early on in the pregnancy. **Amniocentesis** tests analyse cells from the foetus found in the amniotic fluid. A hypodermic needle is used to take a sample, which is checked for chromosome abnormalities, e.g. Down's Syndrome. Chromosome analysis can reveal serious conditions in the foetus.

Amniocentesis carries a risk of miscarriage (1 in 200) and, if an abnormality is detected, parents have to decide whether to continue the pregnancy. Some people think foetal screening offers the unacceptable option of ending an unborn baby's life, and that **termination** is unethical.

Quick Test

1. Name two female sex hormones.
2. What is the job of the testes?
3. Name three enzymes involved in digestion.
4. What is the job of the kidneys?

Key Words Fertilisation • *In vitro fertilisation* • Ovary • Surrogacy

Growth and Repair B5

Organ Donation

Due to disease or trauma, it's sometimes necessary to replace body parts with biological or mechanical parts.

Body parts from **human donors** can biologically replace the heart, lungs, kidney, blood, cornea and bone marrow.

Organs usually come from **dead donors**. A person's organs can be donated if they can't regain consciousness and can't breathe unaided. Some organs, e.g. a kidney, can come from a **living donor**. This is because the donor can live without the organ or tissue they have donated.

Donated organs must be:
- healthy
- the right size and age
- a good tissue match (otherwise the organ will be **rejected**).

Organs can only be donated if the donor is on the organ donor register and if their relatives have given their consent. There's always a shortage of donors.

Ethical issues

There are ethical issues with organ donation. Some people worry about signing up to be an organ donor – the effect it will have on their relatives and on their own body. Some people may not want to donate or receive organs due to religious or personal beliefs. There are many questions surrounding organ donation, e.g. should donors be allowed to receive money for donating organs? Can diseases be passed on to the recipient?

HT — Problems with Organ Donation

If the donated organ isn't a good tissue match, the recipient's immune system will reject it. Organ recipients take **immunosuppressive drugs** for the rest of their lives to prevent rejection. But taking immunosuppressive drugs reduces their ability to fight other infections, making them more at risk of catching other diseases.

Organ Donation Issues

The UK has an **'opt-in'** donor system. Many people don't register as donors, so there's always a shortage of donors and a long wait for transplants. Many people think an **'opt-out'** system would be better. Sometimes the relatives of a person on the **National Register of Donors** don't agree to allow organ donation due to religious or cultural reasons.

In the UK, there's no payment for organ donation. It's been suggested that payment would increase availability. But this could encourage poor people to become donors in order to earn money.

Mechanical Replacements

Mechanical replacements include hip and knee joints, heart, lenses and kidneys. Implants must be:
- small and compact to fit inside the body
- made of materials that will not wear or cause allergic reactions, e.g. metals, plastics.

Some implants, such as pacemakers, need a reliable power supply. Batteries that can be recharged outside the body are now often used.

Some mechanical organ replacements, for example, heart-and-lung machines, kidney **dialysis machines** and mechanical ventilators work outside the body.

Key Words — Immunosuppressive drugs

B5 Growth and Repair

Human Growth

There are five main stages in human **growth**:
1. Infancy (up to 2 years)
2. Childhood (2–11 years)
3. Puberty/adolescence (roughly 11–15 years)
4. Adulthood/maturity (roughly 15–65 years) – the longest stage
5. Old age (over 60–65 years)

The rate of growth is at a maximum when a baby is first born. Growth then slows down gradually during childhood. At puberty, there's another growth spurt. Growth stops in adulthood.

Measuring Human Growth

Human growth is measured in terms of gain in **height** or **mass**. A human foetus grows very quickly in the uterus. Different body parts develop at different rates. The brain and head develop quickly to coordinate the complex human structure and chemical activity.

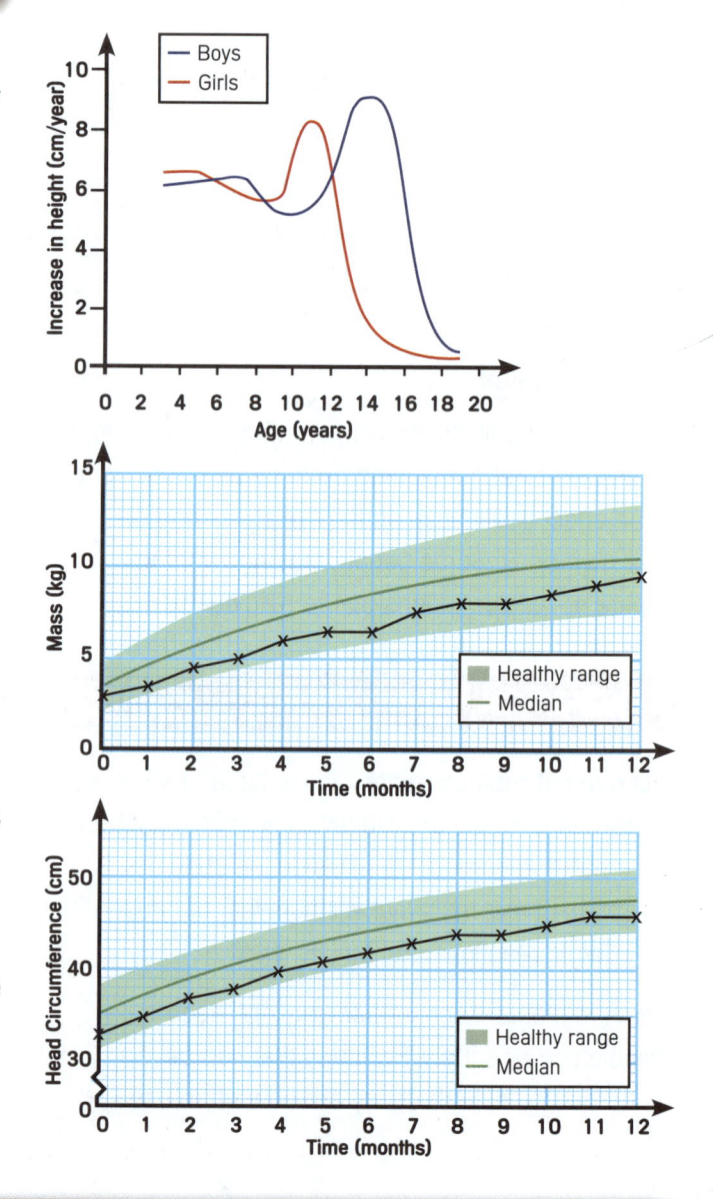

A baby's head circumference, length and mass are measured regularly during the first few months. These measurements are plotted on average growth charts and compared with norms (average values for babies of their age) to indicate whether there are any growth problems. Average growth charts are simply a guide to show a comparison. Babies' growth can be above or below the average and still be totally healthy.

Example

The **mass** and **head circumference** of a baby were measured once a month for a year. The measurements are plotted on the graphs. By comparing the baby's measurements to the normal range, you can see that the baby's measurements were towards the lower end of healthy weight and head circumference, so no cause for concern. If the measurements were consistently above or below the healthy range, then the GP/health visitor may wish to investigate.

Key Words: Growth

Growth and Repair B5

Factors Affecting Human Growth

Your eventual height and mass is determined by:
- inherited information in your **genes**
- your diet
- the amount of exercise you do
- the amount of growth **hormone** you produce
- how healthy you are
- any diseases/conditions you may have had
- hormones.

Diet is very important. A healthy diet contains protein for muscle growth, and calcium and vitamin D for bone growth.

Exercise is needed to encourage muscle growth, and to make bones dense and hard (strong).

Extremes of height are usually caused by genes or by an imbalance in the amount of growth hormone. For example:
- people who don't produce enough growth hormone aren't very tall and are called **dwarfs**
- people who produce too much growth hormone are very tall and are called **giants**.

HT Human growth hormone is produced by the pituitary gland in the brain, which stimulates the growth especially of long bones.

Life Expectancy

Life expectancy has greatly increased in recent years. This is due to:
- healthier diets and lifestyle
- modern treatments and cures for diseases
- better housing conditions, e.g. sewage disposal
- fewer **industrial diseases**, e.g. asbestosis.

HT Problems with Living Longer

Longer life expectancy brings its own problems:
- Elderly people can suffer from **degenerative diseases** such as **arthritis** and **cancer**.
- Elderly people might find it difficult to live independently in their own homes.
- The trend for small families means many elderly people will have no-one to look after them.
- Many pensioners live on a low income so it's difficult for them to maintain a healthy lifestyle.

All these problems reflect on society:
- Hospitals and care homes must cater for the short-term health needs of the elderly, but they also need to consider the residential needs of the increasing population of elderly patients.
- People of working age have to work longer and pay higher taxes to pay the pensions of the elderly population.

Quick Test

1. Give two reasons why life expectancy has increased.
2. What factors must be correct for a successful organ transplant?
3. What are the issues with foetal screening?

Key Words   Gene • Hormone

B5 Exam Practice Questions

1 The diagram shows the apparatus used in an experiment to mimic the workings of the small intestine. The distilled water was tested for starch and sugar at the beginning and end of the experiment. At the start of the experiment neither carbohydrate was present. At the end however, there was a positive test for sugar. Use your knowledge of absorption to explain these results. **[3]**

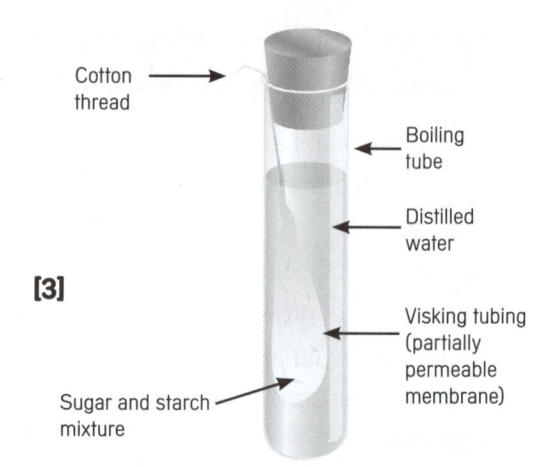

2 Noah has just returned from a skiing holiday, where he fell over and injured himself. Noah had to have an X-ray to see if he had broken any bones. This was his X-ray.

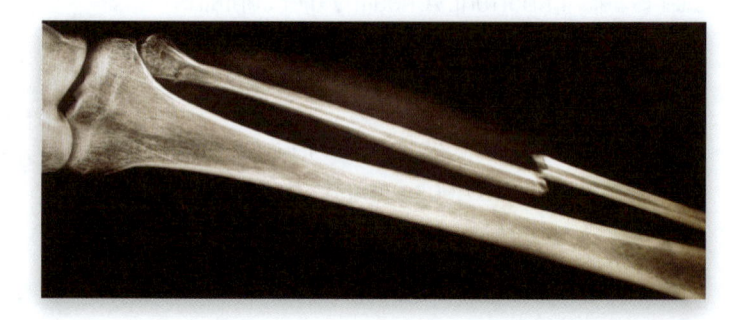

a) What is the name given to this type of fracture? .... **[1]**

b) Noah also complained that his right elbow was painful. **[1]**

  i) What type of joint is the elbow joint?
  ....

  ii) How are bones joined to other bones at joints? Put a (ring) around the correct answer in this list. **[1]**

  Cartilage   **Ligaments**   **Tendons**

3 a) Lee goes for a quick run and manages to run one mile in 7 minutes. When he finishes, he measures his pulse rate every minute for five minutes. His pulse rate returns to normal in five minutes.

Draw a graph to show Lee's pulse rate, starting at one minute. **[2]**

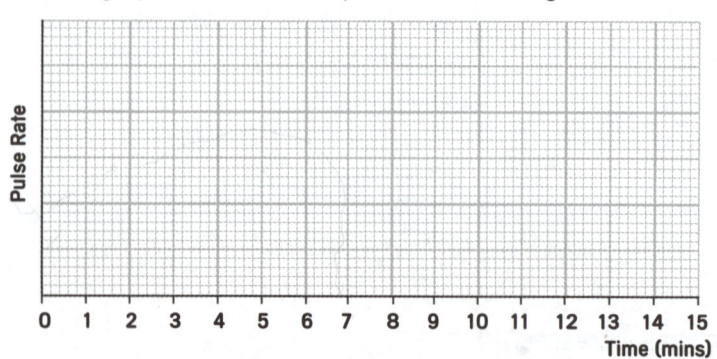

b) Explain why the pulse rate changes during exercise, in the way you have shown on the graph. **[2]**

Exam Practice Questions B5

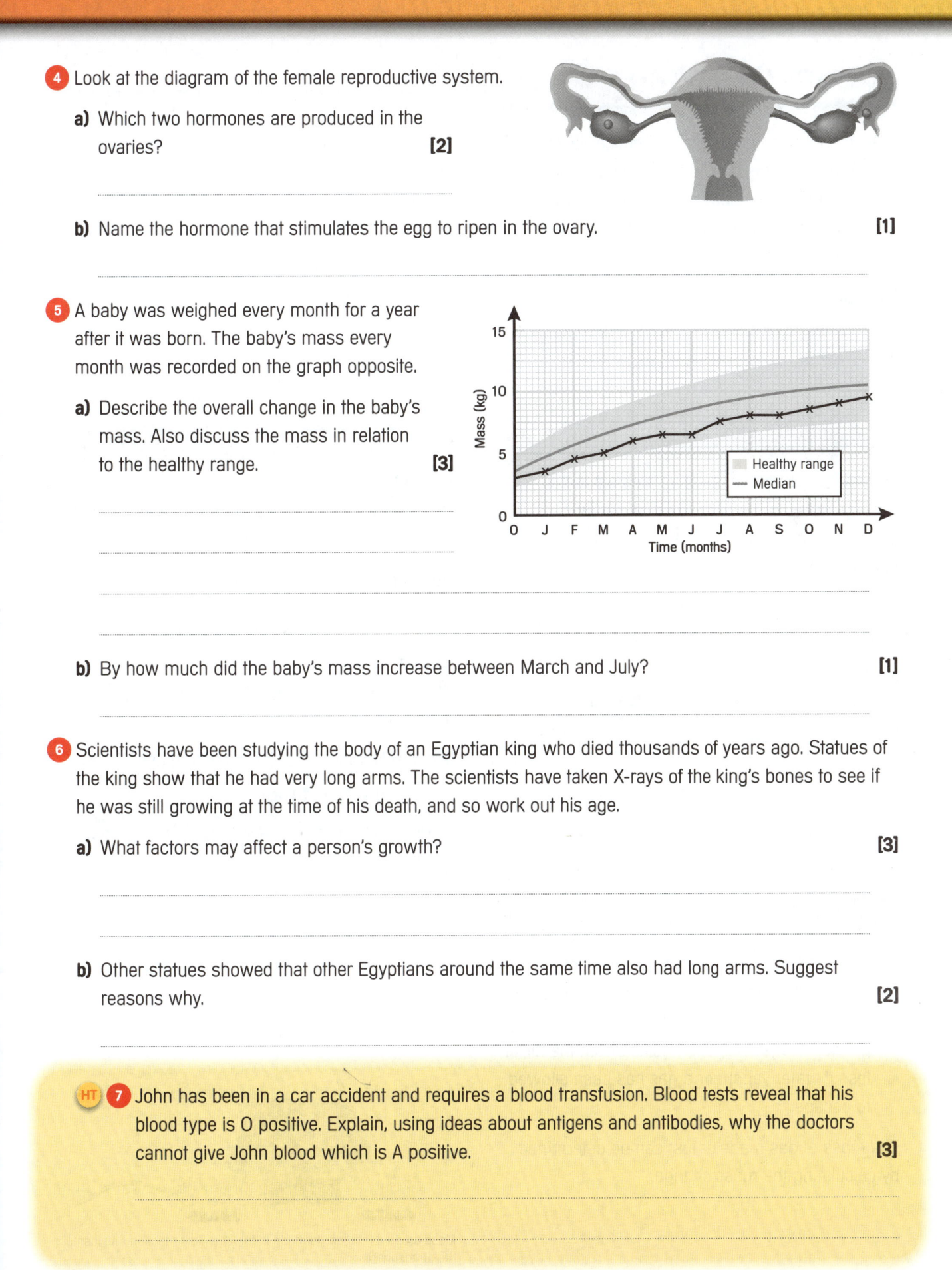

4 Look at the diagram of the female reproductive system.

   a) Which two hormones are produced in the ovaries? **[2]**

   b) Name the hormone that stimulates the egg to ripen in the ovary. **[1]**

5 A baby was weighed every month for a year after it was born. The baby's mass every month was recorded on the graph opposite.

   a) Describe the overall change in the baby's mass. Also discuss the mass in relation to the healthy range. **[3]**

   b) By how much did the baby's mass increase between March and July? **[1]**

6 Scientists have been studying the body of an Egyptian king who died thousands of years ago. Statues of the king show that he had very long arms. The scientists have taken X-rays of the king's bones to see if he was still growing at the time of his death, and so work out his age.

   a) What factors may affect a person's growth? **[3]**

   b) Other statues showed that other Egyptians around the same time also had long arms. Suggest reasons why. **[2]**

HT 7 John has been in a car accident and requires a blood transfusion. Blood tests reveal that his blood type is O positive. Explain, using ideas about antigens and antibodies, why the doctors cannot give John blood which is A positive. **[3]**

29

C5 Moles and Molar Mass

Molar Mass

The amount of substance in a chemical reaction is measured in **moles**. The mass of one mole (the **molar mass**) of any substance is the **relative formula mass** (M_r) in grams (g). Molar mass is measured in g/mol.

Example
What is the molar mass of magnesium hydroxide, $Mg(OH)_2$?

Mg $1 \times 24 = 24$
O $2 \times 16 = 32$
H $2 \times 1 \ = \ 2$
M_r $24 + 32 + 2 = 58$ g/mol

The M_r of $Mg(OH)_2$ is 58, so the mass of 1 mole of $Mg(OH)_2$ is **58g**.

HT Molar Mass, Moles and Mass

The relative atomic mass of an element is the average mass of the atoms of that element compared with a twelfth of the mass of a carbon-12 (^{12}C) atom.

You can use this formula to calculate the number of moles of an element or a compound:

$$\text{Number of moles} = \frac{\text{Mass}}{\text{Molar mass}}$$

Example 1
How many moles of ethanol are there in 230g of ethanol? (The M_r of ethanol is 46.)

$$\text{Number of moles} = \frac{\text{Mass}}{\text{Molar mass}}$$

$$= \frac{230g}{46g} = 5 \text{ moles}$$

Example 2
What is the mass of oxygen in 3 moles of aluminium oxide (Al_2O_3)?

Mass = Number of moles × Molar mass

$= 9 \times 16 = $ **144g**

3 moles of aluminium oxide contains 9 (3 × 3) moles of oxygen.

Conservation of Mass

During a chemical reaction, no mass is lost or gained, i.e. it's **conserved**. But, the mass measured at the end of a reaction might be:
- greater if a gas has been gained from the air **or**
- less if water vapour or a gas has been allowed to escape.

The mass of gas made or lost can be determined by calculating the mass change.

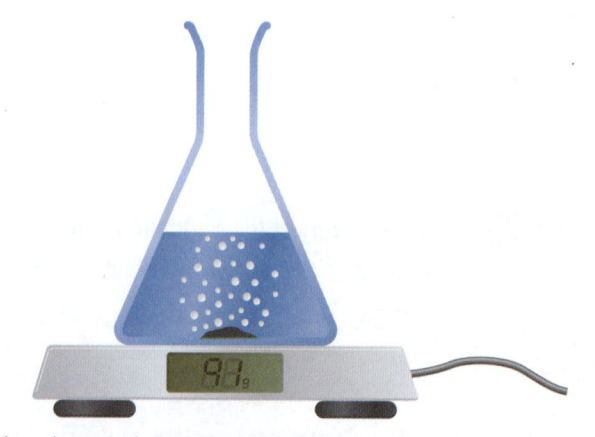

Mass drops as the gas is made in the chemical reaction and lost to the atmosphere.

Key Words Mole • Relative formula mass

Moles and Molar Mass C5

Examples of Conservation

Example 1
When 50g of calcium carbonate is heated in a thermal decomposition reaction, 28g of calcium oxide is made. What mass of carbon dioxide is lost?

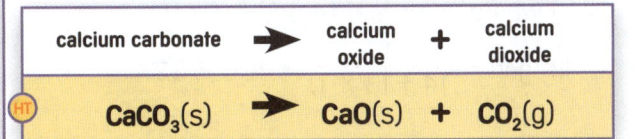

| calcium carbonate | → | calcium oxide | + | calcium dioxide |

$CaCO_3(s) \rightarrow CaO(s) + CO_2(g)$

50g = 28g + Mass of carbon dioxide
Mass of carbon dioxide = 50g − 28g = **22g**

$CaCO_3 \rightarrow CaO + CO_2$

$\frac{50}{100}$ $\frac{28}{56}$ $\frac{22}{44}$

= 0.5 mole   = 0.5 mole   = **0.5 mole**

So, 0.5 mole of carbon dioxide is made.
44 × 0.5 = 22g of carbon dioxide is made.

Example 2
When 12g of carbon is burned in oxygen it makes 44g of carbon dioxide. What mass of oxygen has reacted?

| carbon | + | oxygen | → | calcium dioxide |

12g + Mass of oxygen → 44g

Mass of oxygen = 44g − 12g = **32g**

$C + O_2 \rightarrow CO_2$

$\frac{12}{12}$ $\frac{32}{32}$ $\frac{44}{44}$

= 1 mole   = **1 mole**   = 1 mole

So, 1 mole of oxygen molecules is needed with a mass of 32g.

Reacting Ratios

If you know the reacting masses in a reaction, you can calculate further reacting masses using **ratios**.

Example
The reaction between 160g of copper sulfate and 106g of sodium carbonate produces 124g of copper carbonate and 142g of sodium sulfate. How much copper sulfate and sodium carbonate are needed to produce 372g of copper carbonate?

$CuSO_4(aq) + Na_2CO_3(aq) \rightarrow CuCO_3(s) + Na_2SO_4(aq)$

160g + 106g = 124g + 142g

372g ÷ 3 = 124g, so you just need to multiply all the above masses by the same amount (×3) to find the new set of masses.

(3 × 160g) + (3 × 106g) = (3 × 124g) + (3 × 142g)
= 480g + 318g = 372g + 426g

So, **480g** of copper sulfate and **318g** of sodium carbonate are needed.

N.B. A quick way to check that your calculation is correct is to add the masses of the reactants together to check that the total mass of the reactants is equal to the total mass of the products.

Quick Test

1. What is a mole?
2. What is the molar mass (M_r) of carbon dioxide (CO_2)?
3. Hydrogen will burn in oxygen to make water.
   a) When 4g of hydrogen is reacted with 32g of oxygen, what mass of water is made?
   b) What is the molar mass (M_r) of water?
   c) How many moles of water are made when 8g of hydrogen is reacted with excess oxygen?

C5 Percentage Composition and Empirical Formula

Mass of Elements in a Compound

The **mass** of a compound is made up of the masses of all its elements added together. So, if you know the mass of a compound and the mass of one of the elements, you can calculate the mass of the other element.

Example
80g of copper oxide contains 16g of oxygen. What mass of copper does it contain?

Mass of copper + 16g = 80g
Mass of copper = 80g − 16g = **64g**

Empirical Formula

The **empirical formula** is the simplest whole number ratio of each type of atom in a compound. For example, all alkenes have the empirical formula C_1H_2, or CH_2.

You can work out the empirical formula of a substance from its chemical formula, for example, the empirical formula of ethanoic acid (CH_3COOH) is CH_2O.

You can also calculate the percentage of an element in a compound.

Example
Calculate the percentage of nitrogen in ammonia (NH_3) where A_r for N = 14 and A_r for H = 1.

% nitrogen = $\frac{14}{14 + (3 \times 1)} \times 100$ = **82%**

Quick Test

1. What is the empirical formula for benzene (C_6H_6)?
2. Ammonium chloride (NH_4Cl) can be used as a fertiliser. What is the molar mass (M_r) of this fertiliser?
3. **HT** A hydrocarbon contains 24g of carbon and 4g of hydrogen. What is the empirical formula of this compound?

HT The empirical formula of a compound can be calculated from **either**:
- the percentage composition of the compound by mass **or**
- the mass of each element in the compound.

To calculate the empirical formula:
1. List all the elements in the compound.
2. Divide the data for each element by its A_r (to find out the number of moles).
3. Select the smallest answer from step 2 and divide each answer by that result to obtain a ratio.
4. The ratio may have to be scaled up to give whole numbers.

Example 1
What is the empirical formula of a hydrocarbon containing 75% carbon. (Hydrogen = 25%)

1. Carbon : Hydrogen
2. $\frac{75}{12} : \frac{25}{1}$
3. 6.25 : 25 (÷6.25)
4. 1 : 4

So, the empirical formula is C_1H_4, or **CH_4**

Example 2
What is the empirical formula of a compound containing 24g of carbon, 8g of hydrogen and 32g of oxygen?

1. Carbon : Hydrogen : Oxygen
2. $\frac{24}{12} : \frac{8}{1} : \frac{32}{16}$
3. 2 : 8 : 2 (÷2)
4. 1 : 4 : 1

So, the empirical formula is CH_4O.

Key Words Empirical formula

Quantitative Analysis C5

Volume

The two units commonly used to measure the **volume** of liquids and solutions are:
- cm^3 (cubic centimetres)
- dm^3 (cubic decimetres). $1dm^3$ is equal to $1000cm^3$ and is known as 1 litre.

To convert a volume:
- from cm^3 into dm^3, divide it by 1000
- from dm^3 into cm^3, multiply it by 1000.

Example
Convert $2570cm^3$ into dm^3.

$$\text{Volume in } dm^3 = \frac{\text{Volume in } cm^3}{1000}$$
$$= \frac{2570}{1000} = \mathbf{2.57dm^3}$$

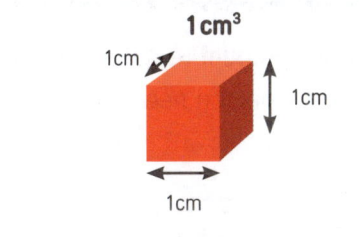

Concentration

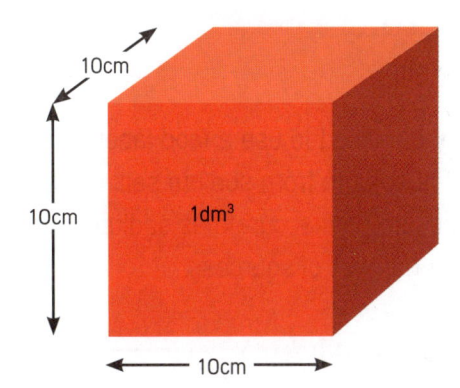

The **concentration** of a solution can be measured in:
- g/dm^3 (grams per cubic decimetre)
- mol/dm^3 (moles per cubic decimetre).

In a concentrated solution, the solute particles are more crowded together than they are in a dilute solution.

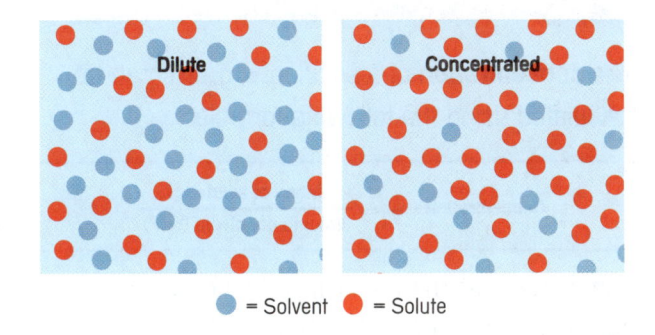

Dilution

A concentrated solution can be made more **dilute** by adding water.

Some concentrated solutions must be diluted before they're used, for example, orange cordial has to be diluted before you can drink it so that it doesn't taste too strong.

It's important to accurately follow the dilution instructions. If a medicine is too dilute then it will not work properly, and if it's too concentrated it may even make you more ill. If baby milk is not diluted correctly then it could harm the baby.

Example
$5cm^3$ of a solution has a concentration of $1mol/dm^3$. How much water should be added to the solution in order to make it have a concentration of $0.1mol/dm^3$?

Since $0.1mol/dm^3$ is ten times smaller than $1mol/dm^3$, the volume of the solution should be ten times greater.

Volume of water added = $9 \times 5cm^3$
$= \mathbf{45cm^3}$

Key Words   Concentration • Dilute

C5 Quantitative Analysis

Guideline Daily Amounts

The **guideline daily amount** (**GDA**) informs you how much of a nutrient a person needs each day for a healthy diet.

You may be asked to read the GDA from a food label.

Vitamins and Minerals	In a 30g serving	%GDA
Salt	0.4g	10%
Vitamin D	1.5µg	30%
Iron	2.4mg	17%
Folic acid	68µg	34%
Niacin	5.5mg	31%
Vitamin B$_1$	0.5mg	34%

HT You may be asked to use a food label to convert the amount of sodium from sodium salt. But the conversion could be inaccurate as sodium ions come from a number of sources.

Example
What mass of sodium ions is in a 30g serving of bran?
1. 0.4g of sodium chloride (NaCl).
2. Number of moles of NaCl = $\frac{0.4}{58.5}$ = 0.0068 moles.
3. There would be 0.0068 moles of sodium ions.

Mass of sodium ions = 0.0068 × 23 = **0.16g**

Concentration in g/dm³ and mol/dm³

The **concentration** of a solution in g/dm³ can be calculated using the following formula:

$$\text{Concentration} = \frac{\text{Mass of solute (g)}}{\text{Volume of solvent (dm}^3\text{)}}$$

The concentration of a solution in mol/dm³ can be calculated using the following formula:

$$\text{Concentration} = \frac{\text{Amount of solute (mol)}}{\text{Volume of solvent (dm}^3\text{)}}$$

First, change the volume to dm³... $\frac{100 \text{cm}^3}{1000}$ = 0.1dm³

$$\text{Concentration} = \frac{\text{Mass of solute}}{\text{Volume of solvent}}$$

$$= \frac{2}{0.1} = \mathbf{20\text{g/dm}^3}$$

Example
2g of sodium chloride is dissolved in 100cm³ of water. What is the concentration (in g/dm³)?

Quick Test

1. Convert 1200cm³ into dm³.
2. What are the two common units of concentration?
3. Explain how you dilute a solution.
4. Why is it important to ensure that medicines are diluted correctly?

Key Words GDA

Titrations C5

Titration

When an acid and an alkali react together, it's known as a **neutralisation** reaction:

acid + alkali → salt + water

You can carry out a **titration** to find out how much acid is needed to neutralise an alkali using this method:

1. Measure the alkali into a conical flask by using a pipette and filler. It is important to use the filler to prevent the acid getting into contact with your skin.
2. Add a few drops of **indicator** to the conical flask.
3. Fill the burette with acid.
4. Record the start volume of acid.
5. Add acid slowly to the alkali until the indicator just changes colour (the end point).
6. Record the end volume of acid.
7. Work out how much acid has been added (final volume − start volume). This is called the **titre**. The titre depends on the concentration of the reactants.
8. To improve the accuracy of the results, repeat the titration until you have consistent (concordant) results, then take an average (mean).

N.B. Sometimes you can put the alkali in the burette, and the acid in the conical flask.

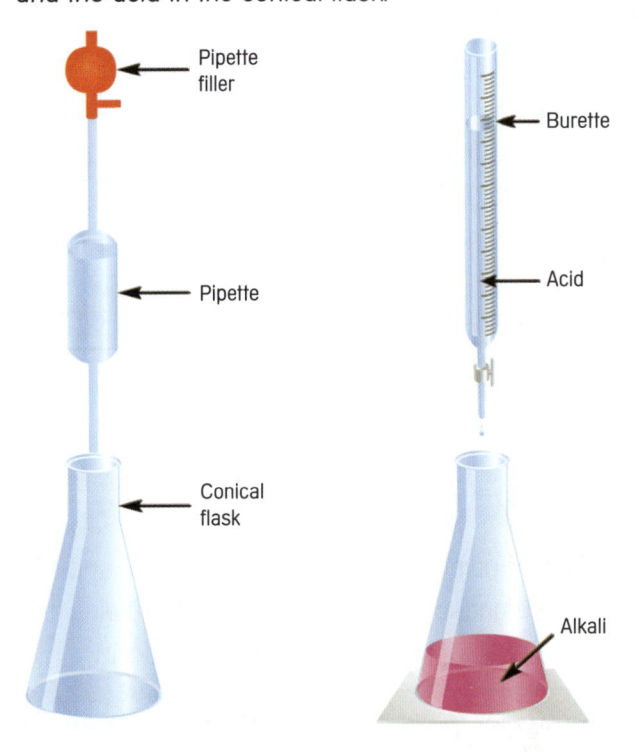

Indicators

Indicators change colour depending on whether they are in acidic or alkaline solutions.

Single indicators, such as litmus, produce a sudden colour change at the end of the titration. This clearly shows the end point.

Universal indicator is a mixture of different indicators, which gives a continuous range of colours. You can estimate the pH of a solution by comparing the colour of the indicator in solution to the pH colour chart.

This table shows the colours of certain indicators in acidic and alkaline solutions:

Indicator	Colour in Acid	Colour in Alkali
Litmus	Red	Blue
Phenolphthalein	Colourless	Pink
Universal indicator	Red	Blue

HT In an acid–base titration, the pH changes very suddenly near the end point, so a single indicator, e.g. litmus, shows the change very clearly.

When a mixed indicator, e.g. universal indicator, is used it's harder to see the end point because it gives a range of colours.

Key Words Neutralisation • Titration • Titre • Indicator

C5 Titrations

pH Curves

pH curves can be drawn to show what happens to the pH in a neutralisation reaction:
- An acid has a low pH. When an alkali is added to it, the pH increases.
- An alkali has a high pH. When an acid is added to it, the pH decreases.

You should be able to read and interpret pH curves (like the one opposite) to work out:
- the titre (the volume of acid needed to neutralise the alkali)
- the pH when a certain amount of acid has been added.

HT You should be able to sketch pH curves for the titration of an acid or an alkali.

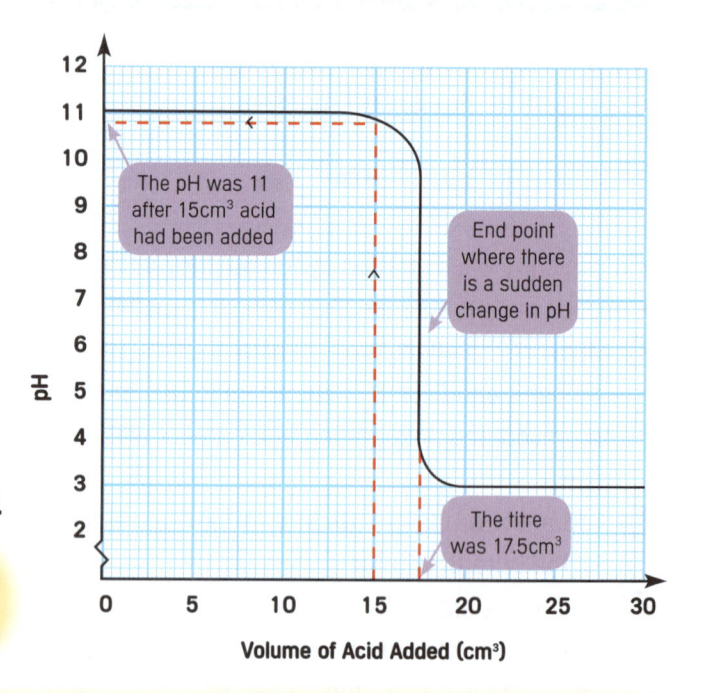

The pH was 11 after 15cm³ acid had been added

End point where there is a sudden change in pH

The titre was 17.5cm³

Concentration Formulae (HT)

At the end point of a titration where the acid and alkali react in a one-to-one ratio, the number of moles of acid is equal to the number of moles of alkali:

Concentration of acid × Volume of acid = Concentration of alkali × Volume of alkali

You can use these formulae to calculate concentration, volume and moles:

$$\text{Concentration (mol/dm}^3\text{)} = \frac{\text{Moles}}{\text{Volume (dm}^3\text{)}}$$

$$\text{Volume (dm}^3\text{)} = \frac{\text{Moles}}{\text{Concentration (mol/dm}^3\text{)}}$$

$$\text{Moles} = \text{Concentration (mol/dm}^3\text{)} \times \text{Volume (dm}^3\text{)}$$

Example
0.025dm³ of a sample of sodium hydroxide (NaOH) is completely neutralised by 0.030dm³ of a 0.1mol/dm³ hydrochloric acid (HCl). What is the concentration of alkali?

sodium hydroxide + hydrochloric acid → sodium chloride + water

NaOH + HCl → NaCl + H$_2$O

Concentration of acid × Volume of acid = Concentration of alkali × Volume of alkali

0.1 × 0.030 = Concentration of alkali × 0.025

$$\text{Concentration of alkali} = \frac{0.1 \times 0.030}{0.025}$$

= 0.12mol/dm³

Quick Test

1. What is an indicator?
2. Describe the changes in pH as an acid is added to an alkali.

Key Words pH

Gas Volumes C5

Measuring Gas Volumes

You can use the following apparatus to collect and measure the **volume** of a gas made in a reaction:
- An upturned measuring cylinder.
- A gas syringe.
- An upturned burette.

You should use this method to measure the volume of gas produced by an experiment:
1. Measure out the reactants.
2. Add the reactants together in a conical flask and start the stopwatch.
3. Record the volume of gas produced at regular time intervals until the volume stops increasing.

A reaction stops when one of the reactants has been used up. The reactant that gets used up first is called the **limiting reactant**.

In a reaction where there is a one-to-one ratio between reactants, the limiting reactant is the one with the smallest number of moles.

The more reactant that's used, the greater the amount of product (in this case, gas) that's produced.

> **HT** More reactants means more reactant particles and so there will be a greater number of collisions, which increase the number of product particles. The number of particles of the limiting reactant determines the maximum number of product particles that can be made.

The amount of gas produced in a reaction is directly proportional to the amount of limiting reactant used.

Apparatus for Collecting and Measuring Volume of Gas made in a Reaction

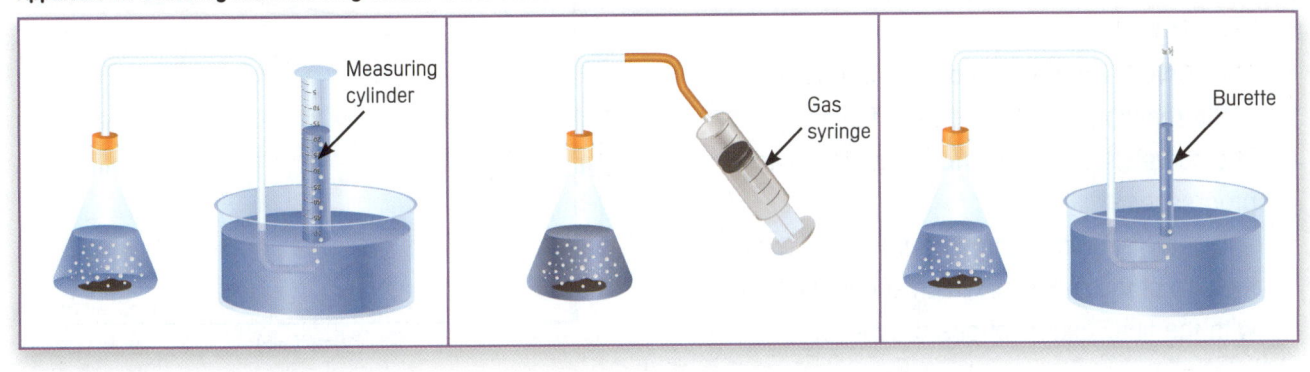

Measuring Gas Masses

The amount of gas made in a reaction can be measured by monitoring the change in mass of a reaction. You should use this method to measure the mass of gas produced by an experiment:
1. Measure the mass of an empty conical flask.
2. Measure out the reactants.
3. Record the total mass of the reactants and the flask.
4. Add the reactants together in the flask and start the stopwatch.
5. Record the mass of the flask and reactants at regular time intervals, until the mass stops changing.

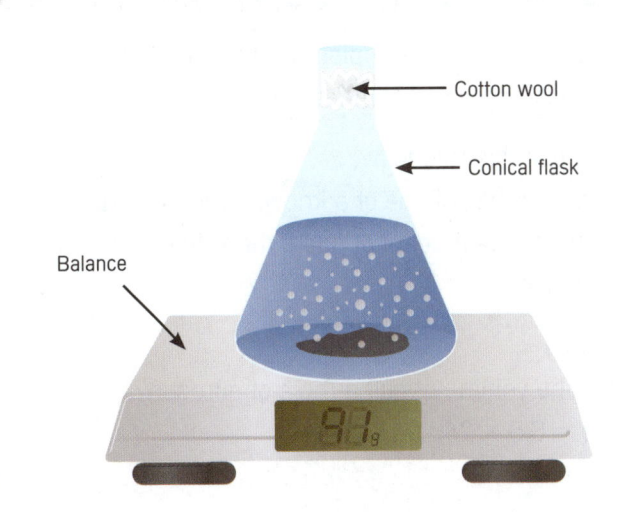

Key Words Limiting reactant

C5 Gas Volumes

Interpreting Graphs of Reactions

Graphs can be used to show the results of a reaction. You can find out the following information from a graph:

1. The total **volume** of gas produced.
2. When the reaction ended.
3. The volume of gas produced at a particular time (or the time at which a particular volume of gas was produced).
4. The point at which the reaction was fastest.

You may be asked to compare the rate of reaction for different reactions by using the gradient.

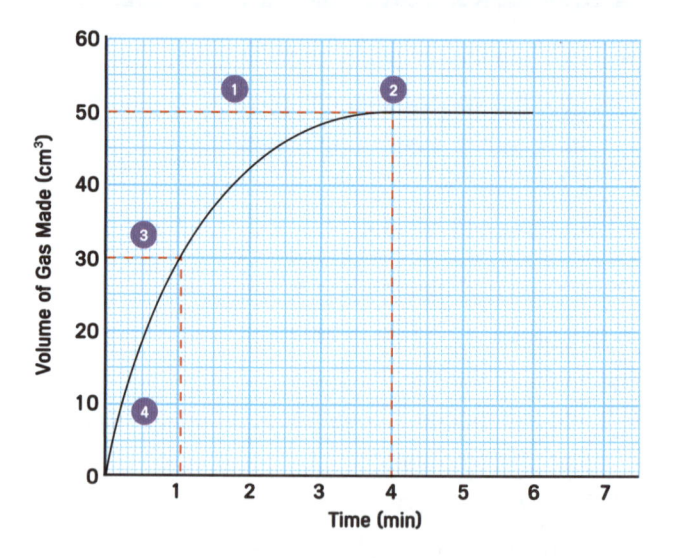

HT Sketching Graphs of Reactions

When you're sketching a graph to show the volume of gas made in a reaction, you should remember the following rules:

- The curve should be steepest at the beginning of the reaction (when the rate is fastest).
- The curve should get shallower as the reaction progresses.
- The curve should become horizontal to show the end of the reaction, which should be level with the final volume of gas produced.

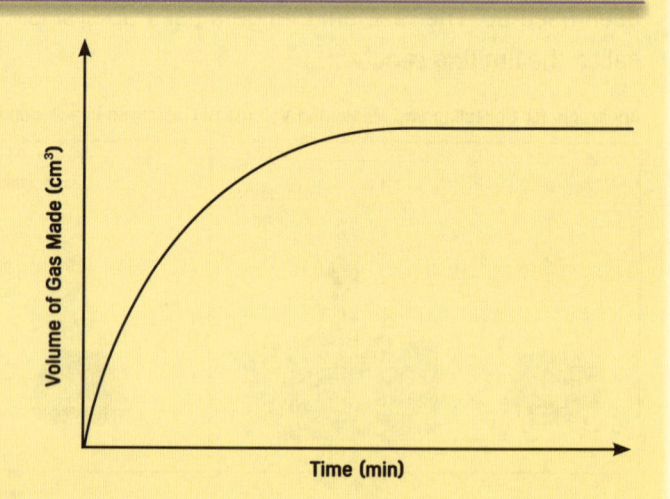

Calculating Volumes and Amounts of Gases

One mole of any gas occupies a volume of **24dm³** at room temperature and pressure.

You can use this rule to:
- calculate the volume of a known amount of gas
- calculate the amount of gas if the volume is known.

Example 1
What is the volume of half a mole of nitrogen?
Volume = 0.5 × 24
    = 12dm³

Example 2
A balloon is filled with oxygen until it has a volume of 6dm³. How many moles of oxygen are in the balloon?

Moles = $\frac{6}{24}$

= **0.25 mole**

Equilibria C5

Reversible Reactions

A **reversible reaction** can go forwards or backwards, under the same conditions. It's represented by ⇌. For example, the reaction between nitrogen and hydrogen to produce ammonia is reversible.

nitrogen + hydrogen ⇌ ammonia
$N_2(g) + 3H_2(g) \rightleftharpoons 2NH_3(g)$

Equilibrium

A reversible reaction can reach **equilibrium** (a balance). This means that the rate of the forward reaction is equal to the rate of the backward reaction. At equilibrium, the amounts and concentrations of reactants and products stay the same, even though reactions are still taking place.

A + B ⇌ C + D
Reactants   Products

The position of the equilibrium can be altered by changing:
- the temperature
- the pressure
- the concentration of reactant(s) and/or product(s).

If the position of the equilibrium lies to the right of the reaction equation, the concentration of the products is greater than the concentration of the reactants.

If the position of the equilibrium lies to the left of the reaction equation, the concentration of the products is less than the concentration of the reactants.

You should be able to read tables or graphs of equilibrium composition to obtain the following information:
- The composition at a particular temperature.
- The composition at a particular pressure.
- The effect of temperature and pressure on composition.

Example

The table and graphs show how altering the reaction conditions can change the equilibrium composition for the reaction to make ammonia.

We can see that percentage of ammonia made falls when the temperature increases.

Pressure (atmospheres)	Ammonia made at 300°C (%)	Ammonia made at 600°C (%)
100	43	4
200	62	12
300	74	18
400	79	19
500	80	20

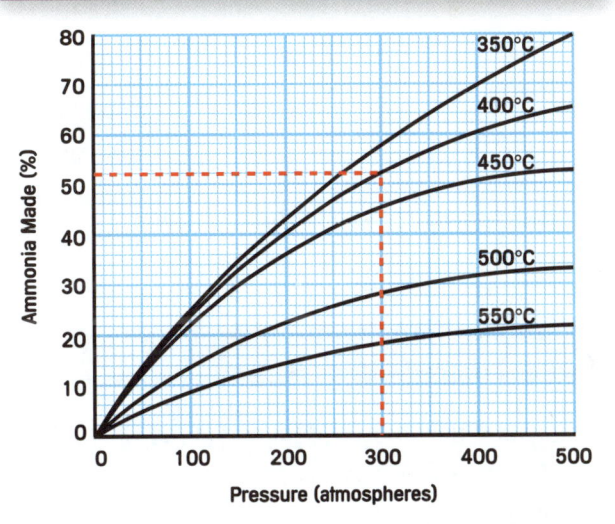

From the table we can see that 200 atmospheres and 600°C is 12%.

From the graph we can see that the percentage of ammonia made at 300 atmospheres and 400°C is 52%.

Key Words: Reversible reaction • Equilibrium

C5 Equilibria

The Contact Process

The raw materials sulfur, air and water are made into sulfuric acid in the **Contact Process**:

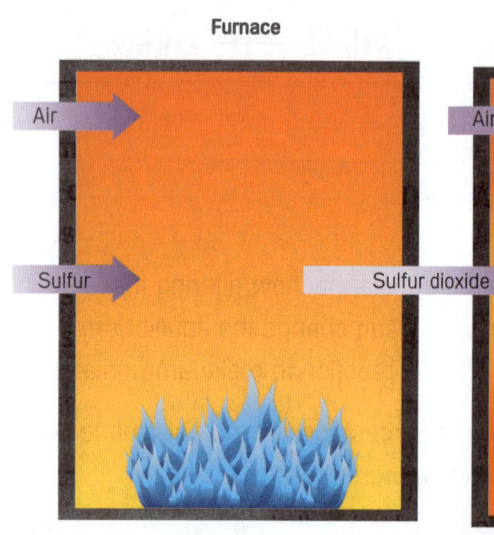

Furnace — Air, Sulfur → Sulfur dioxide
Reactor — Air, Sulfur dioxide → Sulfur trioxide (Catalyst)
Absorber — Water, Sulfur trioxide → Sulfuric acid

1 Sulfur is burned in a furnace to make sulfur dioxide:

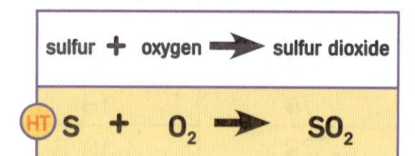

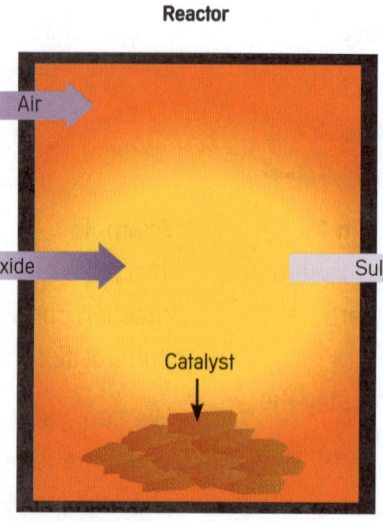

sulfur + oxygen → sulfur dioxide

(HT) $S + O_2 \rightarrow SO_2$

2 The sulfur dioxide combines with oxygen from the air in a reversible reaction to make sulfur trioxide:

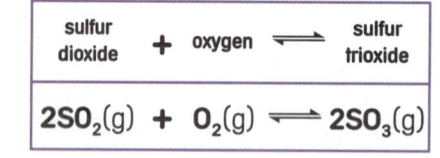

sulfur dioxide + oxygen ⇌ sulfur trioxide

$2SO_2(g) + O_2(g) \rightleftharpoons 2SO_3(g)$

This reaction takes place using a vanadium(V) oxide (V_2O_5) **catalyst**, at a temperature of about 450°C and at atmospheric pressure.

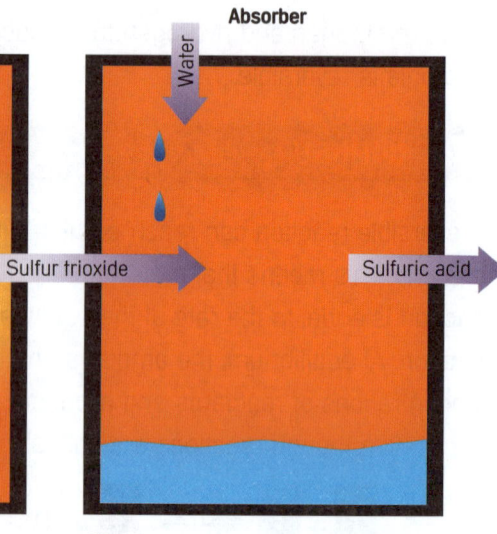

3 Sulfur trioxide is then dissolved in water to make sulfuric acid:

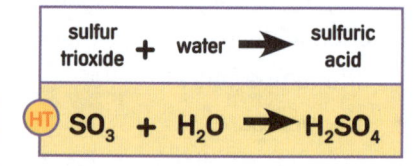

sulfur trioxide + water → sulfuric acid

(HT) $SO_3 + H_2O \rightarrow H_2SO_4$

Uses of Sulfuric Acid

The sulfuric acid that is produced in the Contact Process has many uses, such as the manufacturing of:
- paints and pigments
- soaps and detergents
- fibres
- plastics
- fertilisers.

Key Words: Contact Process • Catalyst

Equilibria C5

Changing Equilibrium Conditions

A reversible reaction will only reach equilibrium if the conditions (such as temperature and pressure) aren't changed and no substance is added or removed. This is known as a **closed system**.

At the start of an equilibrium reaction, the forward reaction will slow down and the backward reaction will speed up until both reactions are at the same rate.

The equilibrium can be moved to the right of the reaction equation by:
- adding more reactant **or**
- removing the product as it's made.

The equilibrium can be moved to the left of the reaction equation by:
- reducing the amount of reactant **or**
- increasing the amount of product.

In a reaction that involves gases, an increase in pressure moves the equilibrium in the direction that has the fewest moles of gas.

Conditions in the Contact Process

A catalyst is used in the reaction to speed up the rate of production of sulfur trioxide but it doesn't change the position of the equilibrium.

Increasing the temperature increases the rate of the reaction but it also reduces the yield and pushes the equilibrium position to the left.

A **compromise** temperature of about 450°C is used to get a balance between yield and rate.

A higher pressure would push the equilibrium to the right and increase the yield. But the extra cost of increasing the pressure isn't worth the small amount of increase in yield because the equilibrium position is well over to the right.

Quick Test

1. What two variables can be used to monitor the amount of gas made in a chemical reaction?
2. What is the symbol used to show a reversible reaction?
3. What four factors can be altered in order to change the position of equilibrium?
4. The Contact Process is used in industry to make sulfuric acid. In the reactor sulfur dioxide is converted into sulfur trioxide. Write a balanced symbol equation for this reaction.

C5 Strong and Weak Acids

Strong and Weak Acids

Acids **ionise** in water to make hydrogen ions (H⁺):
- A **strong acid** ionises completely in water.
- A **weak acid** only partially ionises in water. The ionisation of a weak acid is a reversible reaction, so it makes an equilibrium mixture.

Strong acids, e.g. hydrochloric acid, nitric acid and sulfuric acid, have a lower pH than weak acids, e.g. ethanoic acid, if they're of the same concentration.

Ethanoic acid or hydrochloric acid react with:
- magnesium to produce hydrogen gas
- calcium carbonate to produce carbon dioxide gas.

HT The **concentration** of an acid is determined by how many moles of the acid are dissolved in 1dm³.

The **strength** of an acid is determined by how much it ionises. A strong acid produces more H⁺ ions than a weak acid of the same concentration, because the weak acid does not ionise completely.
- Hydrochloric acid completely ionises:

$$HCl \rightarrow H^+ + Cl^-$$

- Ethanoic acid partially ionises:

$$CH_3COOH \rightleftharpoons CH_3COO^- + H^+$$

If an equal amount of ethanoic acid and hydrochloric acid are used in these reactions, the same volumes of gas will be made. The volume of gas made is determined by the amount of reactants used, not by the acid's strength. But, the reaction with ethanoic acid is slower as there are fewer hydrogen ions than in the same concentration of hydrochloric acid, and so there are fewer collisions.

An acid with more H⁺ ions (i.e. a strong acid) has a lower pH. A weak acid with the same concentration will have a lower concentration of H⁺ ions than a diluted strong acid and so a higher pH.

Hydrochloric acid reacts quicker than ethanoic acid because:
- hydrochloric acid is a stronger acid than ethanoic acid
- hydrochloric acid has a greater concentration of hydrogen ions than ethanoic acid
- the greater concentration of hydrogen ions in hydrochloric acid leads to a higher frequency of collision between hydrogen ions and the other reactant.

Electrolysis of Acids

Acids conduct electricity. A strong acid, such as hydrochloric acid, is a better conductor than the same concentration of a weak acid, such as ethanoic acid. This is because there are fewer hydrogen ions in ethanoic acid to carry the charge.

When hydrochloric acid or ethanoic acid is used in electrolysis, hydrogen gas is made at the negative electrode.

This is because when electricity is passed through the acid, the hydrogen ions are attracted to the negative electrode, where they become hydrogen molecules.

HT The greater the concentration of hydrogen ions in an acid, the greater the electrical conductivity as the ions carry the charge. This is why strong acids, for example, hydrochloric acid, are better conductors than weak acids.

Key Words   Ionise • Strong acid • Weak acid

Ionic Equations and Precipitation C5

Precipitation Reactions

In a solid ionic substance, the ions are in fixed positions, but when they dissolve in water they are free to move about.

A **precipitation** reaction occurs when a **precipitate** (an insoluble solid) is made by mixing two ionic solutions together. The precipitate (the product) is made when ions from one solution collide with ions from the other solution and form an insoluble compound.

You can use this method to make an insoluble compound:

1. Mix the reactant solutions.
2. Filter off the precipitate.
3. Wash the residue in the filter funnel with a little distilled water.
4. Dry the residue (the product) in an oven at 50°C.

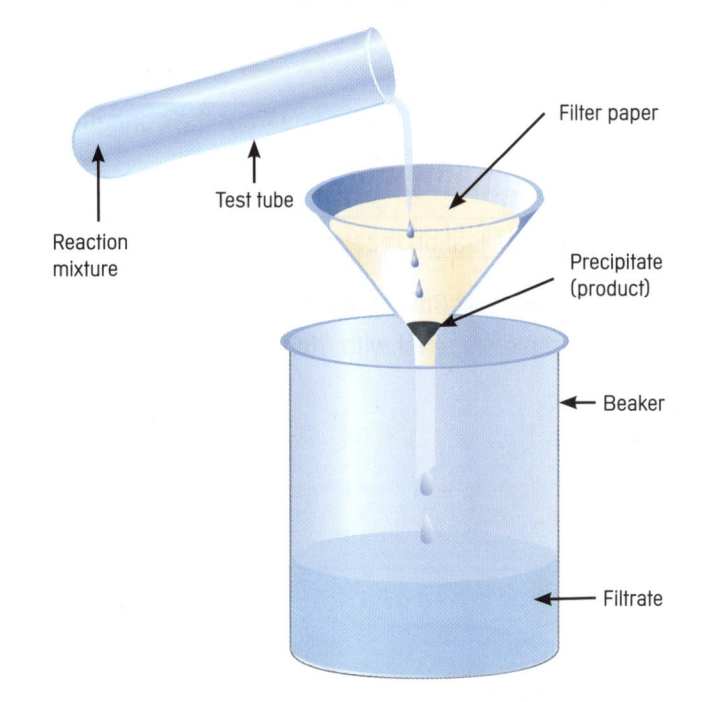

Detecting Ions

Halides are the ions made by the halogens (Group 7 elements). You can use lead(II) nitrate to detect halide ions, e.g.
- chlorides (Cl^-) form a white precipitate
- bromides (Br^-) form a cream precipitate
- iodides (I^-) form a yellow precipitate.

You can detect sulfate ions by using barium chloride solution. It will cause a white precipitate of barium sulfate to form:

sodium sulfate(aq) + barium chloride(aq) → barium sulfate(s) + sodium chloride(aq)

Precipitation reactions are very fast reactions between ions. For example, when sodium chloride and lead nitrate react, the precipitate of lead chloride forms almost instantly:

sodium chloride + lead nitrate → lead chloride + sodium nitrate

HT $2NaCl(aq) + Pb(NO_3)_2(aq) \rightarrow PbCl_2(s) + 2NaNO_3(aq)$

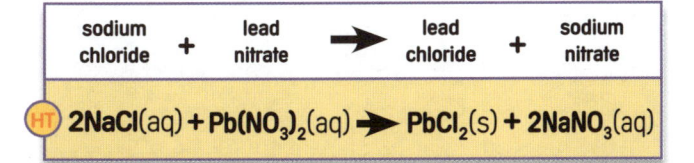

HT The ions involved in this reaction are Na^+, Cl^-, Pb^{2+} and NO_3^-. You can write an ionic equation by picking out the ions that react to form the precipitate, for example:

$$Pb^{2+}(aq) + 2Cl^-(aq) \rightarrow PbCl_2(s)$$

The Na^+ and the NO_3^- ions stay dissolved in the water and don't do anything. So, they are called **spectator ions**.

Quick Test

1. What is a strong acid?
2. Explain how a precipitate is formed.
3. What chemical is used to detect sulfate ions?
4. **HT** Explain why $0.1 mol/dm^3$ of nitric acid would have a lower pH than $0.1 mol/dm^3$ of ethanoic acid.

Key Words Precipitate

C5 Exam Practice Questions

1 Volumes can be measured using different units.

Convert the volume 150cm³ into dm³. [1]

....

2 Titrations can be used to work out the concentration of a solution. What is a titre? [1]

....

3 In a neutralisation reaction acids and bases react together.

Describe how the pH changes when acid is added to an alkali until there is more than enough acid to completely react with the alkali. Tick (✓) the correct answer.

It starts at 7 and falls lower. ☐

It starts at 7 and rises higher. ☐

It starts higher than 7 and falls lower. ☐

It starts lower than 7 and rises higher. ☐

[1]

4 Methane is used as a hydrocarbon fuel in most UK houses for cooking and heating.

What is the volume of two moles of methane gas at room temperature and pressure? [2]

....

5 The Haber process is used to make ammonia. By changing the conditions, the yield can be altered. Use the table below to help you answer the questions that follow.

Pressure (atmospheres)	Ammonia made at 300°C (%)	Ammonia made at 600°C (%)
100	43	4
200	62	12
300	74	18
400	79	19
500	80	20

a) What happens to the yield as the pressure is increased? [1]

....

b) What happens to the yield as temperature is increased? [1]

....

c) What is the yield at 300°C and 400 atmospheres pressure? [1]

....

Exam Practice Questions C5

6 The Contact Process is used to make sulfuric acid.

  a) List the raw materials needed for the Contact Process. [2]

  b) A lower temperature gives a higher yield in the Contact Process.

  Explain why a relatively high temperature of 450°C is used instead. [1]

7 When Group 7 elements react they often become halide ions.

  Which type of halide gives a cream precipitate when tested with silver nitrate solution? [1]

HT

8 Sodium hydroxide has a pH greater than 7 and is an alkali.

  a) How many moles are there in 16g of sodium hydroxide? [2]

  b) What mass of oxygen (A_r = 16) is in 3 moles of sodium hydroxide? [1]

9 A titration is carried out in which the acid and alkali react in a 1 : 1 ratio.

  25cm³ of an unknown concentration of alkali was completely reacted with 22.5cm³ of a 0.2mol/dm³ acid.

  What was the concentration of the alkali? Ring the correct answer.

      0.018mol/dm³   3.6mol/dm³   0.18mol/dm³   0.36mol/dm³

  [1]

10 Hydrochloric acid is a strong acid with a low pH.

  Write a balanced symbol equation to show the ionisation of hydrochloric acid in water. [3]

11 Precipitation reactions can be used to determine which halide ion is present.

  Write a balanced symbol equation for the reaction of potassium iodide (KI) with silver nitrate ($AgNO_3$). [2]

P5 Satellites, Gravity and Circular Motion

Satellites and Gravity

A **satellite** is an object that **orbits** a planet in space. Satellites can be:
- **natural**, for example, the Moon
- **artificial** – they have been put in space by humans.

A satellite is kept in orbit by a **gravitational force**. **Gravity** is a universal force of attraction between masses. Gravity keeps:
- the planets orbiting the Sun
- the Moon orbiting the Earth.

Centripetal force acts towards the centre of a circle; it keeps an object moving in a circle. Gravity provides the centripetal force that keeps a satellite in orbit.

The weight of an object depends on the gravitational force on the surface of the planet.

Weight (N)	=	Mass (kg)	×	Gravitational field strength (N/kg)
w	=	m	×	g

On Earth, gravitational field strength, **g = 10N/kg**

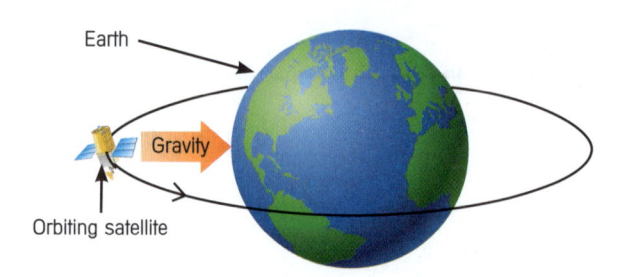

HT The gravitational force between two objects gets weaker as the objects are moved further apart. If the distance is doubled, the force drops to $\frac{1}{4}$. This is called the inverse square law.

Therefore, planets very close to the Sun experience a high gravitational force compared to planets that are further away.

The difference in gravitational force means that:
- planets closer to the Sun travel very quickly and have short orbital periods.
- planets further from the Sun travel very slowly and have long orbital periods.

HT Comets

Periodic comets orbit the Sun in almost-elliptical loops, unlike the planets, which have almost-circular orbits.

When a comet is close to the Sun it has to travel very fast to escape the gravitational force. When the comet is further away, it travels more slowly because the Sun's gravity pulls it back.

The effect is similar to a ball being thrown up into the air: it slows down as it gets higher and speeds up as it gets closer to the Earth.

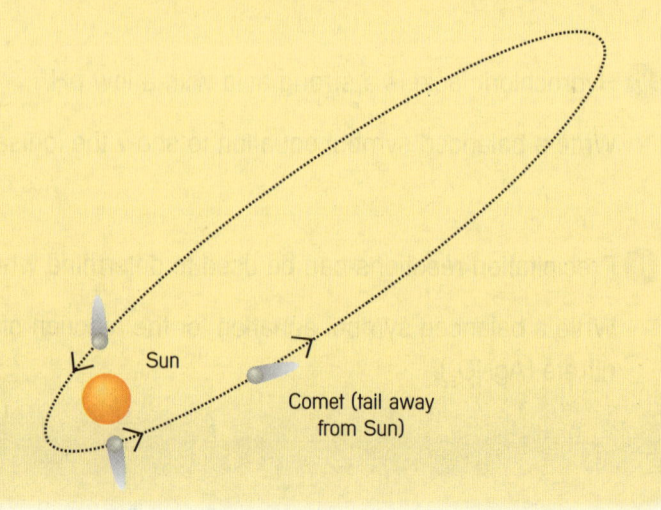

Key Words Satellite • Orbit • Gravitational force • Gravity • Centripetal force

Satellites, Gravity and Circular Motion P5

Artificial Satellites

Artificial satellites can orbit at different heights above the Earth's surface. A satellite's **orbital period** (the time it takes to make one complete orbit) increases with height above the Earth. The height at which a satellite orbits, and its period, determines what it can be used for.

Satellites in **low polar orbit**:
- travel very quickly
- go around the Earth several times each day.

Their uses include:
- imaging the Earth's surface
- weather forecasting
- military uses (e.g. spying).

Geostationary satellites:
- orbit much higher above the Earth
- take 24 hours to complete one orbit
- remain above a fixed position on the Earth's equator.

Their uses include:
- communications, for example, satellite television
- weather forecasting.

Satellites can also be used for scientific research and global positioning systems (GPS).

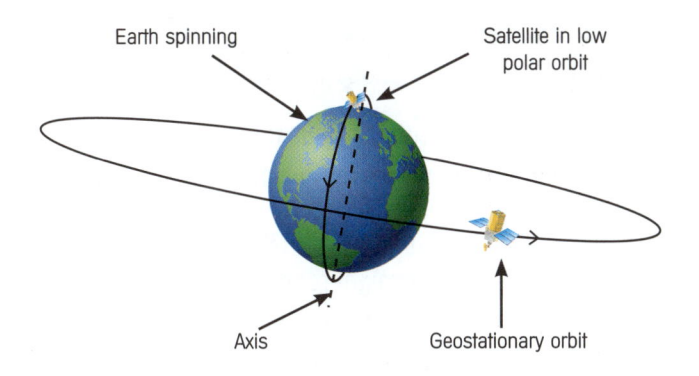

Orbits of Artificial Satellites (HT)

A satellite would naturally travel in a straight line. However, Earth's gravitational force causes it to continually accelerate towards Earth, and prevents it from flying off at a tangent.

The two effects balance, causing the satellite to remain in a circular orbit.

Artificial satellites in low polar orbit feel a strong gravitational force dragging them towards the Earth, so they travel faster than those in high orbits.

The speed of satellites in low orbit must be high enough to balance the gravitational force and keep them moving in a circle.

Geostationary satellites are in high orbits so the gravitational force on them is weak. They move more slowly and have further to travel.

Quick Test

1. Give an example of a natural satellite and an artificial satellite.
2. What happens to the speed of a comet as it travels past the Sun?
3. How long does it take for a geostationary satellite to orbit the Earth?

Key Words   Orbital period

P5 Vectors and Equations of Motion

Scalar and Vector Quantities

Scalar quantities have a **size** only, for example:
- mass
- energy
- speed
- time.

Vector quantities have **size** and **direction**, for example:
- velocity
- force
- acceleration.

Speed

Speed is how fast an object is moving at a particular time. Direction isn't important when measuring **speed**. Speed is a scalar quantity.

The speed of an object can change during the course of its journey.

To calculate the **average speed** for a journey you can use the following equation:

$$\text{Average speed} = \frac{\text{Total distance}}{\text{Total time taken}}$$

Relative Speed

If two objects are moving near to each other, their motion is described in terms of their **relative speed**.

Direction is important when considering motion. Two cars travelling on a straight road will have a higher relative speed if they're moving towards each other than if they're travelling in the same direction.

Example 1
Car A and Car B are travelling towards each other on a straight road. Each car is travelling at 10m/s.

The relative speed of Car A and Car B is 20m/s. That is, if you're in Car A, it will look like Car B is travelling towards you at a speed of 20m/s.

Example 2
Car C and Car D are travelling in the same direction on a straight road. Car D is travelling at 8m/s and Car C is travelling at 10m/s. Every second, Car C will get 2m closer to Car D, which means that Car C's relative speed is 2m/s.

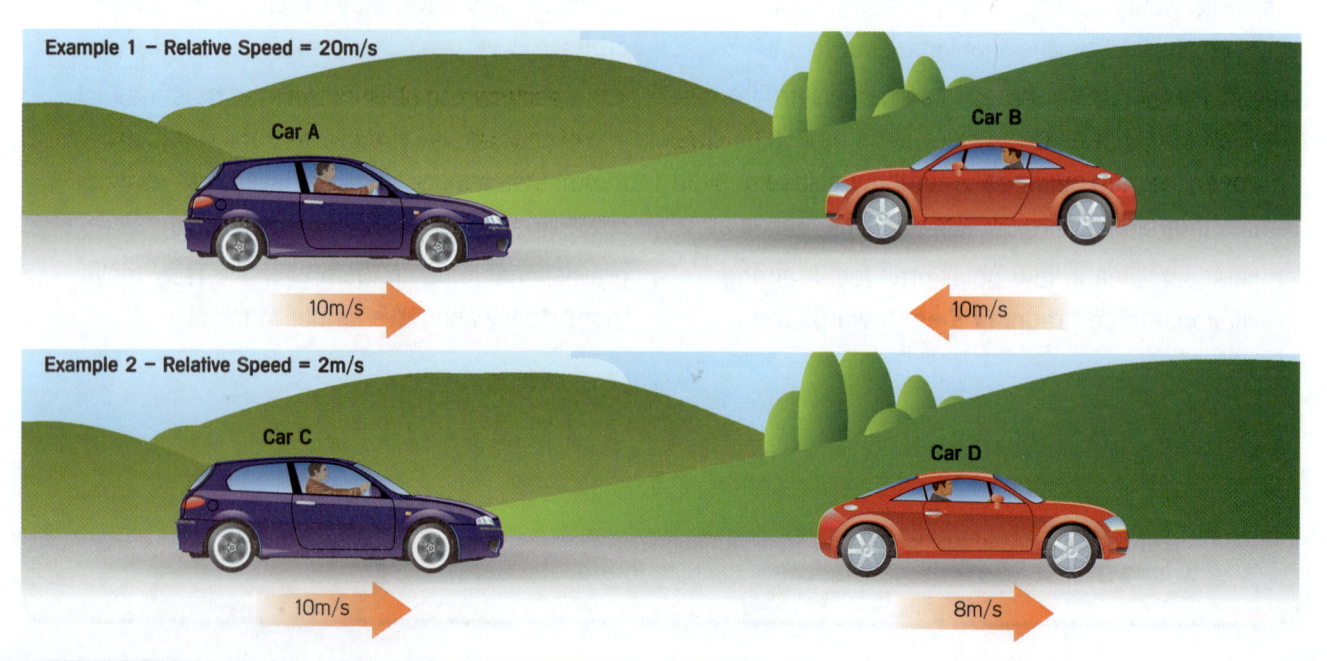

Example 1 – Relative Speed = 20m/s

Car A 10m/s Car B 10m/s

Example 2 – Relative Speed = 2m/s

Car C 10m/s Car D 8m/s

Key Words: Scalar quantity • Vector quantity • Speed • Relative speed

Vectors and Equations of Motion P5

Velocity and Displacement

Velocity is an object's rate of **displacement** (change of distance) in a particular direction. You can calculate velocity and displacement using the following equations:

$$v = u + at$$
$$s = \left(\frac{u+v}{2}\right) \times t$$

where u = initial velocity, v = final velocity, a = acceleration, t = time, s = displacement.

Example
A bike travelling at 5m/s accelerates at 3m/s² for 5 seconds.

a) What is the bike's final velocity?

$v = u + at$

$v = 5 + (3 \times 5) =$ **20m/s**

b) How far did the bike travel whilst accelerating?

$s = \left(\frac{u+v}{2}\right) \times t$

$s = \left(\frac{5+20}{2}\right) \times 5 =$ **62.5m**

(HT) You can also calculate an object's final velocity, displacement, acceleration, or the time it was travelling for, by using the following equations:

$$v^2 = u^2 + 2as$$
$$s = ut + \frac{1}{2}at^2$$

Example 1
A runner starts a race and accelerates at 2.5m/s² for the first 20m of the race. What is the runner's final velocity?

$v^2 = u^2 + 2as = 0^2 + (2 \times 2.5 \times 20) = 100$

$v = \sqrt{100} =$ **10m/s**

Example 2
A car travelling at 20m/s accelerates at 3m/s² for 20 seconds. How far has the car travelled in this time?

$s = ut + \frac{1}{2}at^2 = (20 \times 20) + (\frac{1}{2} \times 3 \times 20^2)$

$s = 400 + 600 =$ **1000m**

Vectors

If two **forces** or velocities are **parallel**, it's possible to calculate their total effect from a **vector diagram**:

- Parallel vectors in the same direction add up:

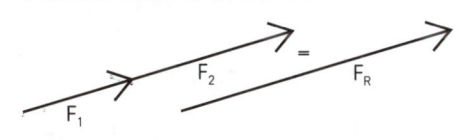

$F_R = F_1 + F_2$

- Parallel vectors in opposite directions subtract.

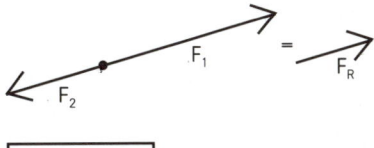

$F_R = F_1 - F_2$

(HT) If two forces or velocities are acting at **right angles** on the same object, you can work out the **resultant force/velocity** by using Pythagoras' theorem.

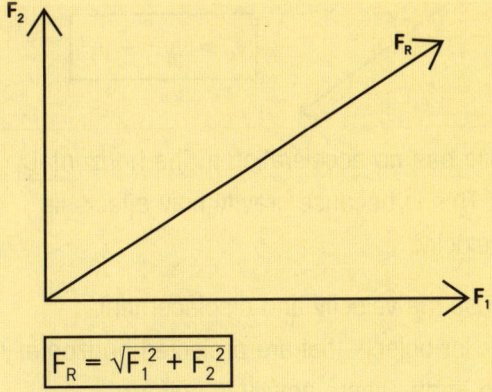

$F_R = \sqrt{F_1^2 + F_2^2}$

Key Words — Velocity • Force

P5 Projectile Motion

Projectile Motion

When objects such as cannon balls or missiles are fired into the air they are called **projectiles**. When moving through the air, the following are all examples of projectiles:
- Golf balls
- Footballs
- Netballs
- Darts
- Long-jumpers.

The path that a projectile takes is known as its **trajectory**. If a projectile is launched horizontally on Earth, and there is no air resistance acting on it, the projectile will have:
- a constant **horizontal** velocity
- a steadily increasing vertical velocity.

The horizontal and vertical velocities are **vectors**. If air resistance is ignored, the only force acting on the projectile is **gravity**.

Earth's gravitational field causes the projectile to accelerate towards the ground, so it only affects the projectile's **vertical** velocity.

Because of the pull of gravity, objects projected horizontally on Earth follow a downward curving path, known as a **parabolic** trajectory.

The horizontal range depends only on the launch angle (measured from the horizontal). Footballs launched at 45° will travel the greatest distance.

HT Calculating Projectile Velocity

The horizontal and vertical velocities of a projectile can be treated as separate vectors. Each vector has its own speed and direction.

The projectile's **resultant velocity** is the **vector sum** of the horizontal and vertical velocities.

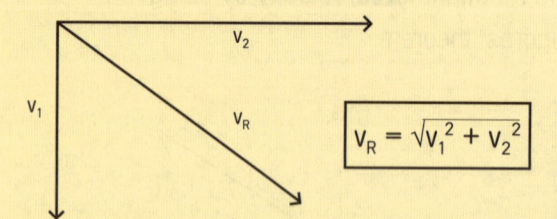

$$v_R = \sqrt{v_1^2 + v_2^2}$$

A projectile has **no** acceleration in the horizontal direction. This is because gravity only affects its vertical velocity.

You can use the velocity and displacement equations for objects that are projected horizontally above the Earth, where gravity is uniform.

Example

A stone is kicked off a cliff with a horizontal velocity of 3m/s. After 3 seconds, it lands in the sea 45m below. What is the **magnitude** (size) of the resultant velocity of the stone when it hits the sea?

Horizontally, the stone's velocity doesn't change.

Vertically, the stone's velocity increases from its initial velocity of 0m/s, due to gravity.

(Remember that acceleration due to gravity is 10m/s².)

$v = u + at = 0 + (10 \times 3) =$ **30m/s vertically**

To find the vector sum of the two velocities, use Pythagoras' theorem:

$v^2 = 3^2 + 30^2$

$v = \sqrt{909} =$ **30.1m/s**

Key Words: Projectile • Trajectory • Gravity • Parabolic

Action and Reaction P5

Actions and Reactions

Every **action** has an equal and opposite **reaction**. When an object collides with another, or two bodies interact, they exert equal and opposite forces on each other. This is **Newton's Third Law of Motion**. For example, when you stand on solid ground:

- you exert a **force** on the ground (your weight)
- the ground exerts an equal and opposite force on you (contact force).

Gravity pulls you down towards the Earth and you are pulling the Earth towards you.

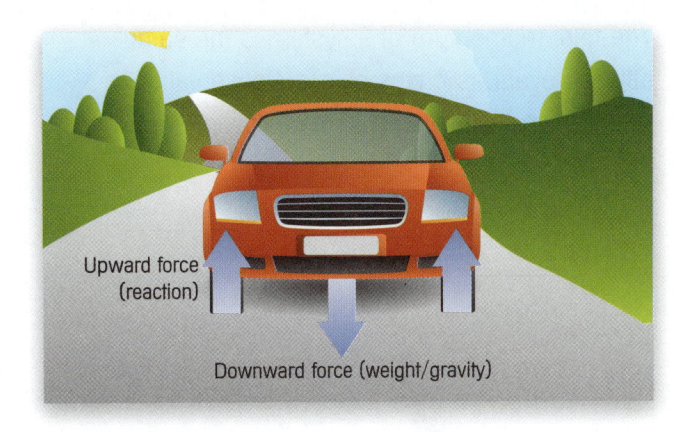

Upward force (reaction)

Downward force (weight/gravity)

Momentum

You can calculate **momentum** using this equation:

$$\text{Momentum} = \text{Mass} \times \text{Velocity}$$

An increase in an object's mass and/or velocity will also increase its momentum.

Calculate the momentum of a person of mass 60kg travelling at 0.5m/s.

Momentum = Mass × Velocity

= 60 × 0.5

= **30kgm/s**

Collisions, Damage and Injury

In a **collision**, the velocities of the objects colliding are parallel.

If Object A hits Object B with a force, then Object B hits Object A with an equal force.

For example:
- if a lorry crashes into a car, then the car hits the lorry with the same force
- if a ball is hit with a racket, then the racket feels the same force from the ball and recoils.

Acceleration is the rate of change of an object's velocity over time. Many injuries in vehicle collisions, and sporting injuries, are caused by rapid acceleration (usually a sudden slowing down) of the body.

Safety features in vehicles reduce injury by spreading out the acceleration over a greater period of time. This means that the passenger's momentum is reduced more slowly.

HT During a collision, two objects exert an equal and opposite force on each other. You need to be able to calculate force, change in momentum, and time taken, using the following equation:

$$\text{Force (N)} = \frac{\text{Change in momentum}}{\text{Time}}$$

Example

A boy of mass 50kg is walking at 2m/s (v_1). A gust of wind blows the boy forward for 2 seconds and he ends up running at 5m/s (v_2). What is the force of the wind?

$$\text{Force} = \frac{\text{Change in momentum}}{\text{Time}} = \frac{mv_2 - mv_1}{t}$$

$$= \frac{(50 \times 5) - (50 \times 2)}{2} = \frac{250 - 100}{2} = \textbf{75N}$$

Spreading a change in momentum over a longer time reduces:
- the forces required to act
- injuries caused by the forces.

Key Words   Force • Momentum • Acceleration

P5 Action and Reaction

Conservation of Momentum

The total momentum of a system is the same after an event as it was before. Conservation of momentum is illustrated in the following table:

Example of Conservation of Momentum	Description
Recoil	The total momentum of a gun and bullet is zero. If the bullet is then fired, the total momentum is still zero. The bullet moves faster than the gun but it has a smaller mass, so their momenta are equal but acting in opposite directions, thus cancelling each other out.
Explosion	Before an explosion, the total momentum is zero. After an explosion, each fragment flies off in a different direction. The momentum of one fragment will cancel out the momentum of another fragment that's travelling in the opposite direction at the same momentum.
Rocket Propulsion	When a rocket's engines fire in space, the rocket speeds up, but the total momentum of the system is conserved. This is because the forward momentum of the rocket is cancelled out by the backward momentum of the gas it fires out.
Collision m_1 m_2 u_1 u_2	During a collision momentum is conserved. If two objects join (coalesce) during the collision, the momentum after the collision must equal the sum of their individual momentums. $$m_1 u_1 + m_2 u_2 = (m_1 + m_2) v$$ (where u and v are initial and final velocities/speeds)

Pressure

Gas particles are in constant motion. As particles collide with the walls of their container they exert a **force** on the wall. Force per unit area is called **pressure**.

The greater the number of collisions between the particles and the wall, the greater the pressure inside the container.

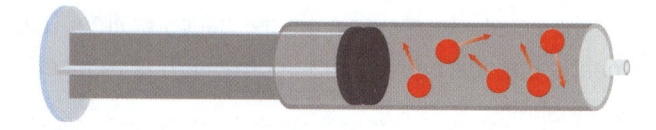

Action and Reaction P5

Pressure (Cont.)

If the gas particles are squashed into a smaller volume:
- the same number of particles will have less space to move in
- each particle will collide with the walls more frequently
- the pressure inside the container increases.

If the temperature of the gas is increased:
- the particles gain energy
- with increased kinetic energy, the particles move more quickly
- each particle will collide with the wall more frequently and collide with more force
- the pressure inside the container increases.

HT As a particle strikes the wall of its container, it undergoes a change in its momentum. This produces a force on the wall.

The size of this force depends upon the length of time that the particle is in contact with the wall (time taken).

$$\text{Force} = \frac{\text{Change in momentum}}{\text{Time taken}}$$

Rockets

At launch, a rocket requires a large force to enable it to accelerate. This force is provided by the exhaust gases. The force pushing the gas backwards out of the exhaust equals the forward force of the gas on the rocket.

The fast-moving particles in the gas collide with the walls of the rocket. This produces a force on the rocket.

HT Rockets used to launch satellites into orbit require very large forces to lift both the rocket and the satellite. Sufficient force is achieved by:
- a large number of particles of exhaust gas
- the particles moving at high speed.

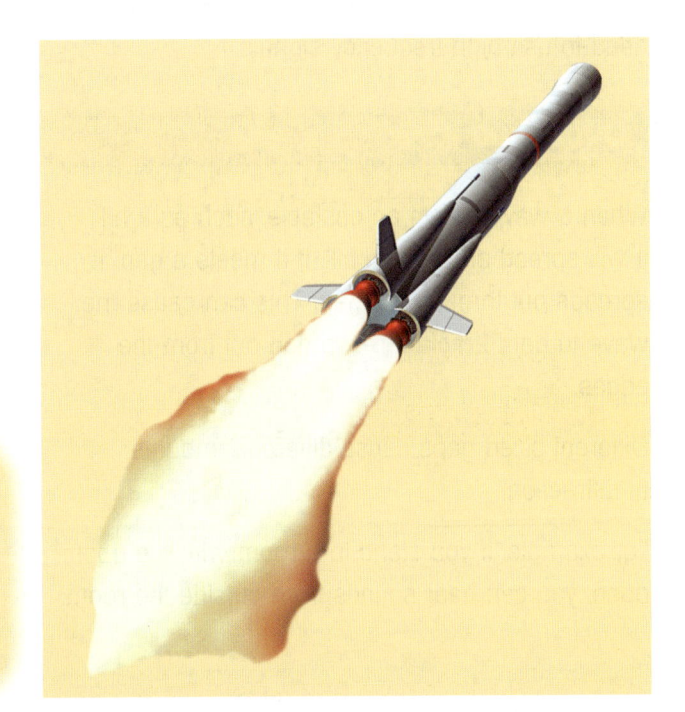

Quick Test

1. List two examples of scalar quantities and two examples of vector quantities.
2. State the equation used to calculate momentum.
3. **HT** What is the result of spreading the change in momentum during a collision over a longer time?

P5 Satellite Communication

Radio Waves

Radio waves have a very long wavelength (1m–10km). Different **frequencies** of **radio waves** are affected by the Earth's atmosphere in different ways:

1. Some frequencies (between 30 MHz and 30 GHz) pass through the Earth's atmosphere (relatively short wavelength).
2. Some frequencies (above 30 GHz) are reduced in strength, or even stopped, by the Earth's atmosphere. They are **absorbed** and **scattered** by rain, dust and other atmospheric effects.
3. Some frequencies (below 30 MHz) are reflected by a part of the Earth's upper atmosphere called the **ionosphere**.

The same frequencies can't be used to send information to all types of satellite. Low orbiting satellites use low frequency signals. Geostationary satellites are much further above the Earth so they need to use high frequency signals.

Microwaves have a higher frequency, and shorter wavelength, than radio waves. They are used to transmit information to orbiting artificial satellites, which then retransmit information back to Earth.

Diffraction

When a wave meets an obstacle, such as a hill, it will spread around the hill. If it meets a gap, it spreads out through the gap. This can cause the wave to be **diffracted**, i.e. spread out from the edges.

Different sized gaps cause different amounts of diffraction.

For example, if you stand in a room with the door open, you can hear sounds from outside the room.

This is because the wavelength of sound is about the same size as a doorway, so the sound waves spread out as they come through the door.

HT The amount a wave is diffracted depends on the size of the gap and the wavelength of the wave:
- Large gaps allow waves to pass straight through without diffracting.
- Diffraction is most obvious when the size of the gap is equal to the wavelength.

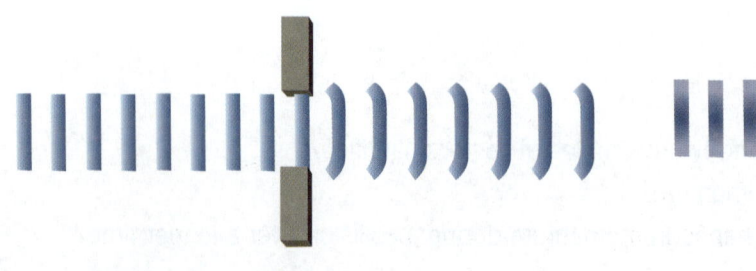

Gap larger than wavelength – slight diffraction

Gap same size as wavelength – increased diffraction

Key Words   Frequency • Ionosphere • Wavelength • Diffraction

Satellite Communication P5

Diffraction of Radio Waves

Diffraction makes radio waves useful for television and radio broadcasts because, by spreading out, the waves can effectively get around obstacles.

Owing to their very long **wavelengths**, it's relatively easy for radio waves to diffract around obstacles and the horizon. This means that long wavelength radio waves have a very long **range**.

The receiving dish and the transmitter must be in exact alignment.

HT The a size of an aerial dish used to receive microwaves must be much larger than the wavelength of those microwaves. This produces very little diffraction of the waves.

When a long wavelength radio wave encounters a hill, the points on the wavefront near the hill set off new waves. These waves are curved, which is why the wave begins to spread round the hill.

Microwaves have a short wavelength, so they don't diffract much around large obstacles. This is why microwaves are only sent in thin beams when transmitting information.

This means that the receiving dish and satellite must be in exact alignment.

Receiving Programmes

Special equipment is needed to receive radio and television programmes. An aerial, such as a metal rod, can be used to pick up a radio signal.

A satellite signal can only be picked up using a 'dish'. The dish is curved to focus all the microwaves onto the receiver at its centre.

Satellites use digital signals because they consist of on (1) and off (0) pulses only. This means they maintain their quality over longer distances and less information is lost during transmission.

Quick Test

1. What is the typical wavelength of radio waves?
2. What effect can the Earth's atmosphere have on radio waves above 30GHz?
3. Why are radio waves refracted as they pass through the ionosphere?
4. **HT** Why do radio waves, but not microwaves, easily diffract around hills?

P5 Nature of Waves

How Light Travels

Light, like all **electromagnetic waves**, is a transverse wave and travels in straight lines. As a result, you see sharp-edged shadows and a solar eclipse when the Moon passes between the Sun and the Earth.

Diffraction and **refraction** can make light look as though it bends.

When light is diffracted, the diffracted waves behave like separate beams of light, and can overlap one another.

Interference

When two waves overlap, it causes **interference**. Interference produces areas of:

- **reinforcement** (where waves add together):

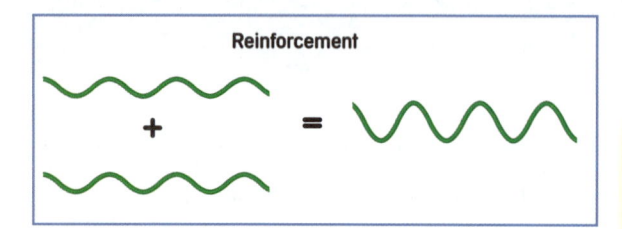

- **cancellation** (where waves subtract from each other):

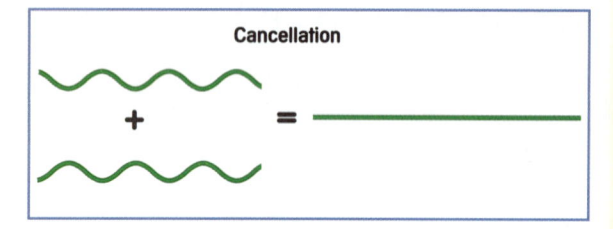

For example, when water waves overlap:
- areas of reinforcement are where the ripples are deeper, because their height is made up of two ripples added together.
- areas of cancellation are where the water's surface is flat, because the peak of one wave fills in the trough of the other.

	Effect of Reinforcement	Effect of Cancellation
Sound waves	Loud areas	Quiet areas
Light waves	Bright areas	Dark areas

A stable interference pattern is only produced when the wave sources are **coherent** (have the same frequency), so light sources are **monochromatic**. Interference patterns are evidence for the wave nature of light.

> **HT** Coherent wave sources:
> - have the same frequency
> - are in phase
> - have the same amplitude.
>
> **Constructive interference** (reinforcement) occurs when identical waves arrive **in phase** at a point. This produces a wave with larger amplitude, so you see bright fringes.
>
> **Destructive interference** (cancellation) occurs when identical waves arrive **out of phase**. The amplitude of the resulting wave is zero, so you see dark fringes. 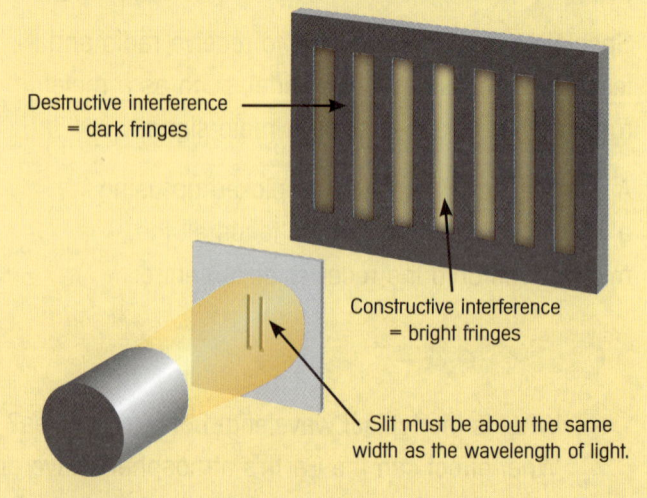
>
> Destructive interference = dark fringes
> Constructive interference = bright fringes
> Slit must be about the same width as the wavelength of light.
>
> Replacing the double slit with a single slit results in a pattern with a much brighter central fringe.

Key Words Electromagnetic waves • Refraction • Interference

Nature of Waves P5

Path Difference

Even though two waves come from the same source, they may have taken different paths to reach an object.

For example, one wave could have reflected off a mirror while the other could have taken a direct path to the object.

If two waves have arrived at a point by different paths, then the **path difference** needs to be calculated. The path difference is:

- an **odd** number of half wavelengths for **destructive interference**
- an **even** number of half wavelengths for **constructive interference**.

Polarisation

Light waves are **electromagnetic**. All electromagnetic waves are **transverse waves**. This means that the **oscillation** of a wave is at 90° to the direction that the wave is travelling.

HT Polarisation is used in some sunglasses to reduce glare from sunlight. The light that gets through the sunglasses is plane polarised and, therefore, less bright.

When light is incident on water, the reflected light is *partly* plane polarised.

Polarising lenses work by absorbing light that's reflected off shiny surfaces (such as water), which have oscillations in certain directions.

Only transverse waves can be **plane polarised**. That is, if a material is a horizontal polariser:

- only horizontal oscillations can get through
- other oscillations are absorbed.

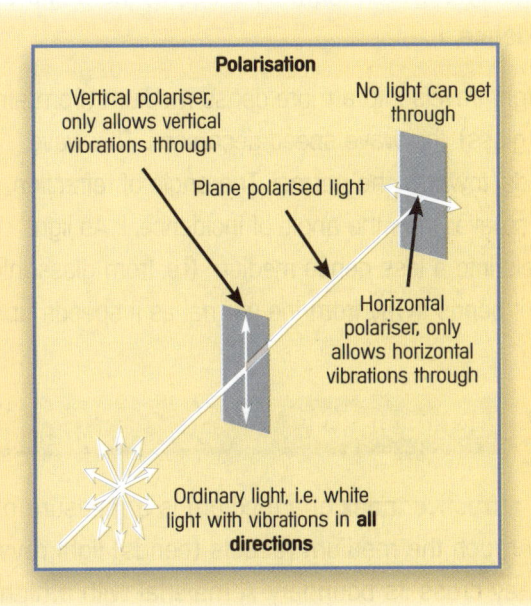

Polarisation

Vertical polariser, only allows vertical vibrations through

No light can get through

Plane polarised light

Horizontal polariser, only allows horizontal vibrations through

Ordinary light, i.e. white light with vibrations in **all directions**

Light – Wave or Particle?

There are two main theories about the nature of light.

During the 17th century, many scientists believed that light behaved like a **particle**. Light travels in straight lines and does not bend around objects. Because of this we observe shadows. Waves are able to bend around objects, so light couldn't be a wave. Reflection can be described in terms of light behaving like a particle. As light strikes a surface it exerts a pressure on the surface (very much like a ball hitting a wall).

But the particle model wasn't universally accepted amongst scientists. Scientists opposing this view believed that light is a series of **waves**. This theory was supported by experiments demonstrating diffraction of waves, interference and dispersion (splitting white light into a spectrum).

Key Words Electromagnetic • Transverse wave • Polarisation

P5 Refraction of Waves

Refraction

A **medium** is a substance that waves can travel through.

A line at 90° to the surface of a medium is known as the **normal**. When light travels from one medium to another at an angle to the normal it changes direction. This is **refraction**.

Refraction occurs at the boundary between two media due to a change in the wave speed as it travels through the different densities.

The angle at which the light ray travels through the second medium is the **angle of refraction, r**. This depends on the angle at which the light hits the boundary between the media, that is, the **angle of incidence, i**.

As light travels into a more dense medium (from air into glass), the wave speed decreases. The wave 'bends' towards the normal. The angle of refraction, r, is smaller than the angle of incidence, i. As light travels into a less dense medium (i.e. from glass into air), it bends away from the normal as it speeds up.

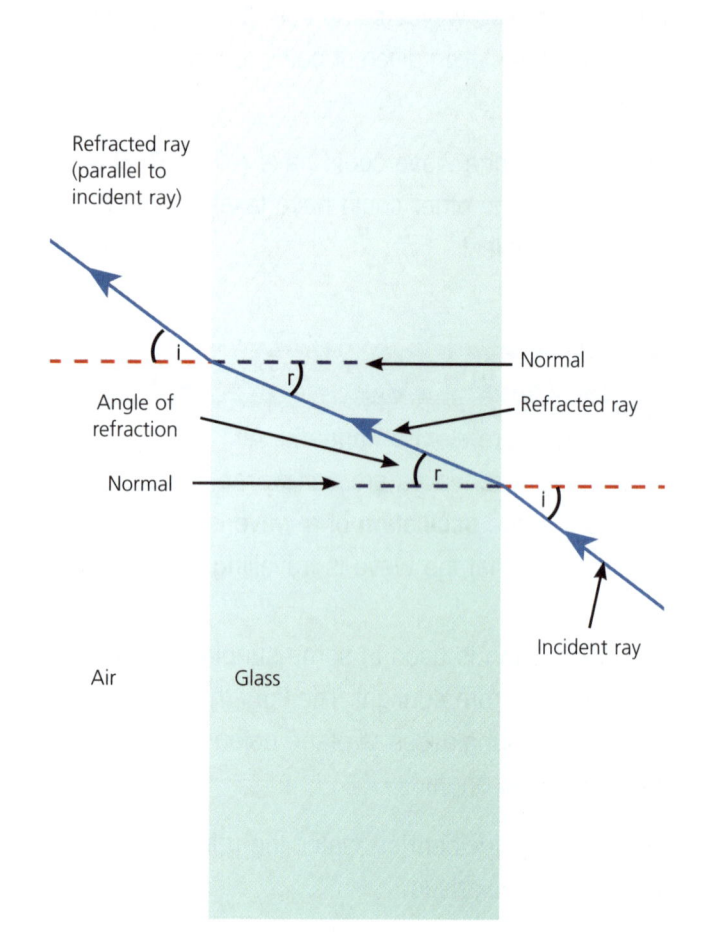

Refractive Index

The **refractive index** of a medium is a measure of how much the medium refracts (bends) light rays as they cross its boundary. A material with a higher refractive index produces a greater degree of bending.

The amount of refraction increases when there's a greater change in the light's wave speed as it passes from one medium to another.

The refractive index, **n**, can be calculated by comparing the speed of light in the medium with the fastest speed that light can travel (i.e. in a vacuum):

$$\text{Refractive index, n} = \frac{\text{Speed of light in a vacuum}}{\text{Speed of light in a medium}}$$

Materials with higher refractive indices have a smaller critical angle.

Material	Refractive Index	Critical Angles (degrees)
Water	1.33	48.8
Glass	1.50	41.8
Diamond	2.42	24.4

Key Words: Refraction • Refractive index

Refraction of Waves P5

HT Refractive Index (Cont.)

Diamond has a high refractive index. All light incident on the diamond–air boundary at an angle greater than 24.4 degrees will undergo **total internal reflection (TIR)**.

This is what produces the sparkling effect of diamonds.

Critical Angle

The **critical angle** is the maximum angle of incidence (measured from the normal) before **total internal reflection** (TIR) occurs. Different media have different critical angles.

Not all light is refracted when it leaves glass or water to travel through air. Some of the light is reflected from the surface:

1. If the angle of incidence is **less than** the critical angle, most of the light is refracted into the air.
2. If light hits the boundary at **exactly** the critical angle, it undergoes maximum refraction, emerging at 90° to the normal.
3. If the angle of incidence is **larger than** the critical angle, no light is refracted, i.e. all the light is **reflected** back into the medium. This is known as **total internal reflection**.

Different media (materials) have different critical angles.

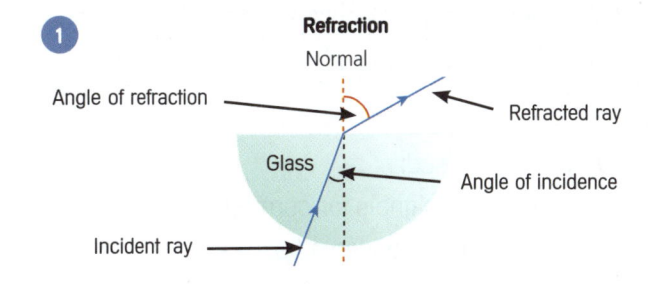

1 Refraction — Normal, Angle of refraction, Refracted ray, Glass, Angle of incidence, Incident ray

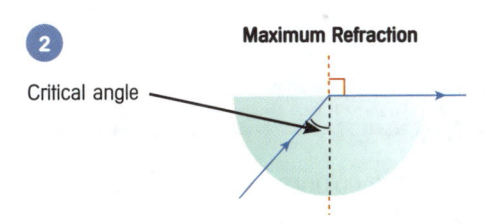

2 Maximum Refraction — Critical angle

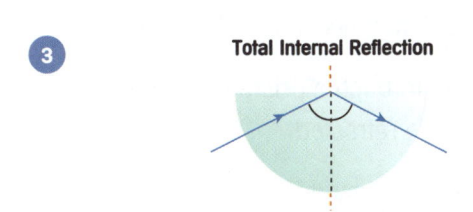

3 Total Internal Reflection

HT Total internal reflection relies on light being refracted away from the normal as the light ray speeds up. Therefore, total internal reflection only occurs when:
- light travels from a medium with a high refractive index into a medium with a lower refractive index
- the angle of incidence is more than the critical angle.

The higher a medium's refractive index, the lower its critical angle. The critical angle, **c**, can be calculated using the following equation:

$$\sin c = \frac{n_r}{n_i}$$

Where: n_r = refractive index of air
n_i = refractive index of medium

Key Words — Critical angle • Total internal reflection

P5 Refraction of Waves

Uses of Total Internal Reflection

Uses of total internal reflection include optical fibres and bike reflectors.

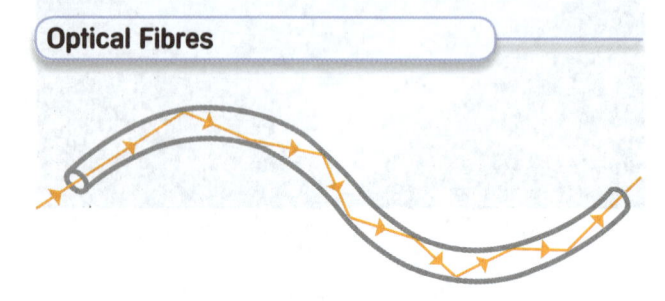

Optical Fibres

Light incident on the glass–air boundary at an angle greater than the critical angle is reflected (TIR). In this way, light travels down the length of the fibre optic cable.

Fibre optics are used:
- to send digital signals for communication
- in endoscopes to observe tissues inside the body.

Bike Reflectors

The light undergoes total internal reflection at the plastic–air boundary and leaves the reflector parallel to the ray of light entering.

Cat's eyes on the road and road signs work in a similar way.

Dispersion

Light is made up of the colours of the **spectrum**. All of the colours travel at the same speed in a vacuum, but at different speeds in other media.

When light travels through a prism it's slowed down, and therefore refracted.

Different colours refract by different amounts:
- Blue/violet light is slowed down the most.
- Red light is slowed down the least.

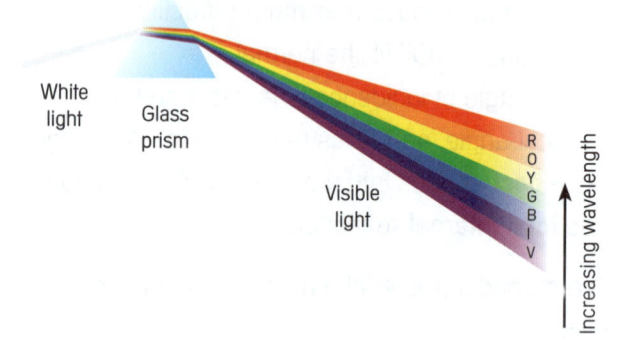

This means that blue light is **deviated** (changes direction) more than red light. This is **dispersion**.

HT The spectral colours have different wavelengths, which is why they are slowed down by different amounts when they travel through a prism.

The colours that have shorter wavelengths are slowed and deviated more than the colours that have longer wavelengths. Therefore, glass has a higher refractive index for the colours that have shorter wavelengths. Blue light has a greater refractive index than red light.

Key Words | Dispersion

Optics P5

Convex Lenses

A **convex lens** is a **converging** lens. When light rays pass through it they meet at a focus.

The **focal length** is the distance between the **centre** of the lens and the **focal point** (focus). Fatter lenses refract light more so they have shorter focal lengths.

Light passing through the optical centre is not refracted. If a beam of light **parallel** to the axis passes through a convex lens, it will pass through the focal point. If a **diverging** beam of light passes through a convex lens, the light will converge but will not hit the focal point. Convex lenses can be used as magnifying glasses, in cameras, projectors and some spectacles.

In cameras and projectors, light passes through the convex lens and converges to create a **real image** on a screen. For the image to be in focus, the lens has to be moved so that the image forms on the screen where the rays from a particular point on the object meet at a point on the screen.

Convex Lens

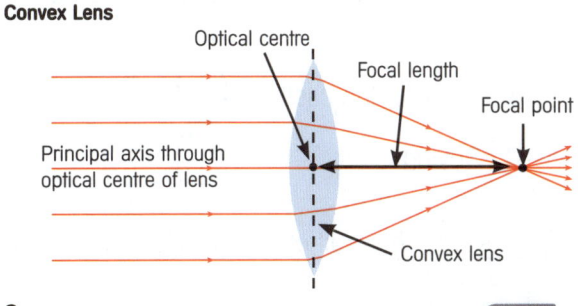

Camera — The image formed is smaller and nearer to the lens than the object.

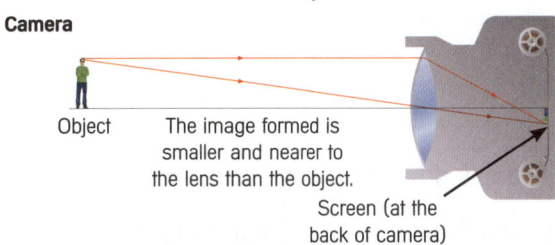

Projector

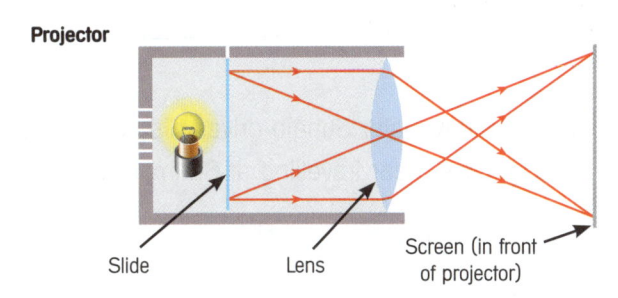

HT Real images can be projected onto a screen and are always **inverted** (upside down). **Virtual images** are the right way up, but they can't be projected onto a screen.

Ray diagrams can be drawn to work out the position and size of an image formed by a convex lens:
1. Draw a ray from the bottom of the object (O), parallel to the axis, through the centre of the lens.
2. Draw a ray from the top of the object through the centre of the lens.
3. Draw another ray from the top of the object (O), this time parallel to the axis and only as far as the lens. Continue the ray from the lens so that it passes through the focal point (F).
4. The point at which the rays join is the top of the image (I).

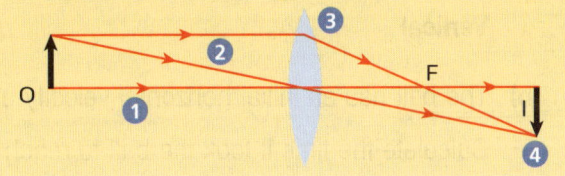

Magnification

Magnification is a measure of how much bigger the image is than the object:

$$\text{Magnification} = \frac{\text{Image size}}{\text{Object size}}$$

Quick Test
1. What is the focal length?
2. Which colour of the spectrum is refracted the most as it passes into a prism?

Key Words   Convex lens • Focal length • Focal point • Real image • Virtual image • Magnification

P5 Exam Practice Questions

1. Satellites are objects that orbit planets in space. They can be natural or artificial.

   a) Which of the following options is not a use of a satellite in low polar orbit? Tick (✓) the correct option. [1]

   A Weather forecasting ☐   B GPS ☐
   C Spying ☐   D Imaging the Earth's surface ☐

   b) Describe the orbit of a geostationary satellite. [2]

2. Suhaib is driving his new car.

   a) The first time he goes out, he takes 10 minutes to travel 6km. What is his average speed in m/s? [2]

   b) A few days later Suhaib drives his new car to his friend's house. He travels at 70km/h and overtakes a car travelling at 60km/h. What is his relative speed? [1]

   c) Is speed a scalar or a vector quantity? Explain your answer. [1]

3. a) Elaine kicks a ball horizontally off the edge of a cliff. Describe what happens to the projectile's velocity in the horizontal direction and in the vertical direction as it falls. [2]

   Horizontal

   Vertical

   b) The ball has an initial horizontal velocity of 6m/s. It hits the ground 18m from the base of the cliff. Calculate the time it took the ball to reach the ground. [2]

   c) The initial vertical velocity of the ball was 0m/s. Calculate the height of the cliff (using g = 10m/s^2). [3]

Exam Practice Questions P5

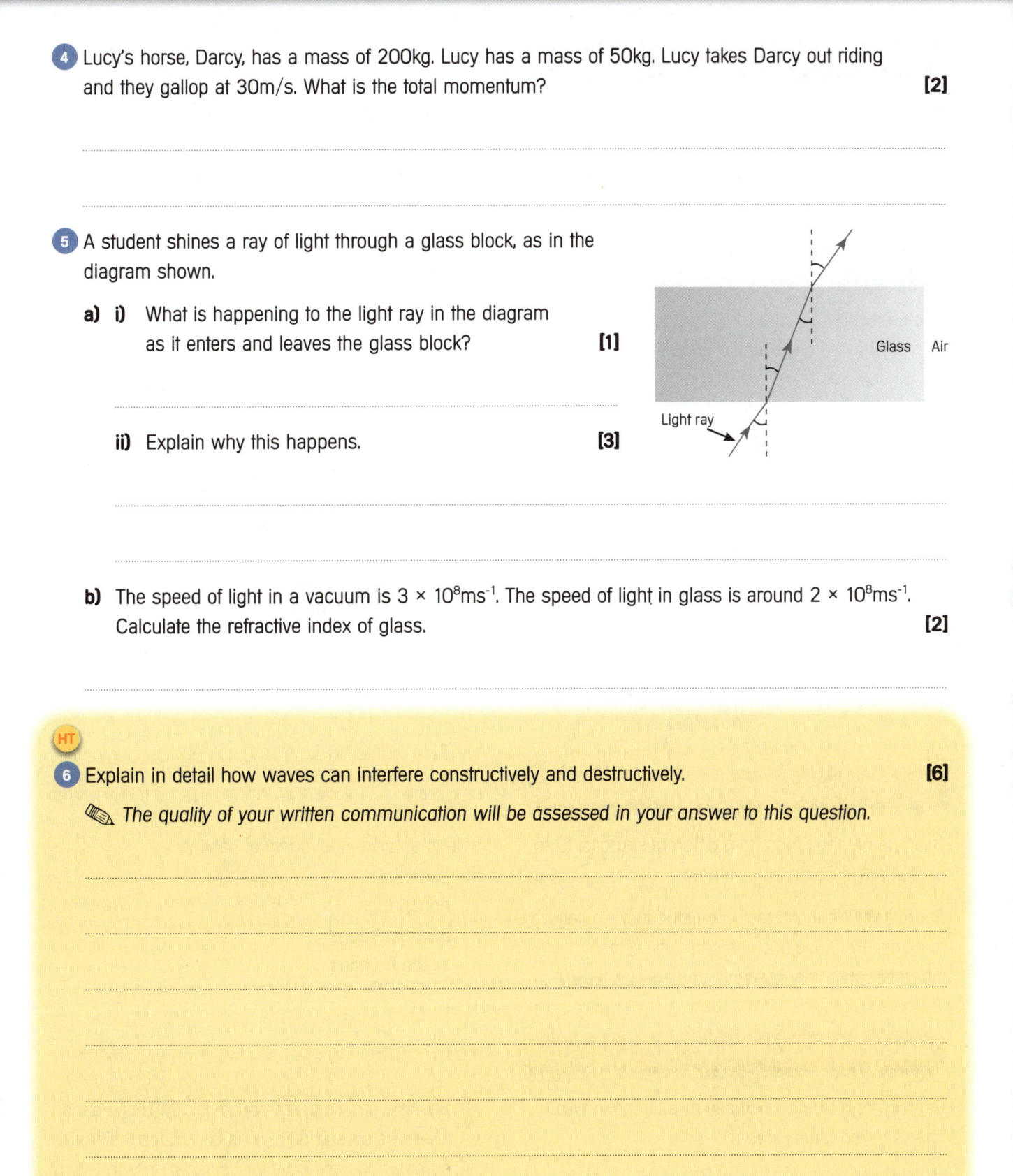

4 Lucy's horse, Darcy, has a mass of 200kg. Lucy has a mass of 50kg. Lucy takes Darcy out riding and they gallop at 30m/s. What is the total momentum? [2]

5 A student shines a ray of light through a glass block, as in the diagram shown.

   a) i) What is happening to the light ray in the diagram as it enters and leaves the glass block? [1]

      ii) Explain why this happens. [3]

   b) The speed of light in a vacuum is $3 \times 10^8 ms^{-1}$. The speed of light in glass is around $2 \times 10^8 ms^{-1}$. Calculate the refractive index of glass. [2]

6 Explain in detail how waves can interfere constructively and destructively. [6]

   The quality of your written communication will be assessed in your answer to this question.

B6 Understanding Microbes

Bacterial Cells

Bacteria are microscopic single-celled organisms. They're smaller and simpler than animal and plant cells. The largest bacteria are only a few microns (i.e. thousandths of a millimetre) long.

Bacterial cells are simpler than plant and animal cells: bacterial cells don't have a 'true' nucleus, mitochondria, chloroplasts or a vacuole.

Describing Bacterial Cells

Bacterial cells:
- may have a flagellum (a whip-like tail) for movement
- have a cell wall to maintain their shape and stop the bacterium from absorbing water and bursting
- have bacterial DNA for cell replication and to control the cell's activities.

A bacterial cell can be classified by its shape:

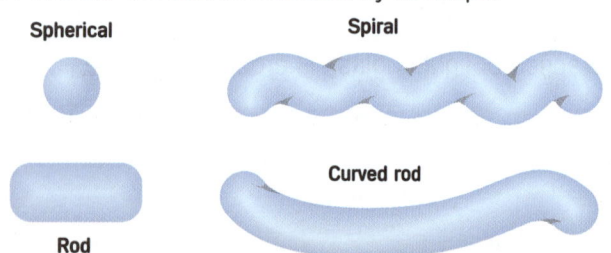

Spherical
Spiral
Curved rod
Rod

E. coli – An Example of a Flagellate Bacillus

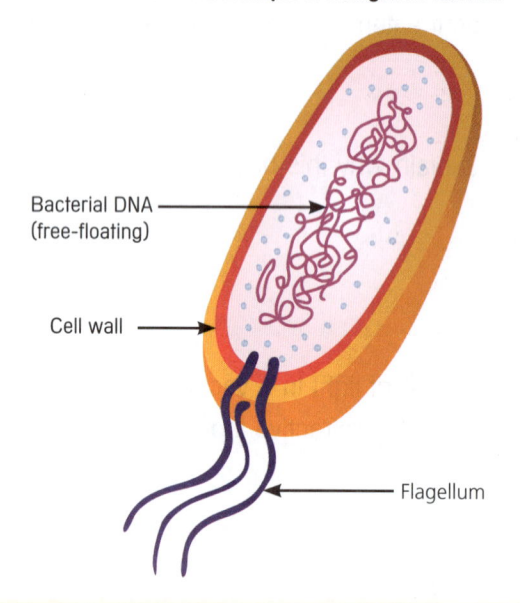

- Bacterial DNA (free-floating)
- Cell wall
- Flagellum

HT Bacterial Food Sources

Bacteria get their food from different sources. Some bacteria feed on organic nutrients.

Some bacteria make their own food in a similar way to plants. Because bacteria can use so many different sources of nutrients and energy, they're able to survive in a variety of habitats, for example:
- hot springs
- acid peat bogs
- inside humans.

Bacterial Reproduction

Bacteria **reproduce asexually** by splitting in two. This is called **binary fission**.

Bacteria reproduce rapidly in the right conditions. They can be grown commercially on a large scale in tanks called **fermenters**.

HT Bacteria grow and reproduce quickly. This means:
- diseases spread quickly as conditions inside the human body are ideal for bacterial growth (warm, moist, food available)
- food can become contaminated by bacteria and the toxic waste produced by bacteria as they feed. Food can spoil very quickly.

Key Words: Bacteria • Flagellum • DNA • Fermenter

Understanding Microbes B6

Viruses

Viruses are not living cells. They can only reproduce in other living cells. They attack specific cells and can infect plant, bacterial or animal cells. They are much smaller than bacteria or fungi.

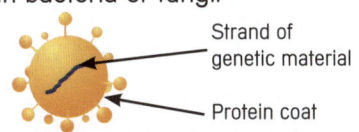

Strand of genetic material
Protein coat

HT To invade a living cell:
1. The virus attaches to a host cell and injects its genetic material into the cell.
2. It uses the cell to make components for a new virus.
3. The host cell splits open to release the virus.

Yeast

Yeast is a single-celled **fungus**. Yeast cells reproduce asexually by **budding**.

Yeast cells reproduce very quickly under the right conditions. They need:
- lots of sugar
- optimum temperature and pH
- the removal of waste products, such as **alcohol**, which poison the yeast.

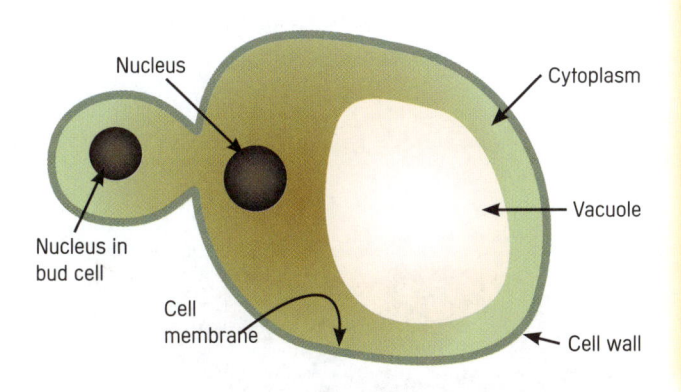

The chromosomes are copied and a new nucleus is made. The new cell 'buds' off the parent. This is known as 'budding'.

HT **Temperature and Yeast Growth**

The growth rate of yeast doubles with every 10°C rise in temperature. So, increasing the temperature increases the rate of **growth**. But, above 40°C, the yeast enzymes are **denatured**, which causes the growth rate to slow down.

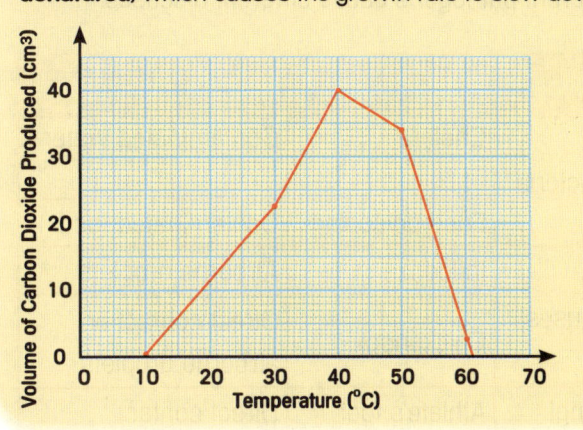

Diagram labels: Nucleus, Cytoplasm, Vacuole, Cell wall, Cell membrane, Nucleus in bud cell

Graph: Volume of Carbon Dioxide Produced (cm³) vs Temperature (°C)

Aseptic Techniques

Aseptic **technique** is the process of growing and transferring bacteria without contaminating the sample by touching or breathing on it, and without any loss of microbes to the surroundings.

Sterile agar plates are prepared with nutrient agar containing the food and water microbes need to grow. Use a sterile swab to wipe across the area you wish to test for microbes. Quickly lift just a corner of the agar plate (just enough to wipe the swab across the surface of the agar). Swiftly replace the lid and seal it down. Incubate in a warm place. After 24 hours, colonies of bacteria will be visible. Do not re-open.

HT It's important to safely handle bacteria by using aseptic technique. This ensures that no unexpected harmful bacteria are grown in large amounts which could make people ill. It safeguards people from being exposed to pathogenic microbes.

Key Words   Virus • Yeast • Fungi • Budding • Alcohol • Aseptic

B6 Harmful Microorganisms

Pathogens

Pathogens are **microorganisms** that cause disease. Some bacteria are pathogens. **Viruses** and **fungi** can also be pathogens.

Pathogens reproduce very quickly once inside the body. This is the disease's incubation period and initially there might not be any symptoms. As they multiply, pathogens produce **toxins**, which start to give the symptoms of the disease, such as fever.

Pathogens can enter your body in different ways:
- Airborne microorganisms enter through your **nose**.
- Microorganisms in contaminated food and water enter through your **mouth**.
- Microorganisms can be injected through the skin, e.g. **insect bites**, **infected needles** or **wounds**.
- Microorganisms can be passed on through the reproductive organs **during sex**.

The body prevents entry of microbes in the following ways:
- The lungs have tiny hairs which trap and waft out air borne microbes
- The stomach has acid which kills microbes that have gained entry through contaminated food or water
- The skin makes sebum, an anti-microbial, oily substance that kills microbes passed on via contact.

If microbes do get into the body via a cut, a scab is quickly made and white cells rush to the area to fight microbes.

Diseases

Different pathogens cause different diseases.

Pathogen	Illness Caused	How it's Transmitted
Bacteria	Cholera	Contaminated water
	Food poisoning	Contaminated food
Viruses	Influenza	Airborne droplets
	Chickenpox	Direct contact or airborne droplets
Fungi	Athlete's foot	Direct contact

Natural Disasters

Natural disasters, like earthquakes, hurricanes or volcanic eruptions, can kill thousands of people.

Many die in the aftermath of a natural disaster due to the rapid spread of diseases such as cholera and food poisoning.

Diseases spread quickly because:
- sewage systems and water supplies can be damaged so drinking water gets contaminated
- electrical supplies can be damaged so fridges and freezers stop working and food goes off
- the energy supply is disrupted, making it difficult to cook food properly
- hospitals and medical supplies get destroyed
- roads may be damaged, making it hard to reach sick or injured people.

Key Words: Pathogen • Microorganism • Toxin

Harmful Microorganisms B6

The Germ Theory of Disease

In the 1860s, **Louis Pasteur** showed that microorganisms in the air were the cause of food decay (not just the air itself, as people had previously thought).

This led to the **germ theory of disease** which explained that microorganisms, passed from one person to another, caused many diseases.

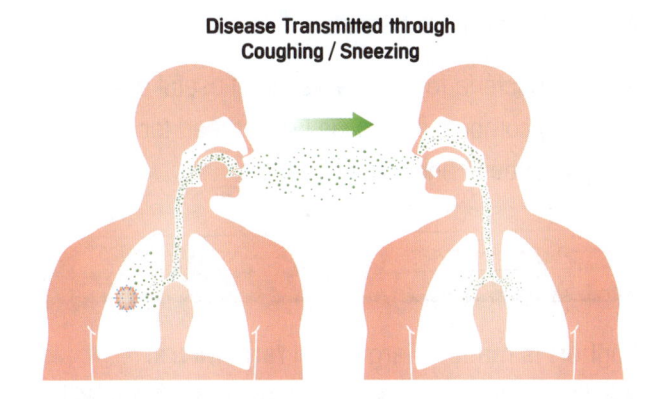

Disease Transmitted through Coughing / Sneezing

The Development of Antiseptics

In 1865, **Lister**, a surgeon, noticed that wounds often became infected after operations.

He realised that spraying wounds with **carbolic acid** prevented wound infection.

Carbolic acid is an **antiseptic** and kills bacteria.

Antiseptics are used today to kill bacteria in wounds on the skin, so preventing the spread of disease.

The Discovery of Penicillin

In 1928, **Fleming** accidentally discovered **penicillin**, an **antibiotic**.

When some of his bacterial culture plates got contaminated with penicillium mould, he noticed that the mould killed the surrounding bacteria.

He used the mould to make the first antibiotic to treat bacterial infections.

Harmful bacteria can be controlled by using antibiotics, but viruses are unaffected by antibiotics. Due to the overuse of antibiotics, some bacteria have developed resistance to them through natural selection.

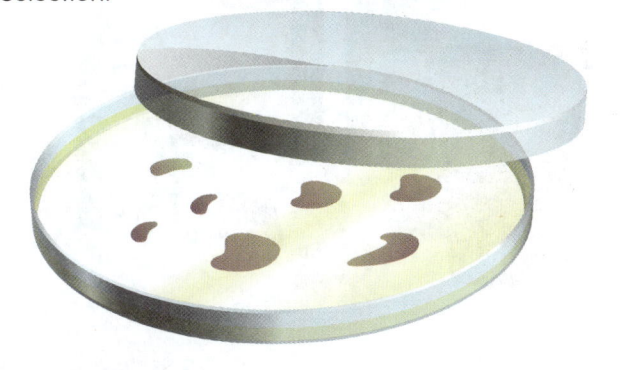

Some strains of bacteria are developing resistance to antibiotics through **natural selection**.

One bacterium may survive the antibiotic treatment due to a genetic change. This bacterium can then rapidly multiply, producing millions of resistant bacterial cells leading to an infection that is resistant to antibiotic treatment. This has become a huge problem recently.

HT To reduce the appearance of bacteria which are resistant to antibiotics, doctors now only prescribe antibiotics where really necessary and patients should always complete the treatment.

Quick Test

1. Describe the structure of a virus.
2. List the main shapes of bacteria.
3. How can microbes enter the body?
4. Which scientist did pioneering work on developing antiseptics?

Key Words Antiseptic • Penicillin • Antibiotics

B6 Useful Microorganisms

Useful Bacteria

Not all bacteria are harmful.

We use bacteria to make a range of useful products including compost and silage (winter feed for cattle), vinegar, cheese and yoghurt.

Making Yoghurt

Yoghurt is made in large steel **fermenters**:

1. The equipment is sterilised using steam to kill any **pathogens**.
2. Raw milk is heated to 80°C to kill bacteria, and then quickly cooled. This is **pasteurisation**.
3. A live bacterial culture is added to the warm milk. The mixture is **incubated** for several hours.
4. The bacteria reproduce and feed on the **lactose** sugar in the milk, producing **lactic acid**, which gives a sharp taste to the yoghurt and thickens and preserves it.
5. The manufacturer **samples** the yoghurt for consistency and flavour.
6. Flavours and colours might be added before packaging.

HT The bacteria *Lactobacillus* feed on the lactose sugar in the milk, breaking it down to produce lactic acid, which gives the yoghurt its taste and texture.

Fermentation

Fermentation is **anaerobic respiration** in yeast. It produces alcohol and is used to make alcoholic drinks.

Sugars are broken down by yeast in the absence of oxygen to produce the alcohol.

Different fruits and seeds are used to provide the **yeast** with sugars and give the drinks flavour.

Carbon dioxide is also produced during fermentation:

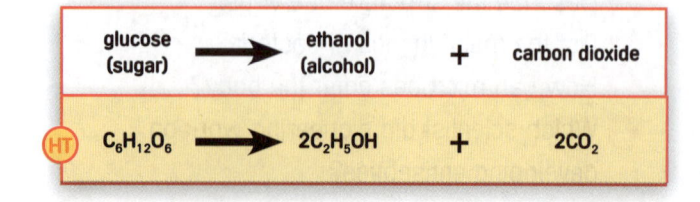

glucose (sugar) $\rightarrow$ ethanol (alcohol) + carbon dioxide

HT $C_6H_{12}O_6 \rightarrow 2C_2H_5OH + 2CO_2$

68 | Key Words | **Fermentation • Anaerobic respiration**

Useful Microorganisms B6

Fermentation (Cont.)

Yeast cells feed on **sugars**. They can respire with oxygen (**aerobic respiration**) or without oxygen (**anaerobic respiration**) to release energy from sugar.

Brewers obviously want yeast to carry out anaerobic respiration as alcohol is a by-product.

Brewing Beer

1. Extracting sugar – barley seeds are mixed with water and allowed to sprout, turning the starch in the seeds into sugars.
2. Hops are added to give flavour to beer.
3. Yeast is added to ferment the sugars into alcohol. The mixture is kept warm so the yeast **reproduces** and **respires**.
4. The tank is sealed so the yeast can respire **anaerobically** producing alcohol. This also stops unwanted microorganisms spoiling the beer.
5. A chemical is added to make the yeast settle, leaving a clear liquid. This is called **clarifying** or **clearing**.
6. The beer is **pasteurised** to kill harmful microorganisms.
7. The beer is bottled or put in sealed casks (casking or bottling).

Yeast must be filtered out (or killed by heat treatment) if the beer's going to be bottled. Otherwise, it would continue to respire, producing carbon dioxide which would make the bottles explode.

Beer is pasteurised by heating to 72°C for 15 seconds, then cooling quickly. This kills harmful microorganisms but doesn't affect the taste much. This needs to be done to bottled beers to prevent spoilage by microbes.

Distilling Spirits

Distillation of alcoholic drinks makes the alcohol more concentrated and is used to produce spirits. Because it produces very strong alcoholic drinks, distillation can only be done on licensed premises; it is a commercial process.

1. The liquid is heated to evaporate the alcohol.
2. The concentrated alcohol is trapped and cooled (condensed) back into a liquid.

The amount of alcohol in brewed drinks is limited because the yeast cells are killed by the alcohol they produce.

Some strains of yeast can tolerate higher concentrations of alcohol so they can be used to brew strong beers.

Quick Test

1. Suggest some useful ways in which bacteria are used.
2. What process is used to increase the alcoholic content of drinks?
3. Is fermentation an aerobic or anaerobic process?
4. What do *Lactobacillus* bacteria do in the yoghurt making process?

Key Words   Pasteurisation • Distillation

B6 Biofuels

Biofuels

Plants grow new plant tissues by using some of the glucose from **photosynthesis** to produce starch and cellulose. This new plant material is **biomass**.

Biomass can be **burned** to release energy to be used as a **fuel**. Some examples of biomass fuels are:
- **fast-growing trees**, e.g. pine burned to release energy
- **manure** or **other waste** – broken down by **bacteria** or **yeast** in a **fermenter** to release methane (**biogas**) which can be used to power electricity generators
- **sugar cane** – broken down by yeast in a fermenter to produce alcohol.

Biogas

When these bacteria feed on dead plant and animal material, they produce waste gases called **biogas**. Biogas contains:
- mainly methane
- some carbon dioxide
- traces of hydrogen, nitrogen and hydrogen sulfide.

> **HT** Biogas is a cleaner fuel than petrol or diesel, but it doesn't produce as much energy as natural gas.
> - Biogas that contains more than 50% methane burns easily and makes a good fuel.
> - Biogas that contains less than 10% methane is explosive.

Biogas Digesters

Biogas (mainly methane) can be made on a large scale using a **continuous flow method** in a **digester**. Organic material is added daily and the biogas is siphoned off and stored. The remaining solid sludge is used as **fertiliser**. The production of biogas is affected by temperature. At low temperatures, little biogas is produced. Above 45°C, no biogas is released.

Biogas digesters are useful in remote areas that don't have access to mains electricity. They can produce biogas from human sewage, which also solves the problem of safe sewage disposal. Biogas can be:
- burned to generate electricity, and to produce hot water and steam for central heating
- used as a fuel for buses and cars.

The rotting of organic material such as dead plants and animal waste occurs mainly in marshes, septic tanks and animal digestive systems. It produces a mixture of gases including methane, thanks to the action of bacteria.

Methane is given off in landfill sites as the microbes feed on the rubbish. This is dangerous as it's explosive. The site may not be safe to use for years.

A Biogas Digester

Gas trapped beneath metal gas holder — Biogas release tap
Waste material — Residual 'digested' sludge

> **HT** At low temperatures, the bacteria reproduce and respire slowly so little biogas is produced. At above 45°C, enzymes in the bacteria are **denatured** and the bacteria are killed. This is why biogas production is so dependent on temperature.

Key Words: Photosynthesis • Biomass • Biogas • Fertiliser

Biofuels B6

Biofuel

Biofuels, such as biogas, are a good alternative to fossil fuels, because burning biofuels produces:
- no increase in greenhouse gas levels
- no soot (particulates).

HT Burning biofuels doesn't cause an overall increase in greenhouse gas levels if:
- they are burned at the same rate as the biomass is being produced
- areas of land are not cleared of other vegetation in order to grow crops for biofuels.

In some areas, the use of large areas of land to produce biofuels is resulting in habitat loss and the potential extinction of species.

Alcohol, made from yeast, can also be used as a clean biofuel. Alcohol doesn't contain as much energy as petrol so it's mixed with petrol or diesel to make **gasohol**, which is used to run cars in countries like Brazil.

HT In countries like Brazil, gasohol is more economically viable because they have little or no oil reserves from which to produce fuel to run cars.

They do, however, have plenty sugar cane and so they ferment this to produce alcohol which is used to make gasohol.

Quick Test

1. Give two examples of fuels from biomass.
2. How can biogas be produced on a large scale?
3. What are the advantages of using biofuels?
4. What is the name of the biofuel used in Brazil to power cars?

Key Words **Biofuel**

B6 Life in Soil

Soil

Soil is a mixture of:
- different sized mineral particles
- **humus** (dead animal and plant material)
- water
- living organisms (e.g. microscopic protozoans, nematode worms, earthworms, insects, slugs, snails, bacteria)
- air (oxygen).

Living organisms need oxygen so they can respire, and water to stay alive. Soil provides both of these.

Plants need soil to grow. Soil provides them with:
- a source of minerals (e.g. nitrates, phosphates)
- water (for **photosynthesis** and **transpiration**)
- anchorage for roots (to hold the plant upright).

There are different types of soil, e.g. sandy, loam, clay. Sandy soil has larger mineral particles than clay soil. Loam is a soil that contains a mixture of clay and sand. If the dead material in soil is largely decomposed it is called **humus**.

HT When there's too much water in the soil, it leads to **waterlogging**: the water fills all the air spaces and excludes oxygen. Pushing holes into the soil aerates it, allowing oxygen to penetrate into it, and helping to drain the excess water.

Some soils are naturally **acidic**. This causes problems for organisms that can't survive in acidic conditions. It also means plants can't absorb minerals easily. So farmers and gardeners add **lime** to acidic soil to neutralise it. Mixing up the soil layers to distribute the lime helps neutralise the acid soil.

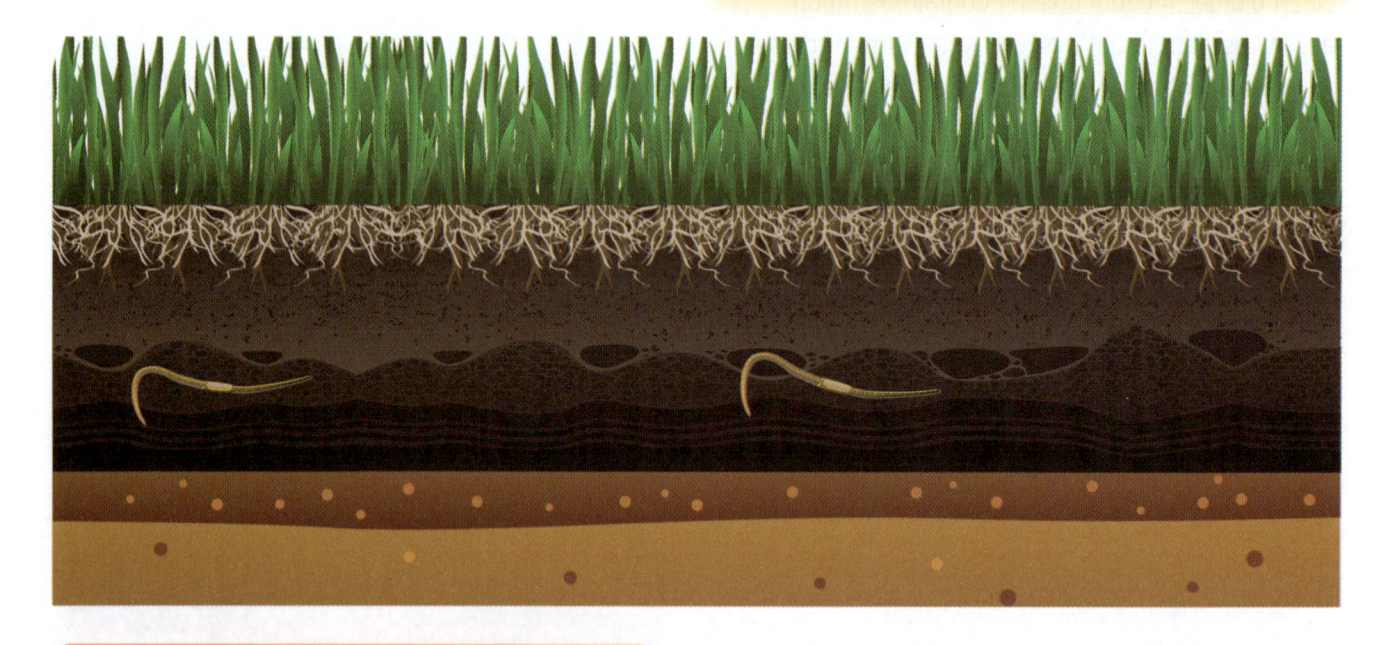

Humus

Humus is often described as the 'life force' of the soil. It helps soil to retain moisture and oxygen, which life in the soil depends on.

As it decomposes, important minerals are released for plant growth.

As humus particle size is quite big it increases the air spaces in soil and, so, the air content.

Key Words Humus • Photosynthesis • Transpiration

Life in Soil B6

Soil Experiments

Different soils can be compared in terms of their water, air and humus content.

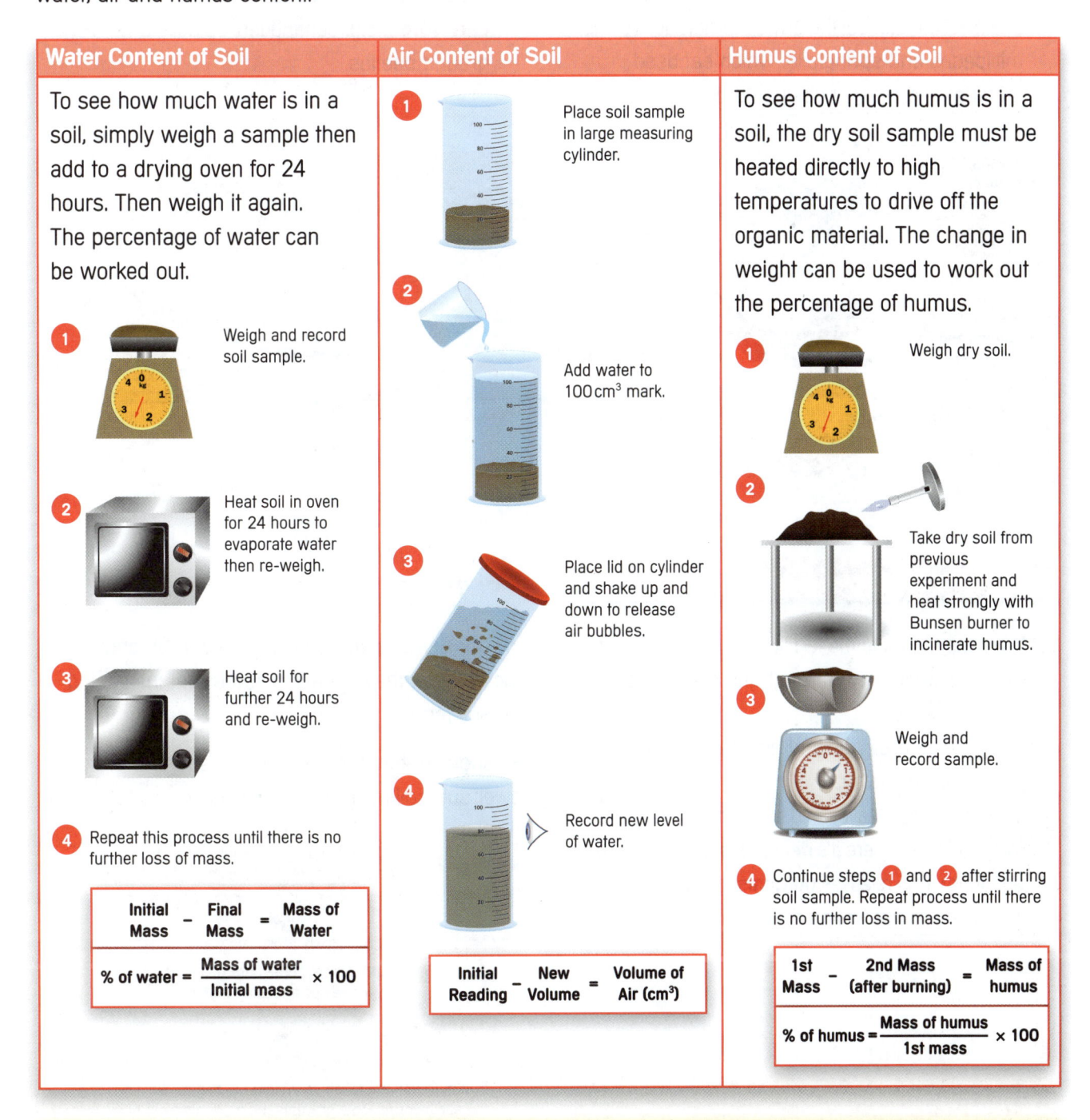

Water Content of Soil

To see how much water is in a soil, simply weigh a sample then add to a drying oven for 24 hours. Then weigh it again. The percentage of water can be worked out.

1. Weigh and record soil sample.
2. Heat soil in oven for 24 hours to evaporate water then re-weigh.
3. Heat soil for further 24 hours and re-weigh.
4. Repeat this process until there is no further loss of mass.

$$\text{Initial Mass} - \text{Final Mass} = \text{Mass of Water}$$

$$\% \text{ of water} = \frac{\text{Mass of water}}{\text{Initial mass}} \times 100$$

Air Content of Soil

1. Place soil sample in large measuring cylinder.
2. Add water to 100 cm³ mark.
3. Place lid on cylinder and shake up and down to release air bubbles.
4. Record new level of water.

$$\text{Initial Reading} - \text{New Volume} = \text{Volume of Air (cm}^3\text{)}$$

Humus Content of Soil

To see how much humus is in a soil, the dry soil sample must be heated directly to high temperatures to drive off the organic material. The change in weight can be used to work out the percentage of humus.

1. Weigh dry soil.
2. Take dry soil from previous experiment and heat strongly with Bunsen burner to incinerate humus.
3. Weigh and record sample.
4. Continue steps 1 and 2 after stirring soil sample. Repeat process until there is no further loss in mass.

$$\text{1st Mass} - \text{2nd Mass (after burning)} = \text{Mass of humus}$$

$$\% \text{ of humus} = \frac{\text{Mass of humus}}{\text{1st mass}} \times 100$$

HT When a dry soil is heated to high temperatures, the humus, which is made of carbon compounds, is converted to carbon dioxide and water. These are given off as gases so the sample weight goes down.

The size and number of pores in the soil determine the air content. When it rains, the water fills the pores, driving out the air.

B6 Life in Soil

Food Webs in Soil

Complex food webs exist in soil. Soil contains:
- **herbivores**, e.g. slugs, snails, wire worms
- **detritivores**, e.g. earthworms, nematode worms, millipedes and springtails, which eat dead material and break it down into humus
- **decomposers**, e.g. fungi, and bacteria which break down the humus
- **carnivores**, e.g. centipedes, spiders and ground beetles.

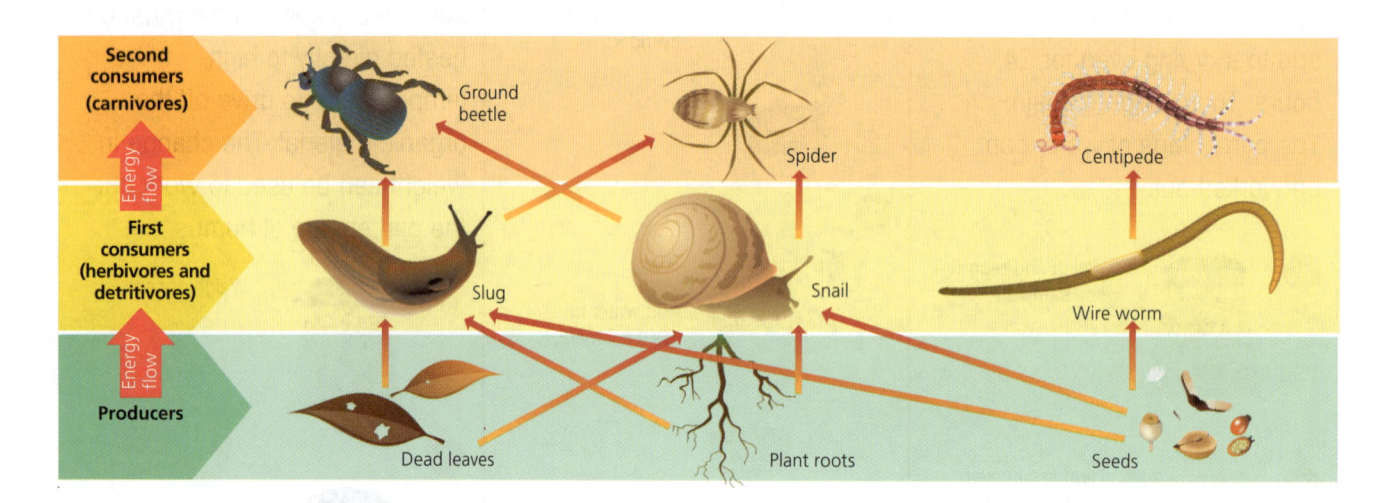

Second consumers (carnivores): Ground beetle, Spider, Centipede
First consumers (herbivores and detritivores): Slug, Snail, Wire worm
Producers: Dead leaves, Plant roots, Seeds
Energy flow

Earthworms

Earthworms increase the fertility and drainage of soil:
- They make burrows through the soil layers, mixing them up.
- They create drainage and air channels (aeration) with their burrows.
- They drag dead leaves and other organic matter into their burrows, where it's **decomposed** by bacteria and fungi. This releases **nutrients** into the soil.
- They help to **neutralise** acidic soil.

HT Charles Darwin studied earthworms and showed that they were very important in keeping the soil fertile.

He showed that they increased the fertility of the lower sub-soil by mixing the soil layers.

> An organic humus layer is formed on top of the soil as a result of decomposition.

> Nutrients (minerals) are released from the decomposing material.

> The nutrients are taken down into the deeper soil layers by earthworms. This prevents the nutrients from being washed away and it also aerates the soil and breaks it up.

Quick Test
1. Describe the main components in soil.
2. What does soil do for plants?
3. Name some herbivores in soil.
4. How can you improve soil?

Recycling is important so that the mineral elements trapped in the bodies of dead organisms can be made available to living organisms.

Key Words: Herbivore • Detritivore • Decomposers • Carnivore

Microscopic Life in Water B6

Life in Water

A wide variety of microorganisms live in water.

Advantages of Living in Water	Disadvantages of Living in Water
• No problem of water shortage or dehydration. • Less variation in temperature. • Water gives more support so organisms grow bigger without huge increases in skeleton size. • Waste is easily disposed of.	• Water is dense so it resists movement. • It might be difficult to control the absorption or release of water from living cells.

Marine Food Webs

Plankton are microscopic plants and animals. **Phytoplankton** (microscopic plants) and **zooplankton** (microscopic animals) live in water. Plankton have limited movement and rely on water currents.

Phytoplankton are the **producers** in aquatic food chains and food webs.

Phytoplankton make sugars by **photosynthesis**. Their growth is affected by temperature, light intensity and availability of minerals like nitrates and phosphates.

In summer, when conditions are good (light, warm, lots of minerals), the plankton grow quickly. In winter (less light, colder, fewer minerals), their growth slows down.

Light intensity and temperature vary at different depths.

An Aquatic Food Web

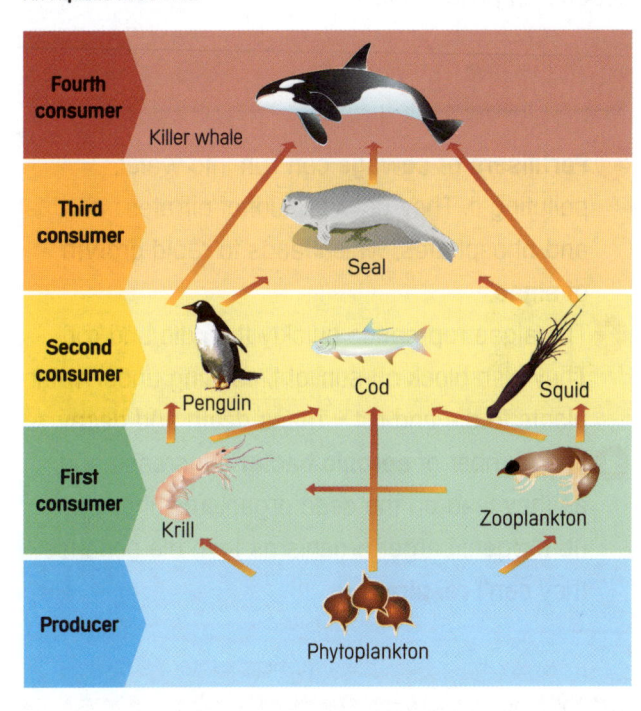

Fourth consumer — Killer whale
Third consumer — Seal
Second consumer — Penguin, Cod, Squid
First consumer — Krill, Zooplankton
Producer — Phytoplankton

HT Grazing food webs are most common in the oceans.

In the ocean depths many organisms rely on **marine snow**. Marine snow is the continuous shower of organic detritus falling from the upper layers of the ocean. It's made mainly of dead and dying plants and animals (e.g. plankton) and faecal material. Most marine snow is consumed by microbes and zooplankton and filter feeding animals. As sunlight can't reach deep sea ecosystems, these organisms rely heavily on marine snow.

Deep in the ocean some bacteria act as producers, making their own food like plants do. They have no light to do this but instead use other chemicals to make glucose. Many food chains in the deep dark ocean rely on these bacteria.

Key Words — Plankton • Producers • Marine snow

B6 Microscopic Life in Water

Water Pollution

Animals, plants and microorganisms are all affected by water **pollution** from:
- sewage
- oil
- PCBs (chemicals used in electrical devices)
- **fertilisers**
- pesticides
- detergents.

Aquatic microorganisms are very sensitive to pollution and pH changes caused by **acid rain**. The variety and number of aquatic microorganisms will depend on pollution levels.

Eutrophication

1. **Fertilisers** or **sewage** can run into water, polluting it. They provide a lot of nitrates and phosphates, which leads to rapid growth of **algae**.
2. The algae reproduce quickly then die and rot. They also block off sunlight, causing underwater plants to die and rot – mass death and decay.
3. The number of **aerobic bacteria** increase and, as they feed on the dead organisms, they use up oxygen. Larger organisms then die because they can't **respire**.

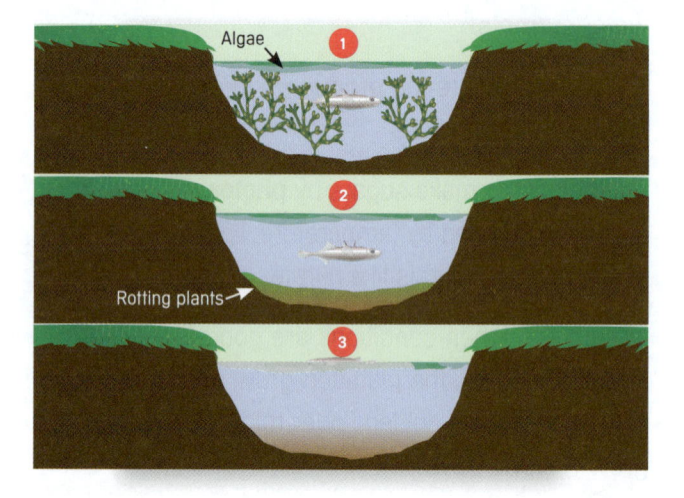

HT Bioaccumulation

Small amounts of toxic chemicals, such as PCBs and DDT, enter the food chain through **plankton**:
- **PCBs** are chemicals used to insulate electrical equipment.
- **DDT** is a powerful persistent insecticide.

If animals eat these chemicals, they can't break them down so they're stored in fat in the body.

Small amounts don't cause any harm, but at each trophic feeding level the chemicals accumulate in the tissues of the animals.

For example, if a whale eats penguins and seals that have eaten contaminated fish, the accumulative effect of the **toxins** can be enough to kill it.

Animals at the top of food chains like whales get a huge dose of these chemicals so they may die.

Key Words — Pollution • Fertiliser • Respiration

Microscopic Life in Water B6

Biological Indicators

Some animal species are very good **indicators** of water's cleanliness. They act as biological indicators for pH and oxygen levels.

For example, some insect larvae like mayfly or stonefly are sensitive to changes in oxygen and can only survive in clean, oxygenated water. Other insect larvae, like bloodworms and rat-tailed maggots, have special adaptations to survive in **polluted**, deoxygenated water.

Counting the total number of indicator organisms and the number of different species (the **biodiversity**) can show how polluted the water is.

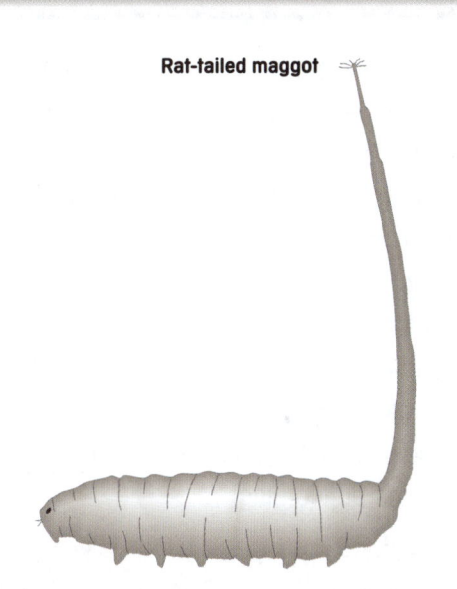

Rat-tailed maggot

HT Problems of Living in Water

Some microscopic organisms, such as amoeba, find it difficult to balance water. This is due to **osmosis**.

An amoeba is a single-celled organism that lives in freshwater. The water is more dilute than the amoeba's **cytoplasm** so water constantly **diffuses** into the cell by osmosis. The amoeba doesn't have a cell wall to prevent it bursting, so it has to use **active transport** to pump the water into **small vacuoles**. These small vacuoles join into one **contractile vacuole** which empties the water out of the cell.

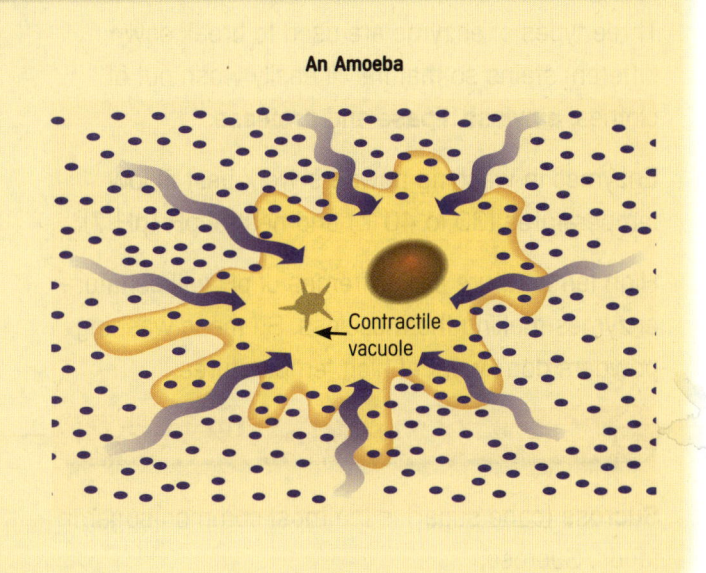

An Amoeba — Contractile vacuole

Quick Test

1. What is phytoplankton?
2. Name some pollutants of water.
3. What is the root cause of eutrophication?
4. HT DDT is a persistent pesticide. What organisms are most at risk from it and why?

Key Words Indicator species • Biodiversity • Active transport • Contractile vacuole

B6 Enzymes in Action

Using Enzymes

Enzymes are biological **catalysts** produced by living cells. They can be extracted from cells and used in a number of ways. For example:

- to separate the curds and whey when making cheese
- to extract juice from fruit
- to alter and improve the flavour of foods
- in medical products, such as **reagent sticks** that test for **glucose** in urine
- in biological washing powders to break down food stains on clothing.

> **HT** In areas with very acidic or very alkaline tap water, the enzymes don't work so well: the extreme pH changes the enzymes' shape, so they can't function. They are **denatured**.

Biological Washing Powders

Biological washing powders contain enzymes. Food, blood and grass stains on clothes are made from large insoluble molecules that are hard to wash away.

Three types of enzyme are used to break down different stains so that they'll easily wash out of clothes: **amylase**, **lipase** and **protease**.

Enzymes in washing powders work best at low temperatures (30 to 40°C) and neutral pH (pH 7).

High temperature and extremes of pH will denature enzymes making them useless. So these washing powders don't work at high temperatures.

> **HT** The soluble products of digestion are easily washed out of clothes.

Enzyme	Insoluble Stain	Soluble Product
Amylase	Carbohydrate, e.g. starch	**HT** Sugars
Lipase	Fat	**HT** Fatty acids, glycerol
Protease	Protein	**HT** Amino acids

Sweetening Food

Sucrose (cane sugar) is the most common sugar in foods. Sucrose:

- is made up of two smaller sugars
- can be broken down using the **sucrase** (or **invertase**) enzyme.

sucrose —invertase→ fructose + glucose

The products are much sweeter than sucrose. They're useful in the food industry for flavouring desserts and sweets without adding much sugar.

> **HT** Foods are sweetened using invertase by converting sucrose into fructose and glucose. These much sweeter products are used to sweeten diet food/low calorie food so less sugar is needed, meaning fewer calories are in the food.

Nutrition Information		
Typical Values	Flora light Per 100g	Flora light Per 10g
Energy	1459kJ/354kcal	146kJ/35kcal
Carbohydrate	2.8g	0.3g
- of which Sugars	trace	trace
Fat	38.0g	3.8g
- of which saturates	9.3g	0.9g
- monounsaturates	9.3g	0.9g
- polyunsaturates	19.0g	1.9g
Sodium	0.5g	0.1g
Salt (based on sodium)	1.3g	0.1g

Key Words Enzyme • Catalyst

Enzymes in Action B6

Lactose-free Milk

Some adults are **lactose intolerant**. This means they don't make the enzyme **lactase**, so they can't break down the lactose sugar in milk. As a result, lactose travels through their digestive system to the large intestine, where bacteria ferment the sugar, producing diarrhoea and gas.

Enzymes can be used to make lactose-free milk. Immobilised lactase enzyme can be added to the milk to break down lactose sugar into smaller sugars – **glucose** and **galactose** – which can easily be absorbed.

Adult cats can't digest cows' milk because they don't produce lactase, so they suffer from the same problems. This is why cat food manufacturers now make lactose-free cat milk.

Immobilised Enzymes

Extracting and purifying enzymes is an expensive business. So it's useful to be able to reclaim the enzymes after the reaction, to reuse them.

This is also important in food preparation because the enzymes mustn't contaminate the final food products.

Enzymes can be immobilised by:
- making them into alginate jelly beads (gel beads)
- putting them on reagent sticks.

They can then be easily separated from the reaction mixture. The mixture is not contaminated with enzymes. Immobilising enzymes in these ways is also useful because it means they can be used in **continuous flow processing**.

To make gel beads, the enzymes are mixed with alginate and the mixture is dropped into calcium chloride solution.

Testing for Sugar

People who have **diabetes** have to test their urine or blood for sugar every day to check blood glucose levels and to ensure they inject the right amount of **insulin**.

The **Benedict's test** can be used to test for sugar, but a large sample of blood or urine is needed. The sample is heated with Benedict's reagent. If the blue reagent turns red, then sugar is present.

Reagent sticks make it easy to test blood sugar. Immobilised enzymes are often incorporated onto reagent sticks e.g. the stick is dipped in urine or blood and changes colour according to the glucose level.

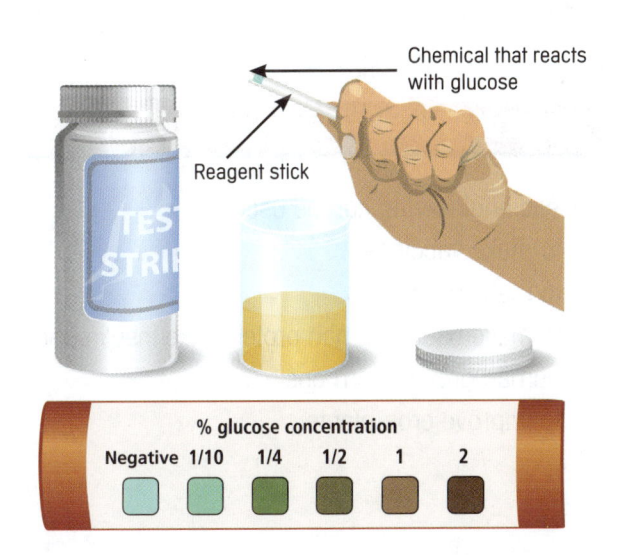

Key Words Diabetes • Insulin

B6 Gene Technology

Genetic Engineering

All living organisms use the same basic genetic code (DNA), so genes can be transferred from one organism to another altering the genetic code.

Genes from one organism can work in another. This is **genetic engineering**.

Section of DNA

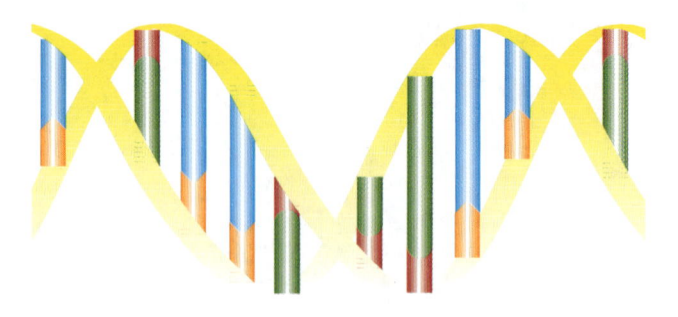

HT The genetic code is universal; the DNA structure for all organisms is the same.

Because of this, genes from one organism can work in another organism, making genetic engineering possible.

Genetic engineering can be used to change the characteristics of bacteria, plants or animals. An organism that has new genes inserted into it is called a **transgenic organism**.

1. The desirable gene in one organism is identified.
2. The gene is removed from the DNA.
3. The DNA of another organism is cut open and the new gene is inserted using enzymes.
4. The new gene works in the transgenic organism.
5. The transgenic organism is **cloned** to produce identical copies.

HT Different enzymes are used in genetic engineering:
- **Restriction enzymes** are used to cut open DNA leaving 'sticky ends'.
- **Ligase enzymes** are used to rejoin DNA strands. The 'sticky ends' rejoin the DNA strands.

Scientists use a technique called **assaying** to identify transgenic organisms because not all the bacteria will take up the new genes. When the new gene is inserted, a 'marker gene', for example, a gene that codes for **antibiotic resistance**, is also inserted.

The bacteria are then grown on an agar plate that contains the antibiotic. The transgenic bacteria can be identified because they survive and grow.

Uses of Genetic Engineering

Genetic engineering can be used:
- to make vaccines
- to make medicines
- to make useful human proteins like insulin and human growth hormone
- to improve crop plants.

Key Words Genetic engineering • Transgenic organism • Clone

Gene Technology B6

Producing Human Insulin

HT The loop of bacterial DNA is known as a **plasmid**. Plasmids are found in the cytoplasm of the bacterial cells.

Human **insulin** is produced using the following method:

1. The human gene for insulin production is identified. It's removed using a special **enzyme** which cuts through the **DNA** in precise places.
2. The enzyme is then used to cut open a loop of bacterial DNA in the cytoplasm.
3. Enzymes are used to insert the section of human insulin gene into the loop.
4. The loop is reinserted into a bacterium which starts to divide rapidly. As it divides, it replicates the loop, and makes insulin.
5. The transgenic bacteria are cultured by cloning in large **fermenters**. Each bacterium carries instructions to make insulin. When the bacteria make the protein, commercial (large) quantities of insulin can be harvested.

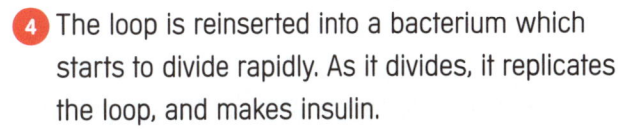

HT Because these loops can be taken up by bacteria, they can be used as vectors in genetic engineering.

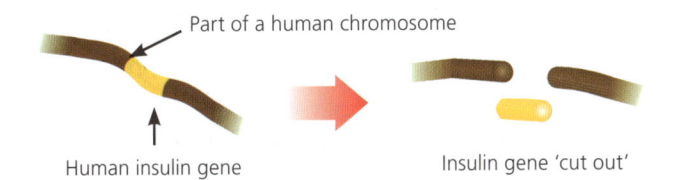

Part of a human chromosome
Human insulin gene
Insulin gene 'cut out'
Ring of bacterial DNA cut open
Human insulin gene inserted into bacterial DNA

DNA Fingerprinting

Each person's DNA is **unique**, so it can be used for **identification** in a technique called **DNA fingerprinting**. For example, blood found at a crime scene can be compared with samples of suspects' DNA.

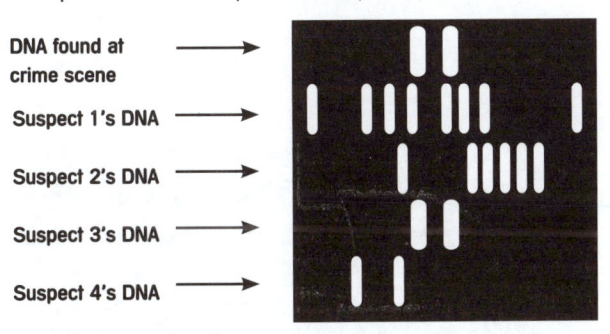

DNA found at crime scene
Suspect 1's DNA
Suspect 2's DNA
Suspect 3's DNA
Suspect 4's DNA

HT To make a DNA fingerprint, a sample of DNA is needed. DNA fingerprinting is carried out in four stages:

1. **Extraction** – DNA is extracted from blood, hair follicles or semen.
2. **Fragmentation** – the DNA is cut into fragments using **restriction** enzymes.
3. **Separation** – the DNA sections are separated using a technique called **electrophoresis**.
4. **Visualising pattern** – the DNA fingerprint is analysed by comparing it with a reference sample, e.g. blood taken from the crime scene.

You can see that the unique DNA fingerprint from the blood sample found at the crime scene matches exactly with the DNA fingerprint of Suspect 3.

Keeping a central database for genetic fingerprints would be very helpful to crime prevention agencies like the Police. It could be used to help solve crimes. But many people don't like this idea, and think DNA is private.

Quick Test

1. How can enzymes be immobilised?
2. What is genetic engineering?
3. Explain why biological washing powders will not work at high temperatures.

Key Words — DNA

B6 Exam Practice Questions

1 Adrian has an intolerance to milk. He has to drink lactose-free milk. He is keen to find out how it is made.

   a) Why is it best to use immobilised enzymes to break down lactose in milk? [1]

   b) Explain why people with diabetes might use immobilised enzymes. [1]

2 After the year 11 prom Sabrina finds some food stains on her dress. Her mum suggests that she should use a biological washing powder to remove the stains. Sabrina reads the following contents on the packet of biological washing powder:

Sodium carbonate to soften water 15%
Perfume 10%
Antifoam agent 5%
Oxidising agents 10%

Soap 45%
Protease enzymes 5%
Brightening compounds 10%

   a) The concentration of enzymes is very low. Why? [1]

   b) Sabrina washes her dress at 60°C. Explain whether you think she was correct to do this. [1]

   c) i) There are three different stains on Sabrina's dress: egg, butter and ketchup. Which one will be removed most easily by the washing powder? [1]

   ii) Explain your answer. [3]

3 Look at this marine food web.

   a) What are the secondary consumers in this food web? [1]

   b) i) What are phytoplankton? [1]

   ii) List the factors that affect the growth of phytoplankton. [3]

82

Exam Practice Questions B6

4 A student wanted to investigate the effect of different cleaning products on the growth of bacteria. She set up five agar plates that were seeded with one type of bacteria. On each plate the student placed four discs that had been soaked in a particular cleaning product. The plates were incubated at 25°C for three days. The student then measured the diameter around the discs where the bacteria hadn't grown. Her results are shown in the table below.

Plate and Cleaning Product	Diameter (mm) Around Each Disc where Bacteria Hasn't Grown				Mean (mm)
	Disc 1	Disc 2	Disc 3	Disc 4	
Plate 1 (soap)	1	2	2	1	1.5
Plate 2 (hand wash)	3	2	2	4	2.75
Plate 3 (kitchen cleaner)	5	4	6	5	5
Plate 4 (bathroom cleaner)	5	5	6	7	
Plate 5 (no cleaner)	0	0	0	0	0

a) Complete the table by calculating the mean diameter where bacteria didn't grow for Plate 4. [1]

b) Which was the most effective product at killing the bacteria? [1]

c) Why did the student use 'Plate 5 (no cleaner)'? [1]

d) How has the student made her results reliable? [1]

HT 5 In the ocean depths, many organisms rely on marine snow. What is marine snow? [1]

6 Describe the process of DNA finger printing. [6]

✎ *The quality of your written communication will be assessed in your answer to this question.*

83

C6 Electrolysis

Electrolysis

The **ions** in:
- an **ionic solid** are fixed and can't move
- an **ionic substance** that is **molten** or in **solution** are free to move.

Electrolysis is a chemical reaction in which an ionic liquid is broken down (**decomposed**) into its elements using an **electric current**. It is a flow of charge produced by moving ions and ions are discharged at the electrodes.

The ionic substance is called the **electrolyte**. It must be molten or in solution as the ions need to be free to move:
- The positive ions (**cations**) move to, and discharge at, the negative electrode (**cathode**).
- The negative ions (**anions**) move to, and discharge at, the positive electrode (**anode**).

Electrons are removed from negative ions.

The electrons then flow around the circuit to the negative electrode and are passed to the positive ions.

Anode (positive electrode)
d.c. power supply
Cathode (negative electrode)
Electrolyte (liquid that conducts and decomposes in electrolysis)

Amount of Substance Produced

The amount of substance made in electrolysis is determined by the size of the current and the length of time it flows for.

More substance is made if:
- a larger current flows
- the current flows for a longer time.

HT The quantity of electricity (Q) passed in an electrolysis reaction can be calculated using the following formula:

Quantity of electricity (coulombs)	=	Current (amps)	×	Time (seconds)
Q	=	I	×	t

One mole of a substance with a 1$^+$ charge will be deposited by 96 500 coulombs. This can be used to calculate how much of a substance will be made from the current, and the time the electricity has been on.

Example
How many moles of silver are deposited when a solution containing Ag$^+$ ions is electrolysed for 24 125 seconds by a current of 2 amps?

Q = I × t
= 2 × 24 125 = 48 250 coulombs

Number of moles = $\frac{48\ 250}{96\ 500}$

= 0.5

Therefore, **0.5 mole Ag$^+$** is deposited.

Key Words Ion • Electrolysis • Electrolyte • Cathode • Anode

Electrolysis C6

Electrolysis of Copper(II) Sulfate

When an electric current is passed through the copper(II) sulfate solution using copper electrodes:
- the positive electrode bubbles as oxygen is made, and the mass decreases because ions move **from** it
- the negative electrode becomes plated with copper and the mass increases because ions move **to** it
- the electrolyte will become less blue as copper(II) sulfate decomposes.

HT In the electrolysis of $CuSO_4(aq)$ with copper electrodes:
- the following reaction takes place at the **cathode**:

$$Cu^{2+} + 2e^- \rightarrow Cu$$

- the following reaction takes place at the **anode**:

$$4OH^- - 4e^- \rightarrow O_2 + 2H_2O$$

The amount of substance produced is directly proportional to the time and the current.

Products of Electrolysis

The table below shows the elements made when certain electrolytes undergo electrolysis.

HT When **aqueous solutions** undergo electrolysis, it's often easier to decompose the water than to decompose the compound that is dissolved in it. This is the reason why hydrogen and oxygen are produced in the electrolysis of electrolytes such as $NaOH(aq)$ and $K_2SO_4(aq)$.

Quick Test

1. Which electrode are positive ions attracted to?
2. What two factors affect the amount of substance made during electrolysis?

Test for hydrogen gas: a lighted splint causes a 'pop!'.
Test for oxygen gas: a glowing splint is re-lit.

Liquid	State	Elements Made	At the Cathode	At the Anode
Aluminium oxide $Al_2O_3(l)$	Liquid	Aluminium, oxygen	**HT** $Al^{3+}(l) + 3e^- \rightarrow Al(l)$	$2O^{2-}(l) - 4e^- \rightarrow O_2(g)$
Lead bromide $PbBr_2(l)$	Liquid	Lead, bromine	**HT** $Pb^{2+}(l) + 2e^- \rightarrow Pb(l)$	$2Br^-(l) - 2e^- \rightarrow Br_2(g)$
Lead iodide $PbI_2(l)$	Liquid	Lead, iodine	**HT** $Pb^{2+}(l) + 2e^- \rightarrow Pb(l)$	$2I^-(l) - 2e^- \rightarrow I_2(g)$
Potassium chloride $KCl(l)$	Liquid	Potassium, chlorine	**HT** $K^+(l) + e^- \rightarrow K(l)$	$2Cl^-(l) - 2e^- \rightarrow Cl_2(g)$
Sodium hydroxide $NaOH(aq)$	Dissolved in water	Hydrogen, oxygen	**HT** $2H^+(aq) + 2e^- \rightarrow H_2(g)$	$4OH^- - 4e^- \rightarrow O_2 + 2H_2O$
Potassium nitrate $KNO_3(aq)$	Dissolved in water	Hydrogen, oxygen	**HT** $2H^+(aq) + 2e^- \rightarrow H_2(g)$	$4OH^- - 4e^- \rightarrow O_2 + 2H_2O$
Sulfuric acid $H_2SO_4(aq)$	Dissolved in water	Hydrogen, oxygen	**HT** $2H^+(aq) + 2e^- \rightarrow H_2(g)$	$4OH^- - 4e^- \rightarrow O_2 + 2H_2O$

C6 Energy Transfers – Fuel Cells

Reacting Oxygen with Hydrogen

The reaction between hydrogen and oxygen releases energy and is an **exothermic** reaction.

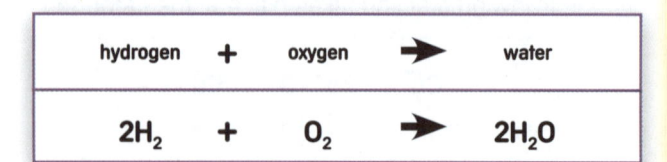

hydrogen	+	oxygen	→	water
$2H_2$	+	O_2	→	$2H_2O$

HT This **energy level diagram** shows the reaction between hydrogen and oxygen:

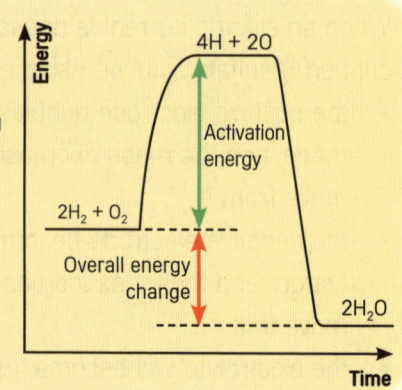

Fuel Cells

Hydrogen can be used as a fuel. When it reacts exothermically with oxygen in a **fuel cell** it makes an **electric current**. The energy from the reaction is used to create a **potential difference** (**pd**).

A fuel cell is very efficient at producing electrical energy. Fuel cells are used to provide electrical power in spacecraft. The water made is **pollution-free**, so it can be used as drinking water for the crew.

The car manufacturing industry is very interested in developing fuel cells as a possible pollution-free method of powering the electric car of the future. Currently, burning fossil fuels in cars produces carbon dioxide, which has been linked to climate change. Also, fossil fuels are non-renewable but there is a plentiful supply of hydrogen from the decomposition of water.

HT In a fuel cell under **acidic** conditions:
1. Each hydrogen atom loses an electron at the **anode** (the positive electrode) to form a hydrogen ion. This is an example of **oxidation**:
$H_2 - 2e^- → 2H^+$
2. The hydrogen ions then move through the electrolyte towards the **cathode** (the negative electrode) and the electrons travel around the circuit. Oxygen gets **reduced** as it gains electrons:
$O_2 + 4H^+ + 4e^- → 2H_2O$

In a fuel cell under **alkaline** conditions:
1. At the **anode**, hydrogen is **oxidised**:
$H_2 + 2OH^- - 2e^- → 2H_2O$
2. At the **cathode**, oxygen gets **reduced** as it gains electrons:
$O_2 + 2H_2O + 4e^- → 4OH^-$

There are many advantages of using a fuel cell:
- They produce less pollution.
- They are very efficient.
- They transfer energy directly.
- They have few stages and are simple to construct.
- They are lightweight and compact.
- They have no moving parts.

HT There are some disadvantages of using fuel cells:
- They often contain poisonous catalysts which have to be carefully disposed of.
- To make the hydrogen fuel, energy is needed. This energy may come from the burning of fossil fuels.

In your exam you may be asked to explain the advantages of using a fuel cell compared to conventional methods for making electricity.

Key Words Fuel cell

Redox Reactions C6

Rusting and Redox Reactions

Rust is a form of hydrated iron(III) oxide. It forms when iron or steel combines with both oxygen (in air) and water. This reaction is an example of a **redox reaction**. A redox reaction involves both **oxidation** and **reduction**. **Oxidation** is the gain of oxygen. **Reduction** is the removal of oxygen.

iron + oxygen + water ⟶ hydrated iron(III) oxide

HT Oxidation involves the loss of electrons. A chemical that removes electrons from another substance is called an **oxidising agent**.

Reduction involves the gain of electrons. A chemical that gives electrons to another substance is called a **reducing agent**.

Rusting is a redox reaction because:
- iron loses electrons (**oxidation**)
- oxygen gains electrons (**reduction**).

Changes can be made using an oxidising agent. These are oxidation reactions because electrons are lost:

$Fe \rightarrow Fe^{2+} + 2e^-$

$Fe^{2+} \rightarrow Fe^{3+} + e^-$

$2Cl^- \rightarrow Cl_2 + 2e^-$

These reactions can be done using a reducing agent. They are reduction reactions because electrons are gained:

$Fe^{2+} + 2e^- \rightarrow Fe$

$Fe^{3+} + e^- \rightarrow Fe^{2+}$

$Cl_2 + 2e^- \rightarrow 2Cl^-$

Preventing Rusting

You can protect iron and steel from rusting by coating them in oil, grease or paint. This stops the water and air coming into contact with the metal. Other methods are as follows:
- **Galvanising** – coating the iron or steel with zinc. This layer stops water and oxygen reaching the iron. Also, zinc can act as sacrificial protection.
- **Alloying**.
- **Tin plating**.

- **Sacrificial protection** – placing a more reactive metal, for example, magnesium, in contact with the iron or steel.

HT **Tin plating** acts as a barrier between the iron and air and water. However, when the tin plating is scratched, the iron will corrode and lose electrons. In **sacrificial protection**, the more reactive metal, e.g. magnesium or zinc, will corrode, losing electrons and protecting the iron.

Displacement Reactions

A more reactive metal will displace a less reactive metal in a reaction. This type of reaction is known as a **displacement reaction**. Magnesium is more reactive than zinc, which is more reactive than iron, which is more reactive than tin.

You can write equations for displacement reactions, e.g.:

magnesium + zinc chloride ⟶ Zinc + magnesium chloride

HT $Mg(s) + ZnCl_2(aq) \rightarrow Zn(s) + MgCl_2(aq)$

HT Displacement is a redox reaction. The metal ion is reduced by gaining electrons and the metal atom is oxidised by losing electrons.

Key Words   Rust • Redox reaction • Oxidation • Reduction

C6 Alcohols

Ethanol and Alcohols

Alcohols are a family of organic compounds containing hydrogen, carbon and oxygen. They are not hydrocarbons.

Ethanol (C_2H_5OH) is an alcohol. Its displayed formula is shown below:

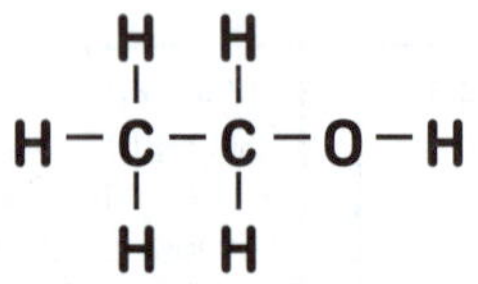

```
      H   H
      |   |
  H — C — C — O — H
      |   |
      H   H
```

Ethanol has many uses, for example, it can be used:
- to make alcoholic drinks
- to make solvents, such as methylated spirits
- as fuel for cars.

HT Alcohols have the general formula $C_nH_{(2n+1)}OH$. For example, pentanol is $C_5H_{11}OH$.

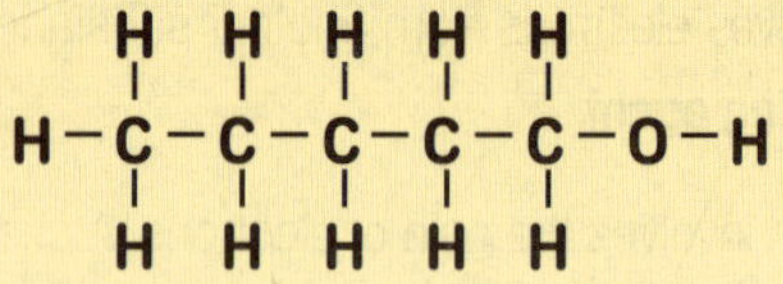

```
      H  H  H  H  H
      |  |  |  |  |
  H — C— C— C— C— C — O — H
      |  |  |  |  |
      H  H  H  H  H
```

Making Ethanol by Fermentation

Ethanol can be made by **fermentation**. Yeast is used to ferment glucose solution.

glucose	→	ethanol	+	carbon dioxide
$C_6H_{12}O_6$	→	$2C_2H_5OH$	+	$2CO_2$

The apparatus used in fermentation prevents air (oxygen) from reaching the fermentation mixture.

The fermentation mixture has to be kept at between 25°C and 50°C for a few days. This is the **optimum temperature** for the enzymes in the yeast to change the glucose into ethanol. This is a renewable method.

Pure ethanol can be extracted from the fermentation mixture by **fractional distillation**.

HT The absence of air from fermentation prevents the formation of ethanoic acid by oxidation of the ethanol.

The temperature of the fermentation mixture has to be kept at between 25°C and 50°C (the optimum temperature) because:
- if it falls below the optimum temperature, the yeast becomes inactive
- if it rises above the optimum temperature, the enzymes in the yeast denature and stop working.

Fermentation

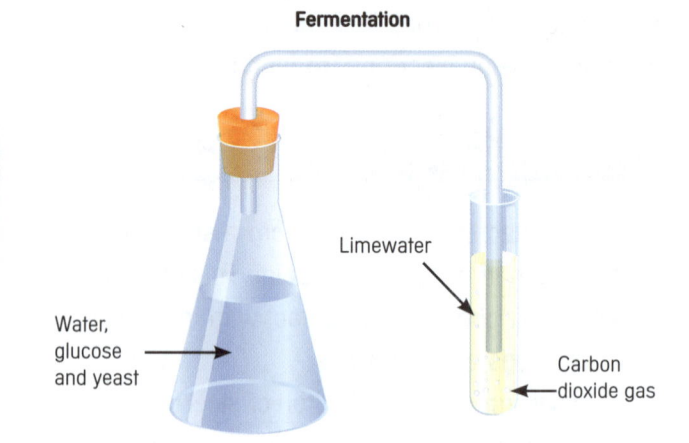

Distillation Equipment

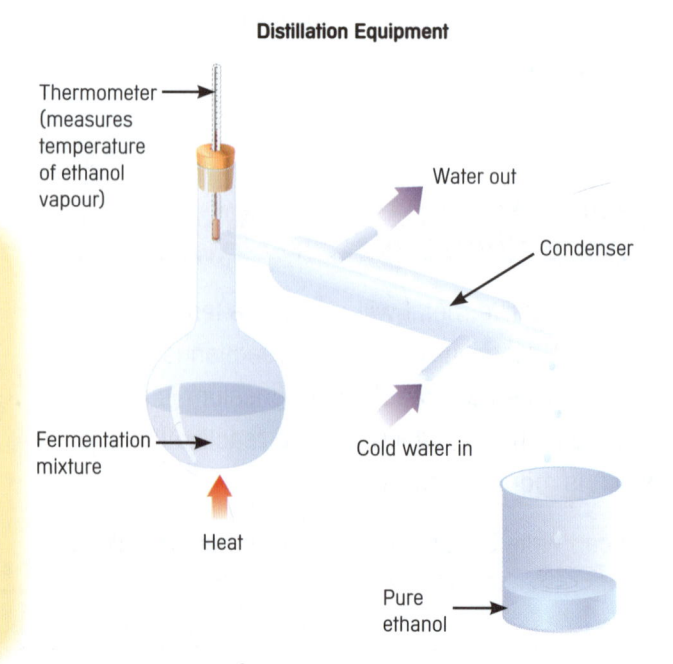

Key Words: **Fermentation** • **Fractional distillation**

Alcohols C6

Making Ethanol by Hydration

The chemical reaction to turn ethene into ethanol is **reversible**:

ethene ⇌ ethanol (hydration / dehydration)

Ethene can be **hydrated** to make ethanol by passing it over a heated phosphoric acid catalyst with steam.

Ethanol made in this way is for industrial use only and is non-renewable.

ethene + water ⇌ (phosphoric acid catalyst) ethanol

$$C_2H_4 + H_2O \rightleftharpoons C_2H_5OH$$

Fermentation or Hydration?

The ethanol made by hydration is **non-renewable** because the ethene will have been made by cracking components of crude oil.

Ethanol made by fermentation is renewable and more sustainable.

HT The two methods of making ethanol have different advantages and disadvantages. These need to be considered before a company chooses which method to use.

It's quicker to produce ethanol by hydration than by fermentation, and ethene is available in large quantities in this country from cracking in oil refineries. This is a continuous process.

Making ethanol by hydration has a 100% atom economy. But fermentation has a higher percentage yield as the reaction is not reversible.

Fermentation is a slow batch process and the ethanol has to be purified by fractional distillation before use. This uses a lot of energy and is expensive.

Quick Test

1. What is galvanising?
2. What can ethanol be used for?
3. **HT** Ethanol can be made by fermenting. Is this production batch or continuous?
4. **HT** Ethanol can be made by hydration. Is this production batch or continuous?

C6 Depletion of the Ozone Layer

Depletion of the Ozone Layer

Ozone (O_3) is a type of oxygen found in a layer high up in the atmosphere (the stratosphere).

Chlorofluorocarbons (**CFCs**) are organic molecules that contain chlorine, fluorine and carbon. CFCs were used as refrigerants and in aerosols because:
- they have a low boiling point
- they are insoluble in water
- they are very unreactive (i.e. chemically inert).

CFCs damage the ozone layer. Hydrocarbons (alkanes) or hydrofluorocarbons (HFCs) are now used as safer alternatives to CFCs.

The depletion of ozone in the atmosphere allows increased levels of harmful ultraviolet (UV) light to reach the Earth, and this can cause:
- increased ageing of the skin and risk of sunburn
- skin cancers
- increased risk of cataracts.

When a CFC molecule is hit by ultraviolet light, a chlorine atom called a **radical** is produced.

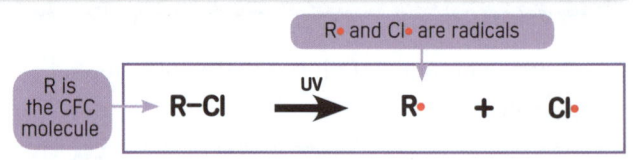

R is the CFC molecule: R–Cl $\xrightarrow{UV}$ R• + Cl•

R• and Cl• are radicals

One chlorine radical can attack and destroy many ozone molecules. This leads to the loss of the ozone layer. Chlorine radicals and CFCs take a very long time to leave the stratosphere.

The international community banned the use of CFCs after they agreed with scientific researchers. The ban started in the developed countries, such as the UK. But, it was a few years before less-developed countries followed suit.

HT When CFCs were first made, they were seen to be very useful, particularly because of their inertness. But, the enthusiasm for their use was dampened when the link between ozone depletion and CFCs was found. Ozone depletion will continue for a few years yet as some countries are still using CFCs, and the inertness of CFCs causes them to stay in the environment for a long time.

HT CFCs' Effect on the Ozone Layer

Ozone filters out harmful ultraviolet light from reaching the surface of the Earth. When ozone absorbs ultraviolet light, the energy in the light causes the **covalent bond** in the ozone molecule to break. The ozone molecule is split into an oxygen molecule (O_2) and an oxygen atom (O). When this happens, the covalent bond can be broken evenly so that each atom retains one electron to form radicals, or unevenly to make **ions**.

When a CFC molecule is hit by ultraviolet light, the C–Cl bond breaks down. One electron from the covalent bond goes to the Cl to make a Cl radical and one electron goes to the main part of the molecule.

When a chlorine radical attacks an ozone molecule:
- the chlorine radical reacts with an ozone molecule to form a chlorine monoxide molecule and an oxygen molecule:

Cl• + O_3 → ClO• + O_2

(This is a radical)

- the chlorine monoxide molecule then reacts with an oxygen atom to produce a chlorine radical and an oxygen molecule:

ClO• + O• → Cl• + O_2

The chlorine radical is **regenerated** by this **chain reaction** and can go on to destroy many more ozone molecules.

Key Words: Ozone • Chlorofluorocarbons • Chain reaction

Hardness of Water C6

Hardness of Water

Water can be hard or soft.
- **Soft** water lathers well with soap.
- **Hard** water doesn't lather with soap.
- Both hard and soft water will lather with a soapless detergent.

Hardness in water is caused by calcium and magnesium ions from dissolved salts. There are two types of hardness in water:
- Permanent hardness.
- Temporary hardness.

Permanent hardness is caused by dissolved substances like calcium sulfate. It can't be destroyed by boiling.

Temporary hardness forms when rainwater comes into contact with rock that contains calcium carbonate, e.g. chalk, marble or limestone. It is caused by dissolved calcium hydrogencarbonate and it can be removed by boiling.

The hardness of the water depends on which rocks the water has flowed over. So the hardness of the water varies across the UK.

Forming and Removing Hardness

Rainwater contains dissolved carbon dioxide, which makes it slightly acidic. When rainwater reacts with rock it makes soluble calcium hydrogencarbonate. This causes temporary hardness:

calcium carbonate + water + carbon dioxide → calcium hydrogencarbonate

When temporary hard water is boiled, the calcium hydrogencarbonate decomposes to form insoluble calcium carbonate, water and carbon dioxide, i.e. the hardness is removed from the water:

calcium hydrogencarbonate → calcium carbonate + water + carbon dioxide

HT $Ca(HCO_3)_2(aq) \rightarrow CaCO_3(s) + H_2O(l) + CO_2(g)$

Limescale

Insoluble calcium carbonate will deposit as **limescale** on the heating element of an appliance, for example, in a kettle.

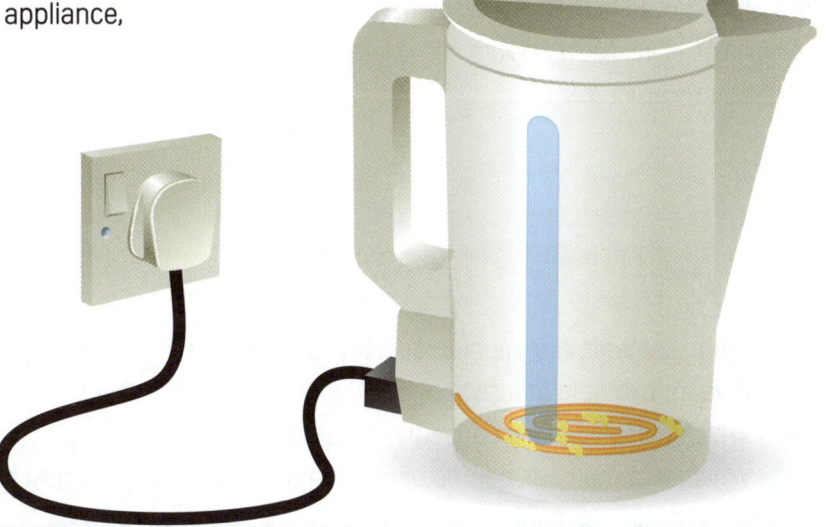

Key Words: Hardness • Limescale

C6 Hardness of Water

Measuring Water Hardness

Hardness in water can be measured by adding soap solution to the water until a permanent lather is produced after it is shaken for five seconds.

The number of drops of soap solution added can be counted, or a burette can be used to measure the volume of soap solution added.

In your exam, you will be expected to interpret data from an experiment to measure hardness in water.

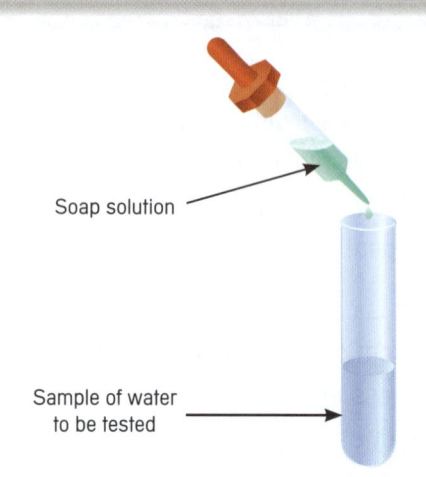

Removing Hardness from Water

You can remove all types of hardness from water by:
- adding washing soda (sodium carbonate crystals)
- passing the water through an **ion-exchange column**.

When hard water is passed through an ion-exchange column, the calcium and magnesium ions swap with the sodium ions, removing the hardness.

The column contains a resin with many sodium ions stuck to it. As the hard water passes over the resin, the calcium and magnesium ions attach to the resin and the sodium ions are released into the water.

HT When washing soda (sodium carbonate crystals) is used to soften water, the calcium and magnesium ions are removed from the water as they form precipitates of insoluble calcium carbonate and magnesium carbonate.

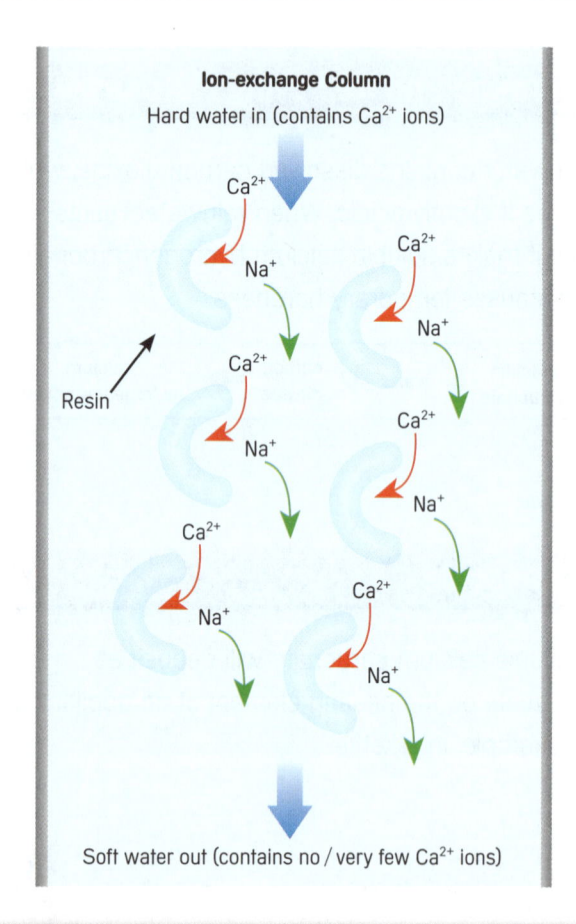

Quick Test

1. What elements are in chlorofluorocarbons (CFCs)?
2. Give an example of a radical that depletes the ozone layer.
3. Which dissolved ions cause the hardness in water?
4. Which two methods can be used to remove permanent hardness from water?

Key Words Ion-exchange column

Natural Fats and Oils C6

Oils and Fats

Oils and fats are **esters** that can be obtained from animals or vegetables.

At room temperature, oils are liquids and fats are solids.

Oils and fats can be:
- **saturated**, i.e. all the carbon-carbon bonds are single bonds (C–C)
- **unsaturated**, i.e. the molecule contains at least one carbon-carbon double bond (C=C).

You can shake an oil or fat with **bromine water** to test if it is saturated or unsaturated:
- If the fat is unsaturated, the bromine water will change from orange to colourless.
- If the fat is saturated, the bromine water will remain orange.

Oil and water are **immiscible**, i.e. they do not normally mix.

You can make an **emulsion** by shaking vegetable oil with water to break down the oil into small droplets that **disperse** (spread out) in the water.

For example:
- milk is an oil-in-water emulsion that is mostly water with tiny droplets of oil dispersed in it
- butter is a water-in-oil emulsion that is mostly oil with droplets of water dispersed in it.

> **HT** Animal oils and fats are often saturated. Vegetable oils and fats are often unsaturated.
>
> It is better for you to have more unsaturated than saturated oils and fats in your diet in order to reduce the build up of **cholesterol** in your body. This is healthier for the heart because cholesterol builds up in the blood vessels, causing the heart to do more work. It can eventually lead to heart disease.
>
> When you are testing oils and fats using bromine water:
> - saturated oils and fats do not react as they have no C=C, which is why the bromine water stays orange
> - the double bonds in unsaturated oils and fats are able to undergo an addition reaction with the bromine water, so the bromine water turns colourless as a di-bromo compound is made.

Using Oils and Fats in Industry

Margarine can be made by reacting unsaturated vegetable oils with hydrogen, using a nickel catalyst. This makes a solid saturated fat, which can then be blended with other ingredients to make it taste and look like butter.

Soap can be made by reacting vegetable oil with hot sodium hydroxide. When this happens, the sodium hydroxide splits up the oil or fat molecules into **glycerol** and **soap** (a sodium salt of a long chain fatty acid). This is called **saponification**.

Oils and fats are very important raw materials for the chemical industry.

There is much interest in how vegetable oils can be converted into **biodiesel** to be used as a renewable replacement for diesel, which is obtained from **crude oil**.

> **HT** This is the word equation for the process of saponification:
>
> fat / oil + sodium hydroxide ➡ soap + glycerol
>
> This reaction can be described as **hydrolysis** because it involves breaking down ester groups in the oil molecule using an alkali.

Key Words — Saponification

C6 Detergents

Washing Powder

The main components of a washing powder have specific jobs:

- **Active detergent** does the cleaning.
- **Bleach** removes coloured stains.
- **Water softener** softens hard water.
- **Optical brightener** makes whites appear brighter.
- **Enzymes** break up food and protein stains in low-temperature washes.

When clothes are washed, the:

- water is the **solvent** (the liquid that does the dissolving)
- washing powder is the **solute** (the solid that dissolves) because it's **soluble** (it dissolves) in water
- resulting mixture of solvent and solute is a **solution**.

Low-temperature washes are used because they:

- can be used to wash delicate fabrics (that would shrink in a hotter wash or have a dye that could run)
- don't denature enzymes in biological powders
- save energy.

Stain Removal

Different solvents dissolve different stains. The table shows which solvents can remove stains.

Although you don't need to learn this information, you might be asked to use similar information to choose which solvent to use to remove a stain. Some stains are **insoluble** (they will not dissolve) in water.

Dry cleaning solvents are used for these kinds of stain. The solvent is a liquid, but it doesn't contain water. This method of cleaning is used when a stain is insoluble in water.

Stain	Solvent
Ball-point pen	Methylated spirits (ethanol) then biological washing powder in water
Blood	Biological washing powder in water
Shoe polish	White spirit then biological washing powder in water
Coffee	Biological washing powder in water
Correcting fluid	White spirit

HT Dry-Cleaning Solvents

The molecules making up a stain are held together by **weak intermolecular forces** (forces between the molecules). There are also weak intermolecular forces between solvent molecules.

The stain will dissolve in a **dry-cleaning solvent** if the intermolecular forces holding it together are overcome. The new intermolecular forces between the stain molecules and the solvent molecules are stronger than the ones between the stain molecules.

Key Words: Solvent • Soluble • Solution

Detergents C6

Washing-Up Liquid

Washing-up liquid contains:
- **active detergent** – to do the cleaning
- **water** – to dissolve and dilute the detergent so that it's easy to pour
- **water softener** – to soften hard water
- **rinse agent** – to help the water drain off the crockery so it dries quickly
- **colour and fragrance** – to make the product more attractive to buy and use.

In your exam, you might be asked to interpret data from an experiment to suggest trends or which detergents washed the most plates.

HT You may be asked to interpret the data to suggest which detergents contain enzymes.

Detergent Molecules

A detergent molecule has a **hydrophilic** head and a **hydrophobic** tail:

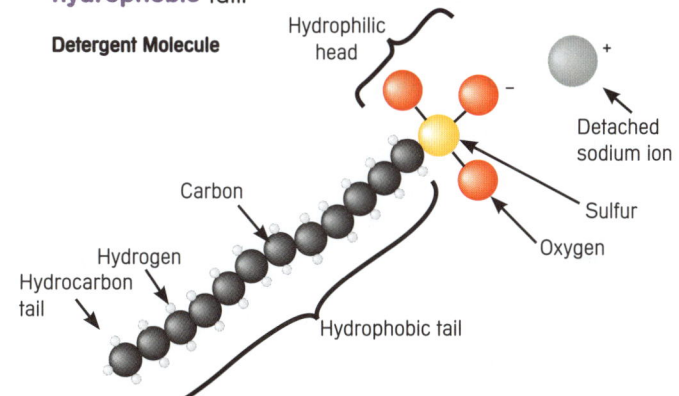

Detergent Molecule

(Diagram labelled: Hydrophilic head, Detached sodium ion, Sulfur, Oxygen, Carbon, Hydrogen, Hydrocarbon tail, Hydrophobic tail)

Quick Test
1. What does saturated mean?
2. What happens when you shake an unsaturated oil with bromine water?
3. What is the name of the chemical reaction to make soap?
4. In a washing machine clothes are often washed with washing powder and water.
   a) What is the solvent?
   b) What is the solute?

HT When detergent molecules dissolve in water:
1. The positively charged **sodium ion** comes away from the 'head' of the detergent molecule.
2. This leaves the molecule head negatively charged, so it's attracted to water molecules. It's known as **hydrophilic (water-loving)**.
3. The hydrocarbon tail is non-polar and so it isn't attracted to water molecules. It's known as **hydrophobic (water-hating)**.

This is how washing-up liquid detergents work:

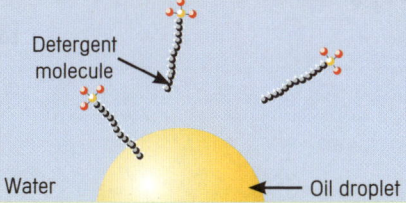

(Diagram showing detergent molecule, water, oil droplet, plate)

The hydrophobic end forms strong intermolecular forces with the oil molecules, causing it to stick to the oil droplet. The hydrophilic end forms strong intermolecular forces with the water.

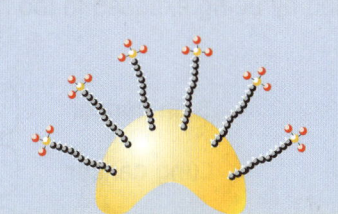

As more and more detergent molecules are absorbed into the oil droplet, the oil is eventually lifted off the plate.

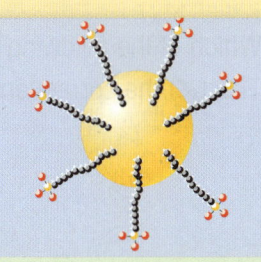

When it is totally surrounded, the oil droplet can be washed away, leaving the plate clean.

Key Words Hydrophilic • Hydrophobic

C6 Exam Practice Questions

1 Electrolysis breaks down an ionic compound into simpler substances.

   a) During electrolysis, positive ions discharge at which electrode? [1]

   b) How do you change an ionic solid into an electrolyte? [2]

   c) What substance is made at the cathode during the electrolysis of copper(II) sulfate solution? [1]

2 A displacement reaction is when a more reactive metal takes the place of a less reactive metal in its compound.

   Complete the word equation for this displacement reaction. [2]

   magnesium + tin chloride → .... + ...

3 Fermentation is a renewable method of making ethanol.

   Ethanol can be used as a fuel and in many industrial processes as a solvent.

   a) Explain why yeast is added during fermentation to produce ethanol. [1]

   b) What type of reaction is used to convert ethene into ethanol? [1]

   c) What catalyst would be used to carry out this reaction? [1]

4 a) The ozone layer is made of O_3 molecules and stops UV light hitting the surface of the Earth.

   Explain why CFCs are harmful to the ozone layer. [2]

   b) Which of the following are caused by being exposed to too much UV light?
   Tick (✓) the correct answer(s). [3]

   Skin cancer ☐
   Lung cancer ☐
   Sunburn ☐
   Cataracts ☐

Exam Practice Questions C6

5) Hard water is made when dissolved magnesium and calcium ions are in water. Write a word equation to show how temporary hardness forms when limestone comes into contact with rainwater. **[2]**

6) Water can be described as hard when it contains certain dissolved metal ions. Explain what causes temporary and permanent hardness and how ion-exchange resin can be used to remove permanent hardness. **[6]**

✎ *The quality of your written communication will be assessed in your answer to this question.*

HT

7) Fat can undergo a chemical change with sodium hydroxide to form soap.

Write a word equation for the saponification of fat. **[1]**

8) Fuel cells can be used to power spacecraft.

a) Write a balanced symbol equation to show the reaction in a fuel cell. **[3]**

b) Explain why the overall reaction in a fuel cell is described as a redox reaction. **[2]**

9) Indicate whether the following reactions are **reduction** or **oxidation** by writing alongside each and explain your answers.

a) $Fe^{3+} \rightarrow Fe^{2+}$ **[1]**

b) $Fe^{2+} \rightarrow Fe^{3+}$ **[1]**

P6 Resisting

Circuit Symbols

The following **symbols** are used to represent components in a circuit:

Fixed resistor	—	Battery	—|---|—	Cell	—||—	Power supply	⊸ ⊸ (DC) / —o∿o— (AC)
Variable resistor		Switch (open)	—⁄ o—	Relay		Bulb	⊗
Diode (current flowing left to right)	—▷|—	Capacitor	—||—	Thermistor		LDR	

Resistors

A **resistor** in a circuit resists the flow of **current**.

A **variable resistor** (rheostat) can have its **resistance** changed. It can be used to:
- control current – increasing the resistance results in a lower current
- vary the brightness of a bulb by varying the current – higher current gives a brighter bulb
- vary the speed of a motor by varying the current – higher current gives greater speed.

HT The resistance of a variable resistor (rheostat) is altered by changing the length of the wire. A longer wire creates a higher resistance.

Variable Resistor used in Dimmer Switch

Ohm's Law

The following units are used for electrical circuits:
- **Voltage** is measured in **volts (V)**.
- **Current** is measured in **amps (A)**.
- **Resistance** is measured in **ohms (Ω)**.

For a given **ohmic** conductor, the current increases as the voltage increases but the resistance remains constant, provided that the temperature doesn't change. In non-ohmic conductors, such as bulbs, the resistance changes.

You can calculate resistance using the following equation:

$$\text{Resistance (Ω)} = \frac{\text{Voltage (V)}}{\text{Current (A)}}$$

Example
A motor requires 12V and a current of 3A to flow through it. What's the motor's resistance?

$$\text{Resistance} = \frac{\text{Voltage}}{\text{Current}} = \frac{12}{3} = \mathbf{4Ω}$$

HT You can rearrange the resistance formula to calculate current or voltage.

Example
Calculate the current in a kettle if the voltage is 230V and the resistance of the heating element is 20Ω.

$$\text{Current} = \frac{\text{Voltage}}{\text{Resistance}} = \frac{230}{20} = \mathbf{11.5A}$$

Key Words: Current • Resistance • Voltage

Resisting P6

Voltage–Current Graphs

The voltage–current graph for an **ohmic conductor** is a straight line. The **gradient** of the graph shows the resistance of the conductor. The steeper the gradient, the higher the resistance.

HT To work out the resistance of an ohmic conductor from a V–I graph, use the following formula:

$$\text{Resistance } (\Omega) = \frac{\text{Change in Voltage (V)}}{\text{Change in Current (A)}}$$

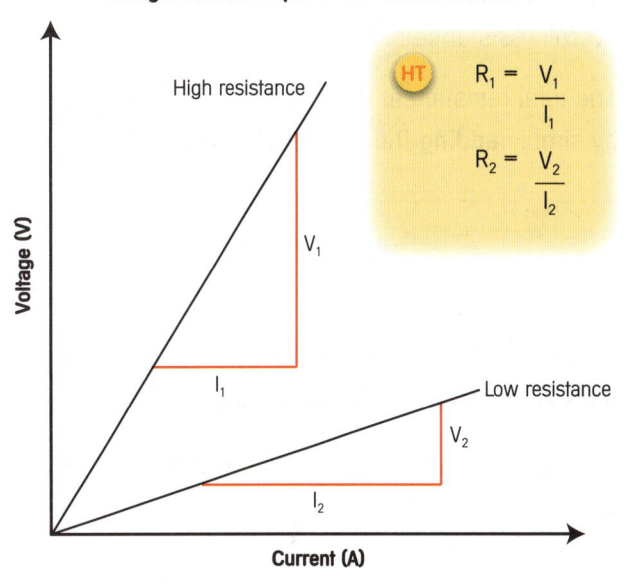

The voltage–current graph for a **non-ohmic conductor** (for example, a bulb) is a curve. The **increasing gradient** shows that the resistance increases as the current increases.

When a wire gets hot, its resistance increases. This means that the hotter a wire gets, the lower the current that can flow through it.

HT As the temperature of a resistor rises, its resistance increases. This is why the V–I graph for a filament bulb is curved. The curve shows an increase in gradient as the current rises, showing that the resistance is increasing.

Voltage–Current Graph for an Ohmic Conductor

HT $R_1 = \dfrac{V_1}{I_1}$

$R_2 = \dfrac{V_2}{I_2}$

Voltage–Current Graph for a Non-Ohmic Conductor

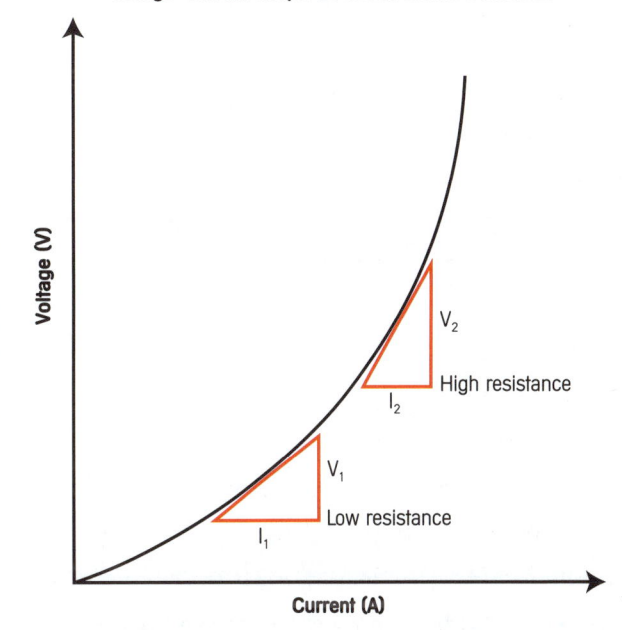

Resistance

An electric current is the flow of charge carriers through a material. In metals the charge carriers are electrons.

As electrons pass along a wire, they collide with atoms (ions) in the metal. This causes the atoms to vibrate more.

As a result:
- the number of collisions increases
- the resistance in the wire increases
- the temperature of the wire increases.

P6 Sharing

Resistors in Series

Two or more resistors in series will increase the overall resistance of the circuit.

The total resistance, R_T, of the circuit can be found by simply **adding** the individual resistances together.

$$R_T = R_1 + R_2 + R_3$$

Example

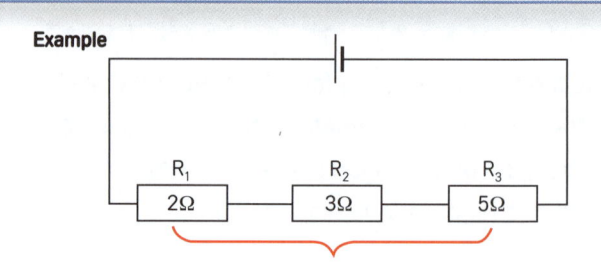

In this example the total resistance, $R_T = R_1 + R_2 + R_3$

$R_T = 2 + 3 + 5$
     $= 10\Omega$

Resistors In Parallel

Resistors in parallel **reduce** the overall resistance of a circuit.

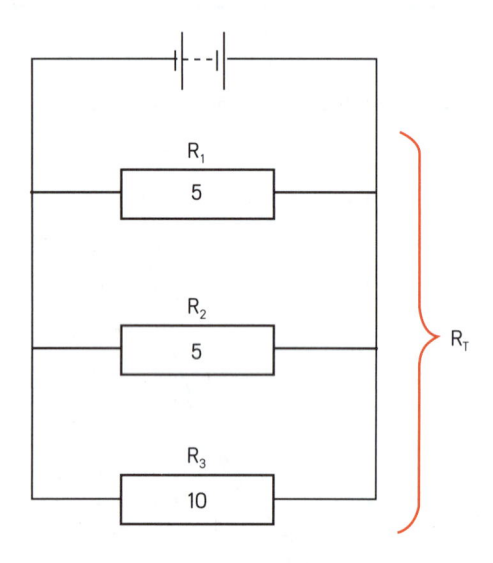

HT The total resistance, R_T, of resistors in parallel is calculated using the following equation:

$$\frac{1}{R_T} = \frac{1}{R_1} + \frac{1}{R_2} + \frac{1}{R_3}$$

In this example the total resistance, R_T, of the circuit is:

$$\frac{1}{R_T} = \frac{1}{5} + \frac{1}{5} + \frac{1}{10}$$

$$= \frac{2}{10} + \frac{2}{10} + \frac{1}{10} = \frac{5}{10}$$

Remember that this value is $\frac{1}{R_T}$, so the answer must be inverted:

$$\frac{1}{R_T} = \frac{10}{5} = 2\Omega$$

Potential Dividers

A **potential divider** can be made of **fixed resistors** that are arranged to produce a required **voltage**, or **potential difference** (pd).

1. In this example, there is a pd across each of the two fixed resistors. If a connection is made across one of the fixed resistors, the pd across that resistor is the output voltage.

2. If a **variable resistor** is used in the potential divider, the exact pd of the output from the circuit can be chosen. The lower the resistance, the lower the pd.

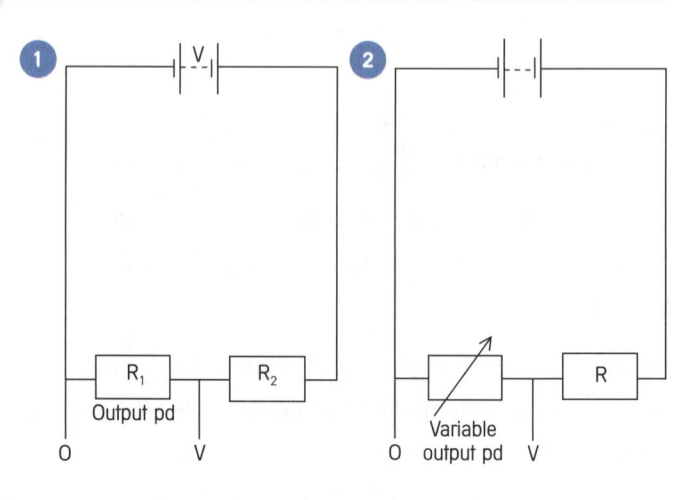

Key Words Potential difference

Sharing P6

Potential Divider Calculator (HT)

If the value of resistor R_2 is much greater than R_1, then the output at Pd will be approximately V (the input Pd).

If the value of resistor R_2 is much less than R_1, then the output Pd across R_1 will be almost zero.

If R_1 and R_2 are both replaced by a variable resistor, then the threshold of the output voltage can be adjusted.

The output pd from a potential divider can be calculated using the following equation:

$$\text{Output pd, } V_{out} = \frac{R_1}{(R_1 + R_2)} \times V_{in}$$

Example

A 20Ω resistor and a 30Ω resistor are connected in series with a 100V supply to make a potential divider. What is the output across the 20Ω resistor?

$$V_{out} = \frac{20}{20 + 30} \times 100$$
$$= 0.4 \times 100 = \mathbf{40V}$$

Using a variable resistor in place of a fixed resistor will give an output pd that can be **adjusted** to provide the voltage required to operate the chosen device.

The voltage can range from zero to almost the total voltage of the circuit.

LDRs and Thermistors

A **light dependent resistor** (**LDR**) changes its resistance in response to different light levels:
- Bright light causes lower resistance.
- Dim light causes higher resistance.

A **thermistor** changes its resistance when the temperature changes:
- High temperature causes lower resistance.
- Low temperature causes higher resistance.

(HT) Using an LDR in place of a fixed resistor in a potential divider gives an output voltage that depends upon light conditions. For example, bright light causes low output voltage because the resistance of the LDR is lower than the fixed resistor. In dim light, the output voltage is high.

Using a thermistor as the variable resistor in a potential divider gives an output voltage that depends upon the temperature. For example, a higher temperature causes a lower output voltage because the resistance of the thermistor is lower than the fixed resistor.

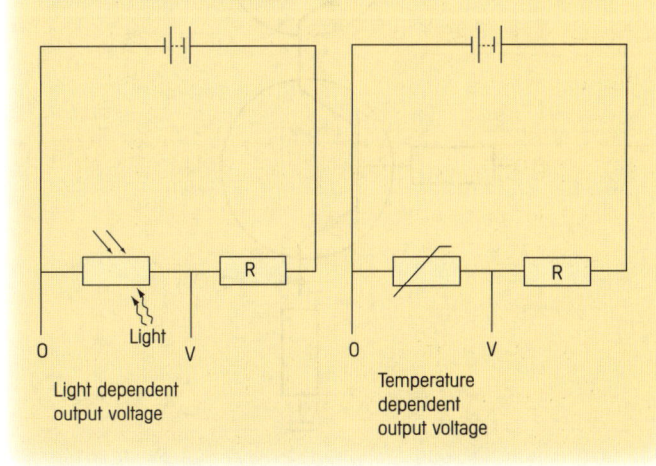

Light dependent output voltage

Temperature dependent output voltage

Quick Test

1. What happens to the resistance of a resistor as its temperature increases?
2. Which combination of two identical resistors has the greatest resistance – series or parallel?
3. What happens to the resistance of an LDR in bright light?

P6 It's Logical

Transistors

The **transistor** is the basic building block of many electrical devices. It is an electronic switch.

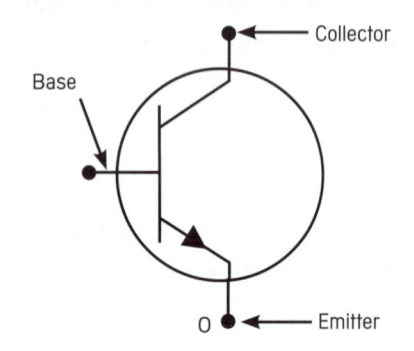

A small base current (I_b) is used to switch on a larger current, which flows through the collector (I_c) and emitter (I_e).

$$I_e = I_c + I_b$$

Millions of these tiny transistors are used in computers and other electrical equipment to speed up processing. They can be connected together to work like **logic gates**.

The two transistors connected together in this circuit produce the same output as an AND gate.

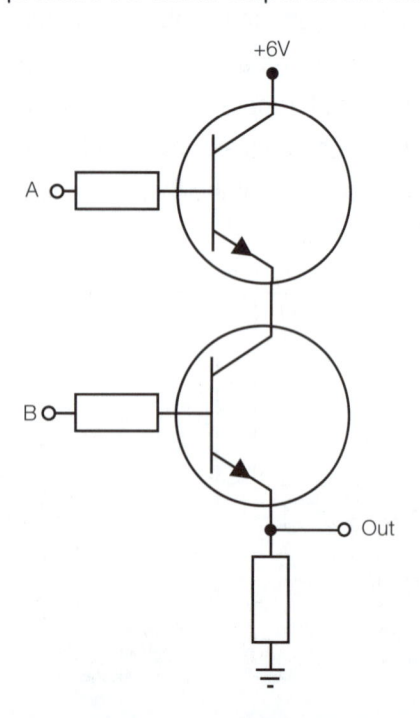

Increasing miniaturisation (making the transistors smaller):
- increases the number of transistors that can be connected in a processor
- means computer processors can be made smaller.

Two factors affect how small transistors can become:
- Smaller components dissipate more heat as a current passes through them.
- As transistors become thinner, they offer less resistance to the electrons due to '**quantum tunnelling**'.

An **npn transistor** can be used as a switch for an LED.

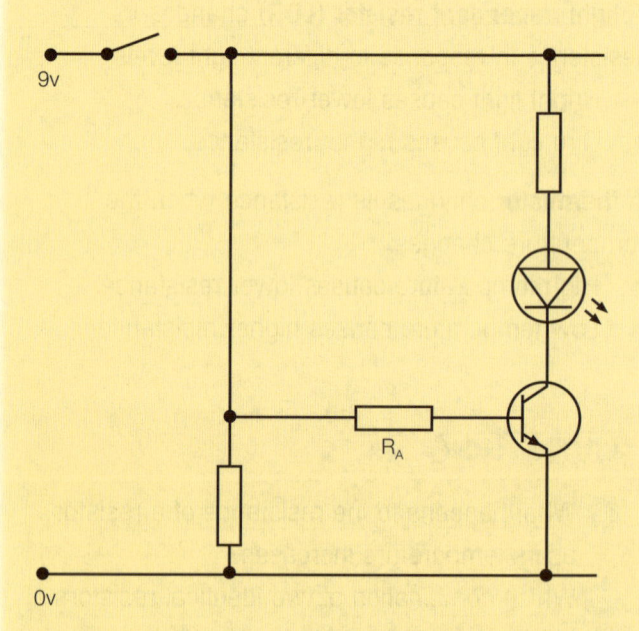

When the switch is closed, a current flows through resistor A to the base. The transistor then allows a current to flow (through the collector and emitter) from +9v to 0v. The LED turns on. Resistors protect the transistor.

A high voltage or current through the transistor will damage the transistor.

It's Logical P6

Inputs and Logic Gates

The input to a logic gate can be:
- a high voltage (about 5V) – called **high**, 1
- a low voltage (about 0V) – called **low**, 0.

The output (Q) of a logic gate is either high or low, depending on its input signal(s).

Switches, LDRs and thermistors can be used in series with fixed resistors to provide input signals for logic gates. In this case, they are being made into potential dividers. A pd, which can be either high (1) or low (0), is fed to the input.

Gate	Truth Table		
NOT gate – gives out the **opposite** of the input.	A	Q	
	0	1	
	1	0	
AND gate – gives a high output if the input on Input A **and** Input B are high.	A	B	Q
	0	0	0
	0	1	0
	1	0	0
	1	1	1
OR gate – gives a high output if Input A **or** Input B is high.	A	B	Q
	0	0	0
	0	1	1
	1	0	1
	1	1	1
NAND gate – an AND gate and a NOT gate in series; the output is the **opposite of an AND** gate.	A	B	Q
	0	0	1
	0	1	1
	1	0	1
	1	1	0
NOR gate – an OR gate and a NOT gate in series; the output is the **opposite of an OR** gate.	A	B	Q
	0	0	1
	0	1	0
	1	0	0
	1	1	0

Key Words — Logic gate

P6 Even More Logical

Thermistors as Inputs for Logic Gates

When a **thermistor** and a fixed resistor are connected in series, a variable potential divider can be produced. This can provide the input to a logic gate that depends upon **temperature**.

> **HT** If the fixed resistor is changed to a variable resistor, the temperature at which the logic gate receives the high input can be set. The voltage output across the variable resistor provides a signal with adjustable threshold voltage to the logic gate.

The example shows a heater control circuit. When the temperature falls, the **resistance** of the thermistor is high. This gives a high input to the AND gate, so the heater is switched on.

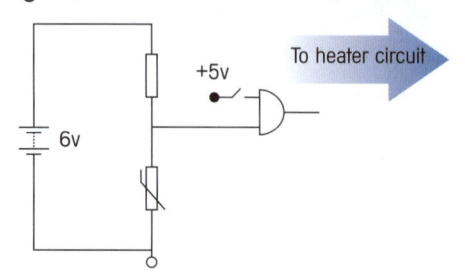

LDRs as Inputs for Logic Gates

When an **LDR** is connected in series to a fixed resistor, it produces a device that can provide the input to a logic gate that depends upon **light conditions**.

The example shows a lighting control circuit. In the dark, the resistance of the LDR is high. This means that the pd on the input of the AND gate is high, so the light switches on.

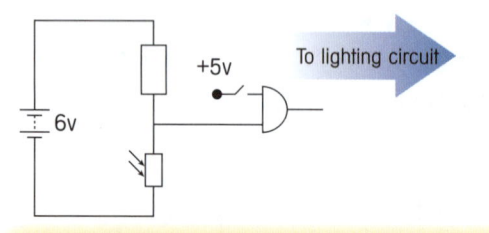

> **HT** If the fixed resistor is changed to a variable resistor, the light level at which the logic gate receives the high input can be set.

LEDs as Outputs

The output from a logic gate can switch on a **light emitting diode** (**LED**). When the logic gate gives a high output, the LED lights up. This could be used to show, for example, when a heater comes on.

> **HT** An LED can be used to indicate the output of a logic gate because it emits light when a voltage is fed to it. An LED only requires a very small current. A resistor is put in series with the LED to ensure that the current flowing through it isn't too large.

Latches and Relays

A **relay** can be used as a switch. A small current in the relay coil switches on a circuit in which a larger current flows.

> **HT** A **relay** is needed in order for a logic gate to switch on a current in a mains circuit, because:
> - a logic gate has a low power output (whereas the mains has a higher power).
> - the relay isolates the low voltage from the high voltage mains.

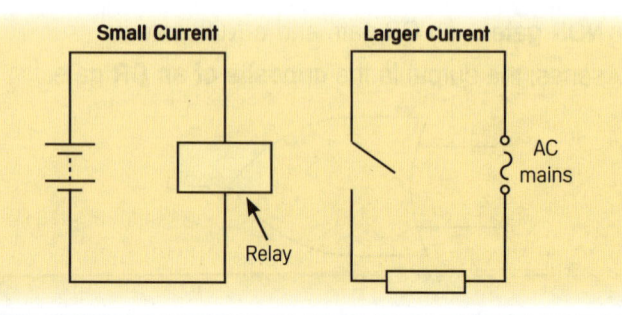

Key Words Resistance • Relay

Even More Logical P6

Complex Truth Tables

You need to be able to complete a truth table for a logic system with up to three inputs made from logic gates, in order to work out what the final output is.

For example, the following diagram and truth table show a logic system consisting of an AND gate connected to an OR gate.

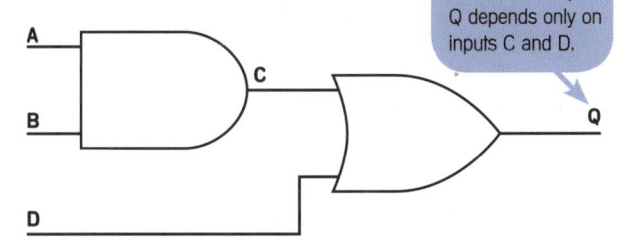

Remember output Q depends only on inputs C and D.

A	B	C	D	Q
0	0	0	0	0
0	0	0	1	1
0	1	0	0	0
0	1	0	1	1
1	0	0	0	0
1	0	0	1	1
1	1	1	0	1
1	1	1	1	1

HT In your exam you may be asked to work through the truth table of a logic system with up to four inputs made from logic gates:

1. Set up the inputs, (A, B, C, D, etc.) and then fill in the truth table using **binary**.
2. Work out the output for a logic gate for each pair of inputs.
3. Repeat the process for each logic gate until the final outputs have been found.

The following example is for a logic system consisting of an OR gate and an AND gate connected to a NOR gate.

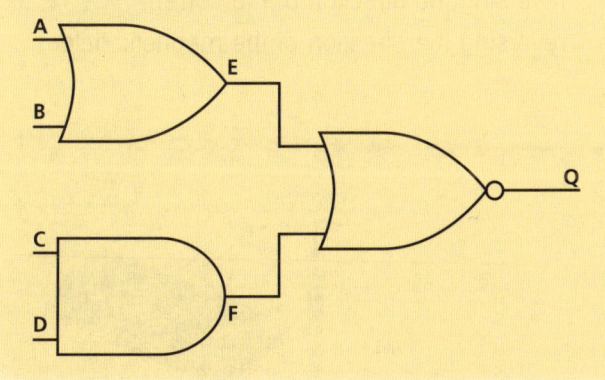

A	B	C	D	E	F	Q
0	0	0	0	0	0	1
0	0	0	1	0	0	1
0	0	1	0	0	0	1
0	0	1	1	0	1	0
0	1	0	0	1	0	0
0	1	0	1	1	0	0
0	1	1	0	1	0	0
0	1	1	1	1	1	0
1	0	0	0	1	0	0
1	0	0	1	1	0	0
1	0	1	0	1	0	0
1	0	1	1	1	1	0
1	1	0	0	1	0	0
1	1	0	1	1	0	0
1	1	1	0	1	0	0
1	1	1	1	1	1	0

Quick Test

1. What value must both inputs to an AND gate have so that the output is high?
2. **HT** What is the job of a relay?
3. **HT** Which gate can be used in place of a NOT and an OR gate together?

105

P6 Motoring

Magnetic Field Around a Wire

A straight wire carrying an electric current has a circular **magnetic field** around it. The magnetic field is made up of **concentric circles**.

If the wire is put near a magnet, the two magnetic fields interact and the wire can move.

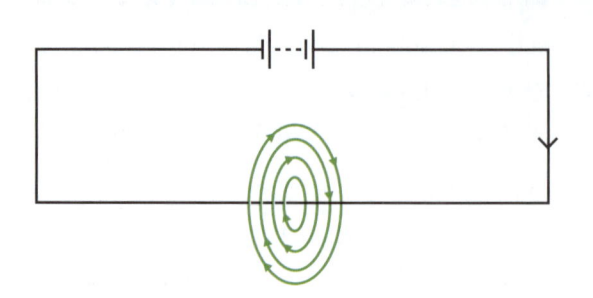

Magnetic Field Around Coils

The magnetic field around a **rectangular coil** forms straight lines through the centre of the coil:

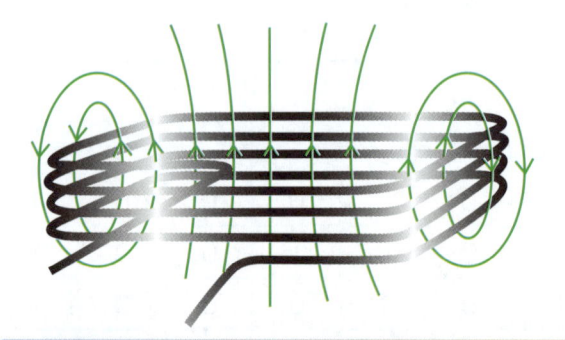

The magnetic field around a **solenoid** looks like the magnetic field around a bar magnet:

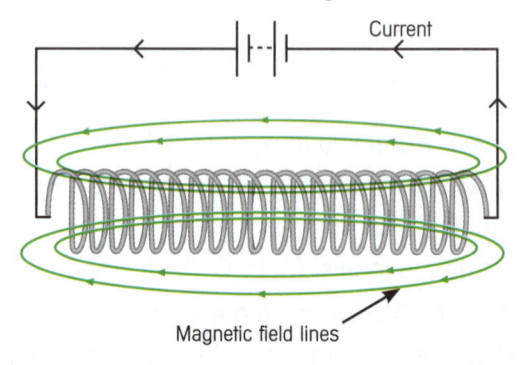

Wires Moving in Magnetic Fields

If a current-carrying wire is placed in a magnetic field it experiences a force and moves. This is called the **motor effect**.

For a current-carrying wire in a magnetic field to experience the maximum **force**, it has to be at **right angles** to the magnetic field.

The direction the wire moves in depends upon:
- the direction of the current
- the direction of the magnetic field.

The direction the wire moves in can be reversed by:
- reversing the direction of the current
- reversing the direction of the magnetic field.

HT Fleming's Left Hand Rule

Fleming's Left Hand Rule can be used to predict the direction of the force on a current-carrying wire.

The rule states that if:
- your first finger points in the direction of the magnetic field, N to S, **and**
- your second finger points in the direction of the current, + to −, **then**
- your thumb will point in the direction of the force on the wire.

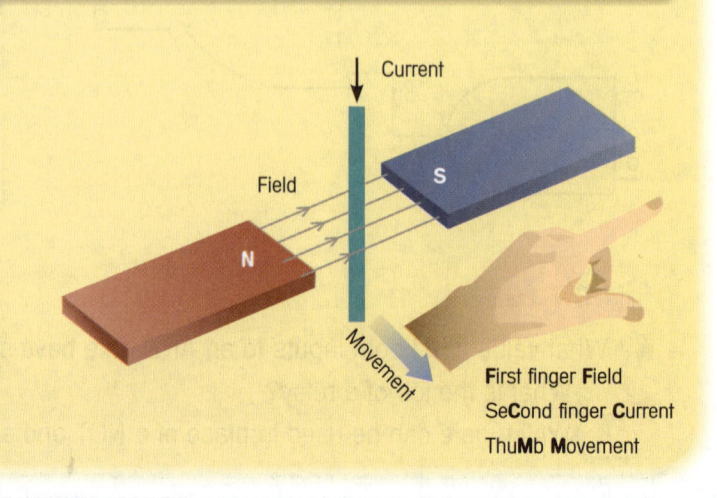

First finger **F**ield
Se**C**ond finger **C**urrent
Thu**M**b **M**ovement

Key Words Magnetic field • Force • Fleming's Left Hand Rule

Motoring P6

Coils Rotating in Magnetic Fields

A simple **direct current** (**DC**) electric **motor** works by using a current-carrying coil.

When a current-carrying coil is placed in a magnetic field, it will **rotate** in the following way:

1. The current flowing through the coil creates a magnetic field.
2. The magnetic field of the magnet and the magnetic field of the coil interact.
3. Each side of the coil experiences a force in an opposite direction because the current is flowing in opposite directions in the two parts of the coil.
4. The forces combine to make the coil rotate.

Electric motors transfer energy to the device (load). Some energy is wasted to the surroundings, often as heat.

Electric motors are found in many devices, such as:
- washing machines
- CD players
- food processors
- electric drills and electric lawnmowers
- windscreen wipers.

The speed of a motor can be increased by:
- increasing the size of the electric current
- increasing the number of turns on the coil
- increasing the strength of the magnetic field.

HT The direction of the current affects the direction of the force on the motor coil.

The current must always flow in the same direction (DC) relative to the magnet in order to keep the coil rotating.

This is achieved by using a **split-ring commutator**.

A split-ring commutator changes the direction of the current in the coil every half turn.

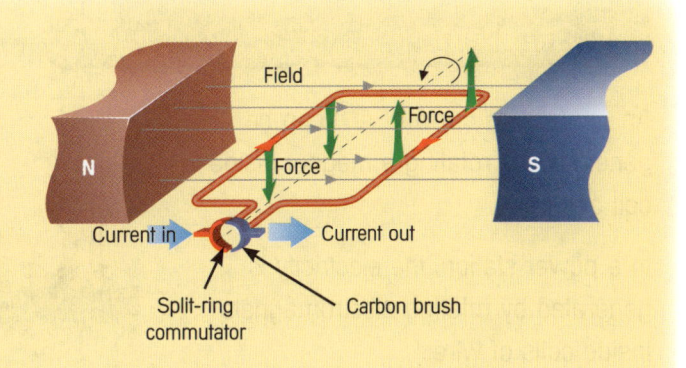

Radial Fields

Because the maximum force is produced when the coil and the magnetic field are at right angles, curved pole pieces are used to give a **radial field**.

The effect of the radial field is that the magnetic field lines and the coil are always at the correct angle to give maximum force.

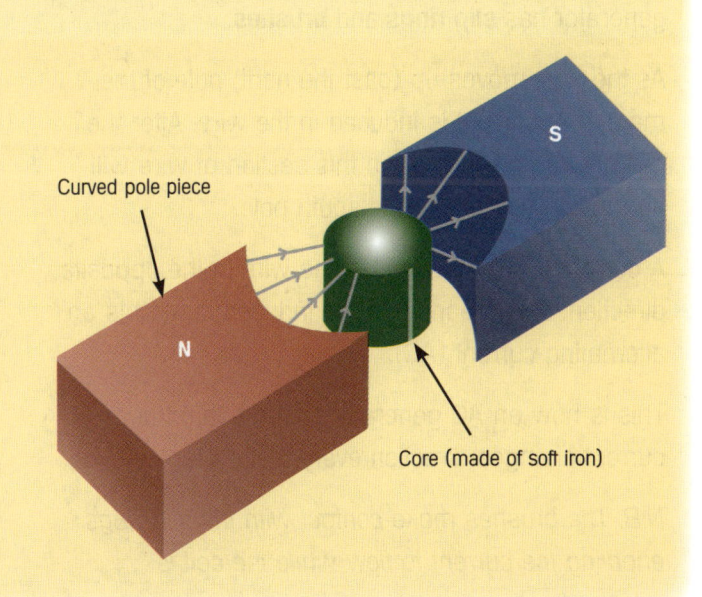

Key Words   **Direct current**   107

P6 Generating

Generating Electricity

Generating electricity is known as the **dynamo effect**. Electricity can be generated by moving a wire near a magnet, or a magnet near a wire.

In the UK, mains electricity is generated at 50 hertz (50Hz). This means the current goes back and forth along the wire 50 times each second.

DC Generator

A DC generator is a DC motor working in reverse. Instead of feeding a voltage to the coil and watching it move, the coil is moved to produce a voltage.

A DC generator enables energy to be stored for later use.

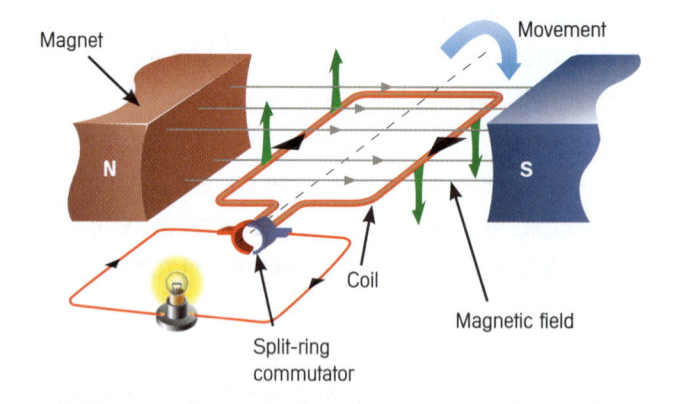

AC Generator

An **alternating current (AC)** can be generated by rotating a magnet inside a coil of wire.

In a power station, the electricity is generated by rotating electromagnets inside coils of wire.

HT Where a DC generator has commutators, an AC generator has **slip rings** and **brushes**.

As the wire moves up (past the north pole of the magnet) a current is induced in the wire. After the coil has turned half a turn this section of wire will be moving down past the south pole.

A current is now induced in the wire in the opposite direction. This means that the induced current is an alternating current (AC).

This is how an AC generator ensures that the current changes direction every half cycle.

N.B. The brushes make contact with the slip rings, enabling the current to flow while the coil is rotating freely.

N.B. You'll need to be able to label the diagram of an AC generator (below) in the exam.

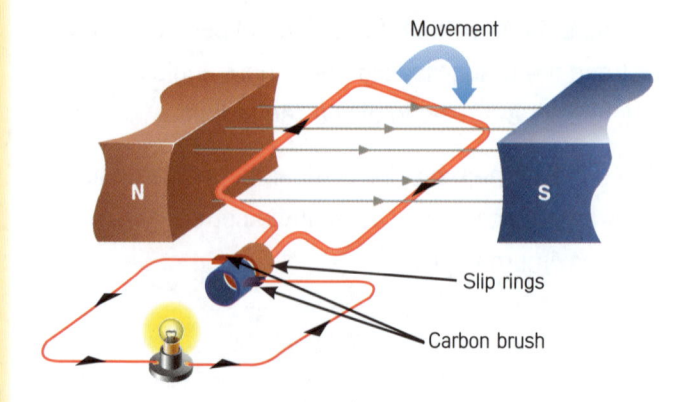

108 | Key Words | Dynamo effect • Alternating current

Generating P6

Inducing Voltages

A **voltage** is induced:
- across a **wire**, when the wire moves relative to a magnetic field
- across a **coil**, when the magnetic field linking the coil changes.

Reversing the direction of the changing magnetic field also changes the direction of the induced voltage.

The voltage induced can be increased, as shown in the table.

HT The induced voltage depends upon the rate at which the magnetic field changes.

The rate of change of the magnetic field can be increased by increasing the speed of movement.

❶ increasing the speed at which the magnet or coil moves/rotates (this also increases the frequency of the AC).	
❷ increasing the number of turns on the electromagnet's coils.	
❸ increasing the strength of the magnetic field.	

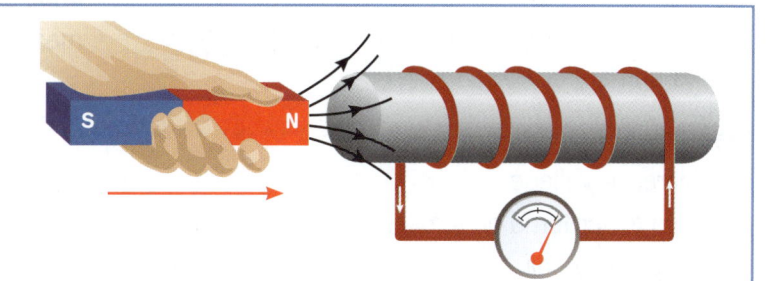

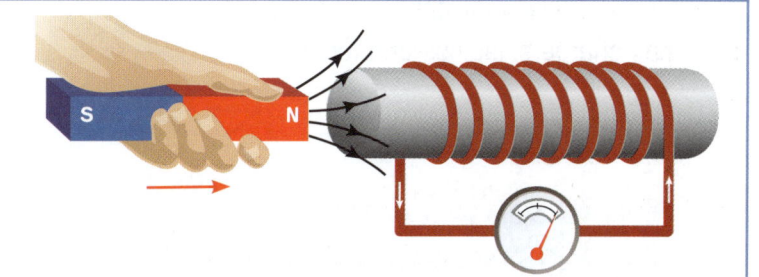

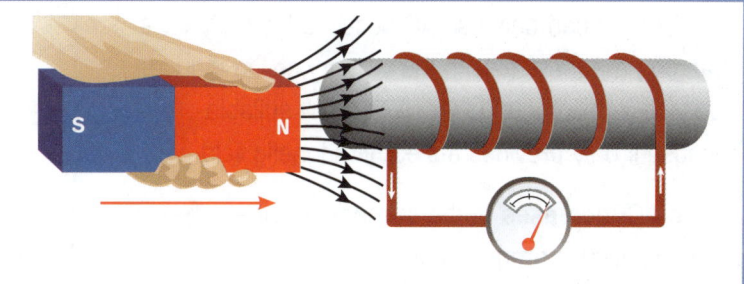

Quick Test

1. When a current-carrying wire is placed in a magnetic field it experiences a force and moves. What is this called?
2. What is meant by the dynamo effect?
3. At what frequency is mains electricity generated in the UK?

Key Words Voltage

P6 Transforming

Transformers

A **transformer** is made of two coils of wire wound onto an iron core.

The two coils of wire aren't connected to each other. This enables the transformer to change the size of an alternating voltage.

A transformer only works with AC. It **doesn't** change AC to DC.

Step-up transformers:
- increase voltage
- have more turns on the secondary coil than on the primary coil.

Step-down transformers:
- decrease voltage
- have fewer turns on the secondary coil than on the primary coil
- are used in everyday applications, such as phone chargers, laptops and radios.

HT The voltage on the secondary coil can be calculated from the voltage on the primary coil (and vice versa) using the following equation:

$$\frac{\text{Voltage across primary coil}}{\text{Voltage across secondary coil}} = \frac{\text{No. primary turns}}{\text{No. secondary turns}}$$

Example
A laptop runs on 12V. If it's to be plugged into the mains (230V), a transformer is needed. If the transformer has 960 turns on the primary coil, how many turns does it have on the secondary coil?

$$\frac{V_p}{V_s} = \frac{N_p}{N_s}$$

$$N_s = \frac{N_p \times V_s}{V_p}$$

$$= \frac{960 \times 12}{230} = \mathbf{50 \text{ turns}}$$

HT Transformers and AC

Transformers can only use AC because they rely on a **changing** magnetic field in the primary coil to induce a voltage in the secondary coil. DC isn't suitable because it only provides a **steady** magnetic field.

As the AC **increases** in the primary coil, the magnetic field it produces grows and cuts through the wire of the secondary coil. This induces a current (to try to cancel out the magnetic field from the primary coil).

The current or voltage in a transformer can be calculated using the transformer equation opposite.

NB. This only applies if the transformer is 100% efficient.

$$V_p I_p = V_s I_s$$

Where: V_p = voltage in primary coil
I_p = current in primary coil
V_s = voltage in secondary coil
I_s = current in secondary coil

Example
If a current of 0.3 amps is supplied to a transformer in a laptop at a voltage of 230 volts, what current is fed to the laptop after the voltage has been stepped down to 12 volts?

$$V_p I_p = V_s I_s$$

$$230 \times 0.3 = 12 \times I_p$$

$$I_p = \frac{230 \times 0.3}{12} = \mathbf{5.75A}$$

Key Words: Transformer

Transforming P6

Transformers in the National Grid

When overhead power cables carry current, they get hot so energy is wasted as heat. This power loss can be reduced by reducing the current. The power loss in transmission relates to the current **squared**.

HT Power loss = (Current²) × Resistance

In a step-up transformer, if you increase the voltage, the current automatically decreases. Therefore, step-up transformers are used to increase the voltages from power stations to supply the National Grid.

Step-down transformers are used in sub-stations in order to reduce the voltages for domestic and commercial users.

HT The transformer equation shows that the power input to a transformer is equal to the power output of a transformer.

This means that in a step-up transformer, when the voltage is increased, the current is decreased in the same proportion. As a lower current will reduce power loss during transmission, using a step-up transformer at the power station reduces the energy lost as the current flows along the overhead cables.

A step-down transformer reduces the voltage to a safer level for consumers (but increases the current).

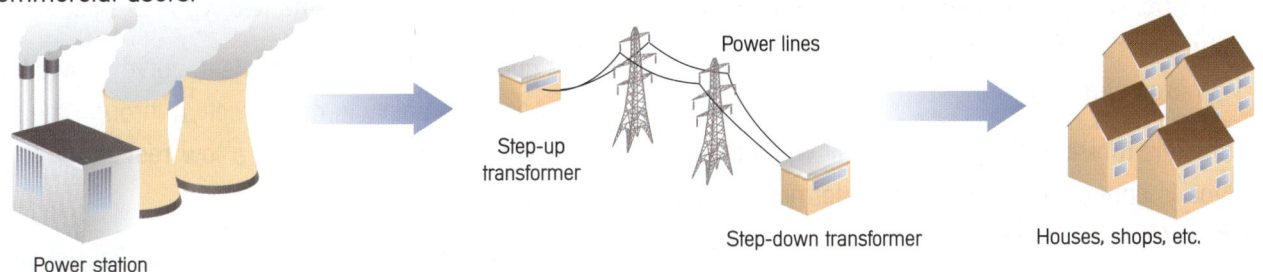

Power station → Step-up transformer → Power lines → Step-down transformer → Houses, shops, etc.

Isolating Transformers

An **isolating transformer** is used in some mains circuits, for example, bathroom shaver sockets, to make them safer.

In an isolating transformer, the two coils aren't connected to each other. This means that the user is isolated from the mains supply.

It's particularly important to use isolating transformers in areas such as bathrooms, so there's less chance of electrocution where there is water present.

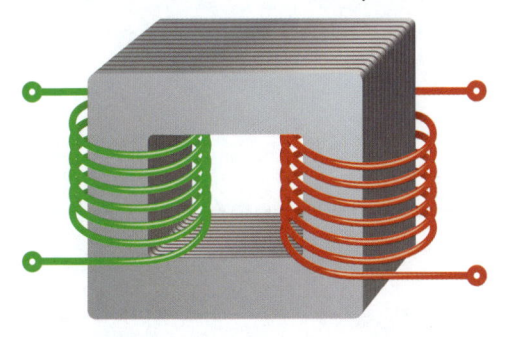

HT An isolating transformer has equal numbers of turns on the primary and secondary coils. This makes no difference to the voltage.

The benefit of an isolating transformer is that it keeps the two halves of the circuit separate. Therefore, there is less risk of contact between the live parts (connected to the mains) and the earth lead (connected to the body of, for example, a shaver).

Quick Test

1. What type of transformer decreases voltage?
2. **HT** Write the transformer equation.

P6 Charging

Diodes

A silicon **diode** is a device that allows current to flow through it in one direction only.

A **current–voltage characteristic** can be drawn for a diode by plotting the current through the diode against the voltage across the diode.

From the example opposite, it can be seen that the current flows through the diode in one direction but not in the opposite direction.

Current flows through the diode in this direction only.

Current–Voltage Characteristic Curve

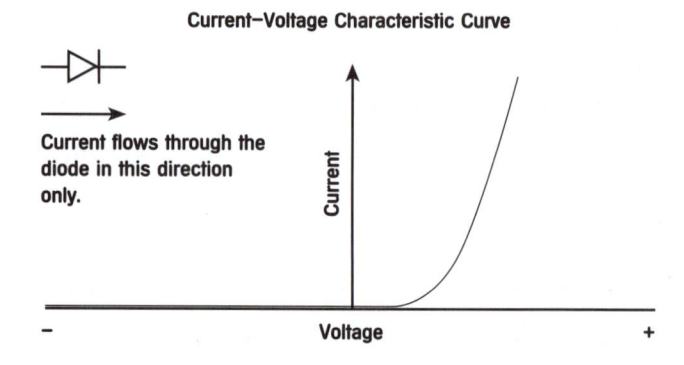

HT A silicon diode is made of two types of silicon:
- **n-type**, which contains extra electrons (so has extra negative charge carriers)
- **p-type**, which has holes where there should be electrons (so the holes are like positive charge carriers).

A diode is **forward biased** in a circuit when the n-type is connected to the negative terminal of the battery. Current can flow because:
- the electrons can flow towards the holes
- the holes can flow towards the electrons.

If the diode is **reverse biased** ('backwards'), the current can't flow. This is because the electrons seem to drop into the holes and are unable to get past the layer between the two types of silicon.

The current–voltage characteristic curve shows that current flows easily in one direction through the diode. This is because it has a **low resistance** to current in this direction.

Current doesn't flow easily in the opposite direction because the diode has a **high resistance** to current flow in the reverse direction.

Half-Wave Rectification

If alternating current is passed through a single diode, the diode will allow the current flowing in one direction to pass through and will stop the current flowing in the opposite direction. This is **half-wave rectification**.

You should recognise half-wave rectification from a voltage–time graph.

Unrectified Wave

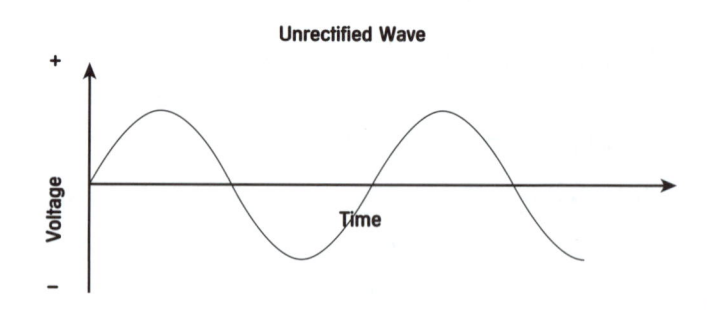

Half-Wave Rectified AC

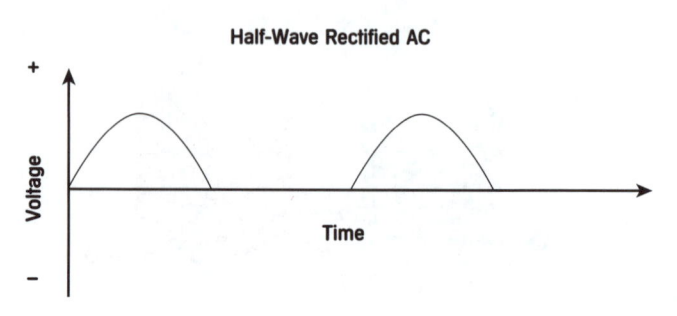

Key Words

Diode • Half-wave rectification

Charging P6

Full-Wave Rectification

A group of four diodes can be connected together to make a **bridge circuit** to give **full-wave rectification**.

You should recognise full-wave rectification from a voltage–time graph.

HT A bridge circuit can supply full-wave rectification of AC. For each half of the AC cycle, there are two diodes that can pass the current, and send it to the output:
- Positive half cycle – current passes P, B, load, C then Q.
- Negative half cycle – current passes Q, D, load, A then P.

During each half cycle, the current passes through the load in the **same direction**.

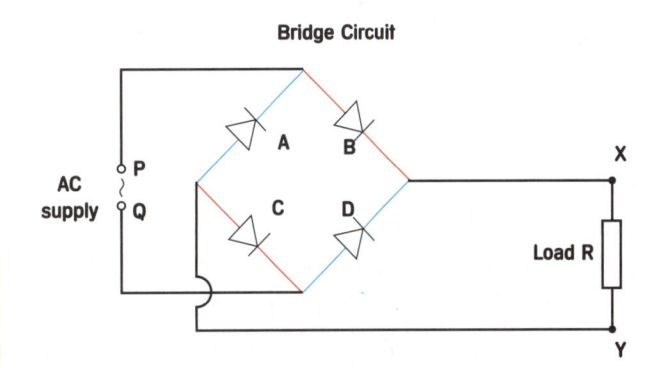

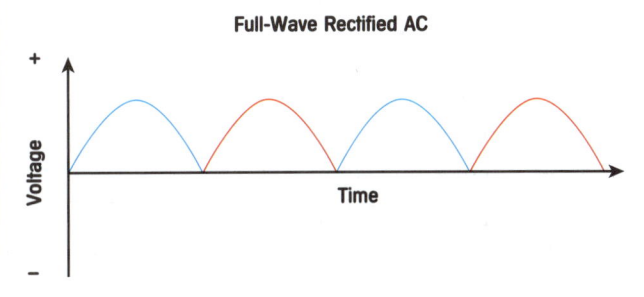

Capacitors

A **capacitor** stores charge that can be discharged later.

When current flows in a circuit containing an uncharged capacitor, the charge is stored on the capacitor and its pd increases.

When a charged capacitor is connected to a conductor, the capacitor behaves like a **battery**. The capacitor **discharges**, sending its stored current through the conductor.

HT When a charged capacitor is connected to a conductor, the flow of current from the capacitor to the conductor isn't steady. Instead the current flow decreases as the charge on the capacitor decreases.

As the charge on the capacitor decreases, the pd across the capacitor also decreases. This means that the pd across the conductor has decreased and so the current flowing decreases. This continues until the capacitor is fully discharged.

Simple Smoothing

A capacitor connected across a varying voltage supply produces a more **constant** (smoothed) output. This is useful for devices that need a more constant voltage supplied to them.

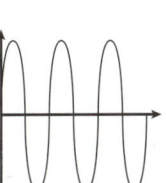

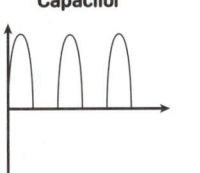

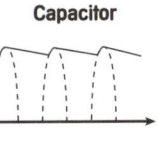

HT A capacitor **smoothes** the output by discharging when the pd falls to a certain level, putting more charge into the circuit. This boosts the current so that it remains constant.

When the pd in the circuit is high enough, the capacitor charges up again. It remains charged until the pd falls and the capacitor has to make up the difference once more.

Key Words — Full-wave rectification • Capacitor

P6 Exam Practice Questions

1 a) Three resistors with values 8Ω, 12Ω and 20Ω, are connected in series. Calculate their total combined resistance. **[1]**

b) The resistors are now connected so that the 20Ω resistor was in one branch of a parallel circuit and the 8Ω and 12Ω resistors were connected in series with each other in the other branch of the circuit. Calculate the total resistance of this combination. **[3]**

2 Describe how you would increase the speed of an electric motor. **[3]**

3 a) What does the gradient of a voltage-current graph represent? **[1]**

b) Describe the difference in resistance between the two ohmic conductors. How do you know? **[2]**

ID# Exam Practice Questions P6

4 a) How many diodes are required to produce full-wave rectification of an AC input? [1]

b) What is the name of the component used to 'smooth' a varying output voltage? [1]

5 A hairdryer powered by 230V has a resistance of 20Ω. How much current passes through the hairdryer? [2]

6 a) Explain how transformers are used in the National Grid. [4]

b) How is an isolating transformer different from a step-up or step-down transformer? [2]

HT 7 Describe the benefits of miniaturisation of transistors and the limits affecting miniaturisation. [4]

8 A combination of logic gates is shown below. Construct the truth table for this combination of logic gates. [4]

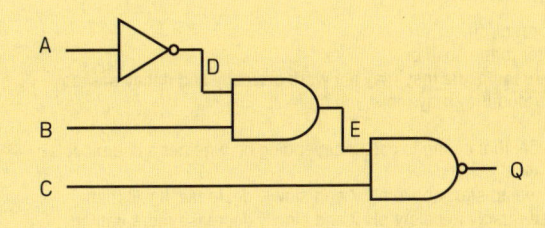

A	B	C	D	E	Q

Answers

Fundamental Chemical Concepts

Quick Test Answers
Page 9
1. electrons
2. nucleus
3. an atom that has lost or gained an electron.
4. The different types of atom in a compound; the number of each type of atom; where the bonds are in the compound.

B5 The Living Body

Quick Test Answers
Page 11
1. Ball and socket, hinge.
2. These muscles are in pairs and do opposite things. When one contracts the other relaxes.
3. Secretes synovial fluid.
4. It may cause further injury, especially to the spine.

Page 14
1. Amoeba   2. Closed
3. There are two circuits: heart to lungs and back; and heart to body and back.
4. Impulses from the SAN cause atria to contract and stimulate the AVN, impulses from the AVN cause ventricles to contract.

Page 19
1. **Any four from:** Irregular heart beat; Hole in the heart; Damaged or weak valves; Coronary heart disease; Heart attacks.
2. Haemophilia   3. Asbestosis   4. A, B, AB, O

Page 24
1. Oestrogen and progesterone
2. Produce sperm, produce testosterone
3. Carbohydrase, protease, lipase.
4. Clean the blood. Filter the blood reabsorbing water and useful substances.

Page 27
1. **Any two from:** Healthier diets/lifestyle, modern treatments, better housing, fewer industrial diseases.
2. Correct size and age, tissue match and same blood group.
3. Risk of miscarriage, decision of whether to continue with the pregnancy.

Answers to Exam Practice Questions
1. No starch molecules as they are too large **[1]**; Sugar present as molecule is small **[1]**; Therefore able to diffuse through partially permeable membrane **[1]**.
2. a) Simple
   b) i) Hinge joint   ii) Ligaments
3. a)

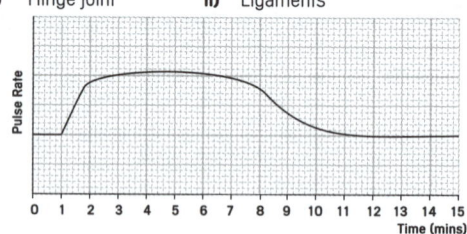

   [1 for increased heart rate for 7 mins; 1 for heart rate returning to start point after a further 5 minutes]
   b) To supply oxygen **[1]** and glucose **[1]** to the respiring muscles.
4. a) Oestrogen and progesterone
   b) FSH / follicle-stimulating hormone
5. a) The baby's mass increased consistently **[1]** apart from in June and September when it dipped slightly **[1]**. The baby's mass stayed within the healthy range. **[1]**
   b) 2.5kg
6. a) **Any three from:** Genes; Diet; Growth hormone; Disease; Exercise.
   b) **Any two from:** They may be family members / related; There may be a genetic link; Growth hormone problem may have been inherited
7. Transfused blood possesses A antigens; John's blood has Anti-A antibodies; Antibodies will recognise A antigens as 'non-self/foreign'; A antigens are on red blood cells **[Any two for 2]** Cells carrying SA antigen will be *agglutinated*. **[1]**

C5 How Much? (Quantitative Analysis)

Quick Test Answers
Page 31
1. A measurement of the amount of substance.
2. 44g/mol
3. a) 36g b) 18g/mol c) 4 moles

Page 32
1. CH
2. 53.5g/mol
3. CH_2

Page 34
1. 1.2 dm^3
2. g/dm^3 or mol/dm^3
3. Add water to the solution.
4. If they are too dilute they may not work correctly and if they are too concentrated they may make you more ill.

Page 36
1. A chemical that changes colour depending on whether a chemical is acid or alkali.
2. The pH would start above pH 7 and slowly decrease. It will then decrease rapidly to below pH 7 and slowly decrease more until it reaches a steady level at a pH of less than 7.

Page 41
1. Measure the volume of gas made, or the mass lost.
2. ⇌
3. Temperature; Pressure; Concentration of reactants; Concentration of products.
4. $2SO_2 + O_2 \rightleftharpoons 2SO_3$

Page 43
1. An acid that completely ionises in water.
2. A precipitate is made when ions from two different solutions collide and react to make an insoluble product.
3. Barium nitrate.
4. Ethanoic acid does not completely ionise, whereas nitric acid does. This means that nitric acid releases more H^+ and so has a lower pH.

Answers to Exam Practice Questions
1. 0.15dm^3
2. The volume of acid or alkali added from a burette that just neutralises the test solution. (Final volume – Start volume on the burette)
3. It starts higher than 7 and falls lower **should be ticked**
4. 48dm^3 (2 × 12 = 24) **[1 for calculation, 1 for correct answer]**
5. a) Yield increases
   b) Yield decreases
   c) 79%
6. a) Sulfur, air, water. **[All three named for 2]**
   b) The reaction would be too slow if it were cooler. It is a compromise between rate and yield.
7. A bromide.
8. a) 16 ÷ 40 = 0.4 moles **[1 for calculation, 1 for correct answer]**
   b) 3 × 16 = 48g
9. 0.18mol/dm^3
10. $HCl \rightarrow H^+ + Cl^-$ **[All correct for 3]**
11. $KI + AgNO_3 \rightarrow KNO_3 + AgI$ **[All correct for 2]**

Answers

P5 Space for Reflection

Quick Test Answers

Page 47
1. Natural – moon; Artificial – **Any one from:** Communication; Weather; Military satellite.
2. It increases.
3. 24 hours

Page 53
1. Scalar – **any two from:** Mass; Energy; Speed; Time. Vector – **any two from:** Velocity; Force; Acceleration.
2. Momentum = Mass × Velocity
3. It reduces the force required to act and reduces the injuries caused.

Page 55
1. 1m–10km
2. It reduces their strength or stops them.
3. They travel more slowly through the ionised gas in the ionosphere.
4. Radio waves have very long wavelength.

Page 61
1. The distance between the centre of the lens (optical centre) and the focal point.
2. Blue / violet light

Answers to Exam Practice Questions
1. a) B **Should be ticked**.
   b) They orbit high above he Earth; They take 24 hours to complete one orbit; In fixed position above Earth's surface **[Any two for 2]**
2. a) Average speed = $\frac{\text{Total distance}}{\text{Total time taken}} = \frac{6000}{600} = 10\text{m/s}$ **[1 for calculation, 1 for correct answer]**
   b) 70 − 60 = 10km/h
   c) Scalar, because it has size only.
3. a) **Horizontal** – Constant velocity; **Vertical** – Projectile accelerates.
   b) Speed = $\frac{\text{distance}}{\text{time}}$
      Time = $\frac{\text{distance}}{\text{speed}}$
      Time = $\frac{18}{6}$
      Time = 3s **[1 for calculation, 1 for correct answer]**
   c) s = ut + $\frac{1}{2}$at²
      s = (0 × 3) + ($\frac{1}{2}$ × 10 × 3²)
      s = 0 + 45
      s = 45m **[2 for calculation, 1 for correct answer]**
4. Momentum = Mass × Velocity = (200 + 50) × 30 = 7500kg m/s **[1 for calculation, 1 for correct answer]**
5. a) i) It is being refracted.
      ii) The waves travel from one medium to another; This causes the wave speed to decrease; and the wave to change direction.
   b) Refractive index = $\frac{\text{speed of light in vacuum}}{\text{speed of light in medium}}$
      Refractive index = $\frac{3 \times 10^8}{2 \times 10^8} = \frac{3}{2}$
      Refractive index = 1.5 **[1 for calculation, 1 for correct answer]**
6. **This is a model answer, which demonstrates QWC and therefore would score the full 6 marks:** Waves can interfere constructively, which is known as constructive interference or reinforcement. This happens when identical waves arrive at a point in phase. The result is a wave with a larger amplitude and bright fringes can be seen. Waves can also interfere destructively, which is known as destructive interference or cancellation. This happens when identical waves arrive at a point out of phase. The result is a wave with an amplitude of zero, and dark fringes can be seen.

B6 Beyond the Microscope

Quick Test Answers

Page 67
1. A protein coat, surrounding a strand of genetic material.
2. Spherical, rod, spiral, curved rod.
3. Through the nose (airborne microbes), mouth (contaminated food and water), skin (insect bites, cuts, needles), reproductive organs (unprotected sex).
4. Lister

Page 69
1. Making yoghurt, cheese production, vinegar production, silage production, and composting.
2. Distillation
3. Anaerobic
4. Breakdown of lactose, and production of lactic acid.

Page 71
1. **Any two from:** Alcohol, biogas, wood.
2. In a digester.
3. Alternative to fossil fuels, no net increase in greenhouse gases, no particulates produced.
4. Gasohol.

Page 74
1. Mineral particles, dead material, living organisms, air, water.
2. Provides minerals, source of water and anchorage.
3. Slugs, snails, wireworms.
4. By draining it and aerating it.

Page 77
1. Microscopic plants.
2. Oil, Sewage, PCBs, fertilisers, pesticides and detergents.
3. Fertiliser run-off into water system.
4. Organisms at the top of food chains like whales. This is because they get a huge dose of the chemical as they are at the top of the food chain.

Page 81
1. In gel beads; On reagent sticks.
2. Inserting genes from one organism into another to alter the genetic code.
3. Because the enzymes are denatured by the high temperatures. Their shape is changed so the 'key' no longer fits the 'lock'.

Answers to Exam Practice Questions
1. a) It is easier to separate the enzyme from the milk; No need to separate the enzyme and milk; Milk not contaminated; Enzyme protected in bead; It can be reused. **[Any one for 1]**
   b) To measure the glucose level in their blood.
2. **Any one from:** Enzymes are not destroyed; Enzymes work at low concentrations / only tiny amounts are needed.
   b) No, the temperature was too high / Heat destroys / denatures enzymes.
   c) i) Egg
      ii) There is protease in the washing powder; Egg is a protein; Protease breaks down egg.
3. a) Penguin, cod, squid **[All three named for 1]**
   b) i) Microscopic plants.
      ii) Temperature; Light; Availability of minerals **[All three named for 3]**
4. a) $\frac{5 + 5 + 6 + 7}{4} = \frac{23}{4} = 5.75$mm
   b) Plate 4 (bathroom cleaner)
   c) As a control that the student could compare her results against.
   d) By repeating her investigation four times.
5. The continuous shower of organic detritus falling from the upper layers of the ocean.
6. **This is a model answer, which demonstrates QWC and therefore would score the full 6 marks:** DNA fingerprinting has four main stages. A sample of DNA must first be obtained; DNA can be extracted from hair follicles, blood or semen. The DNA is then cut into fragments using restriction enzymes. A technique called electrophoresis separates the DNA fragments so that the sample can be analysed by comparing it with a reference sample, e.g. blood found at a crime scene. The analysis will show whether the DNA matches the reference sample.

Answers

C6 Chemistry Out There

Quick Test Answers
Page 88
1. Negative electrode (cathode).
2. Size of current and the time it flows for.

Page 89
1. Coating iron or steel in zinc.
2. To make alcoholic drinks, solvents or as a fuel for cars.
3. Batch
4. Continuous

Page 92
1. Chlorine, fluorine and carbon.
2. A chlorine atom, Cl•
3. Magnesium and calcium ions.
4. Add washing soda (sodium carbonate crystals), or pass the water through an ion-exchange column.

Page 95
1. All the carbon-carbon bonds are single bonds.
2. The bromine water turns from orange to colourless.
3. Saponification.
4. a) Water b) Washing powder

Answers to Exam Practice Questions
1. a) Cathode / negative electrode.
   b) Melt **[1]** or dissolve it. **[1]**
   c) Copper.
2. Tin; Magnesium chloride
3. a) This contains the enzymes to carry out the reaction.
   b) Hydration.
   c) Phosphoric acid.
4. a) CFCs break down and release chlorine atoms (radicals) **[1]** which destroy ozone molecules and make the ozone thinner. **[1]**
   b) Skin cancer; Sunburn; Cataracts **should be ticked**
5. calcium carbonate + water + carbon dioxide → calcium hydrogencarbonate **[All correct for 2]**
6. **This is a model answer, which demonstrates QWC and therefore would score the full 6 marks:** Temporary hardness is caused when rain water reacts with calcium carbonate to form dissolved sodium hydrogencarbonate. Dissolved magnesium and calcium ions cause permanent hardness. When hard water is passed through an ion-exchange resin, the calcium and magnesium ions are attracted to the resin and are swapped for sodium ions.
7. fat + sodium hydroxide → soap + glycerol
8. a) $2H_2 + O_2 \rightarrow 2H_2O$ **[All correct for 3]**
   b) Because the reactions involve both reduction **[1]** and oxidation. **[1]**
9. a) Reduction as electrons have been added.
   b) Oxidation as electrons have been removed.

P6 Electricity for Gadgets

Quick Test Answers
Page 101
1. Resistance increases.
2. Series
3. It decreases.

Page 105
1. Both inputs 'high' or 1.
2. It uses a small current to switch on a large current.
3. NOR gate

Page 109
1. The motor effect.
2. Generating electricity.
3. 50Hz

Page 111
1. Step-down transformer
2. $V_p I_p = V_s I_s$

Answers to Exam Practice Questions
1. a) $R_T = 8 + 12 + 20$
      $R_T = 40\Omega$
   b) Resistance of 8Ω and 12Ω resistors combined = 20Ω
      $\frac{1}{R_T} = \frac{1}{20} + \frac{1}{20}$
      $\frac{1}{R_T} = \frac{2}{20}$
      $R_T = \frac{20}{2}$
      $R_T = 10\Omega$ **[2 for calculation, 1 for correct answer]**
2. Increase number of coils; Increase magnetic field; Increase electric current.
3. a) Resistance.
   b) Ohmic conductor B has a greater resistance; Because it has a greater gradient.
4. a) Four
   b) Capacitor
5. Current = $\frac{Voltage}{Resistance} = \frac{230}{20} = 11.5A$ **[1 for calculation, 1 for correct answer]**
6. a) Step-up transformers are used from power stations to supply the National Grid; to increase voltage so that current is reduced in overhead power lines; However, the voltage is too high for domestic and commercial users so step-down transformers are used in sub-stations; to reduce the voltage before it reaches homes and offices.
   b) An isolating transformer has an equal number of turns **[1]** on the primary and secondary coils **[1]**. (Voltage out equals voltage in)
7. Benefits: Increases the number of transistors that can be connected in a processor; Means computer processors can be made smaller. **[2]**
   Limitations: Smaller components give out more heat as a current passes through; The thinner they are, the less resistance they offer (quantum tunnelling). **[2]**
8.

A	B	C	D	E	Q
0	0	0	1	0	1
0	0	1	1	0	1
0	1	0	1	1	1
0	1	1	1	1	0
1	0	0	0	0	1
1	0	1	0	0	1
1	1	0	0	0	1
1	1	1	0	0	1

[$\frac{1}{2}$ mark for every correct row]

Glossary

Acceleration – the rate at which an object changes its velocity.

Aerobic respiration – respiration using oxygen, which releases energy and produces carbon dioxide and water.

Alcohol – waste product made by yeast, following anaerobic respiration.

Alveoli – tiny air sacs in the lungs where gas exchange occurs.

Amino acids – building blocks of proteins.

Anaerobic respiration – releasing energy from glucose in living cells in the absence of oxygen to produce a small amount of energy very quickly.

Anode – the positive electrode.

Antagonistic muscles – a pair of muscles that work together to create movement: when one contracts the other relaxes.

Antibiotics – medication used to kill bacterial pathogens inside the body.

Anticoagulant – drugs used to prevent blood clotting.

Antiseptic – a chemical that kills microorganisms, but is safe to use on skin.

Artery – large blood vessel with narrow lumen and thick elastic walls (carries blood away from the lungs).

Asbestosis – a lung disease caused by inhaling asbestos particles.

Aseptic – sterile conditions which prevent contamination.

Asthma – an illness that stops people breathing properly due to a narrowing of the airways.

Bacteria – microscopic, single-celled organism with no nucleus.

Biodiversity – the variety of living organisms in an ecosystem.

Biofuel – a fuel produced by a living organism.

Biogas – fuel produced from the anaerobic decomposition of organic waste.

Biomass – the mass of matter in a living organism.

Bronchi – the branches of the trachea (windpipe).

Bronchioles – the small branches of the bronchi.

Budding – reproducing asexually by 'budding' off the parent.

Carnivore – an animal that hunts and eats other animals.

Cartilage – smooth, connecting tissue that covers the ends of bones in a joint.

Catalyst – a substance used to speed up a chemical reaction without being chemically altered itself.

Cathode – the negative electrode.

Centripetal force – the external force towards the centre of a circle required to make an object follow a circular path at a constant speed.

Chitin – material that is used in exoskeletons.

Chlorofluorocarbons (CFCs) – inert chemicals used as refrigerants and propellant gases; have been shown to damage the ozone layer.

Cholesterol – a type of fat that builds up in the arteries.

Circulatory system – a system of tubes and a pump to move fluids around a body. In humans, this consists of the heart and blood vessels.

Clone – a genetically identical offspring of an organism.

Clot – a mass or lump of coagulated blood.

Concentration – a measure of the amount of substance dissolved in a solution.

Contact Process – the process used to make sulfuric acid.

Convex lens – a lens that causes light rays passing through it to meet at a point (converge).

Critical angle – the largest incident angle at which refraction can occur.

Data – information collected from an experiment/investigation.

Decomposers – organisms that break down dead plants or animals into simpler substances.

Deoxygenated – blood with no or little oxygen.

Detritivore – an organism that feeds on dead organisms and the waste of living organisms.

Diabetes – a disease caused by the failure to control blood sugar levels due to the inability of the pancreas to secrete insulin.

Diffraction – the spreading out of a wave as a result of passing an obstacle through a gap.

Diffusion – the net movement of particles from an area of high concentration to an area of low concentration.

Digestion – the process of breaking down food into smaller soluble particles that can pass through the gut wall and into the blood.

Dilute – to reduce the concentration of a substance using water.

Dispersion – (of light) the separation of light into different wavelengths, which represent the colours of the rainbow (visible spectrum).

Distillation – a process used to separate liquids by evaporation followed by condensation to produce a pure liquid.

DNA (deoxyribonucleic acid) – the nucleic acid molecules that make up chromosomes in cells and carry genetic information.

Echocardiogram – a medical test which uses sound waves that echo against structures in the heart to build up a detailed picture of the heart.

Glossary

Egestion – the removal of undigested food and waste from an animal's body.

Electrocardiogram – a tracing of the electric currents that initiate the heart beat; used to diagnose heart conditions.

Electrolysis – the breaking down of a liquid or dissolved ionic substance using electricity.

Electrolyte – an aqueous or molten substance that contains free-moving ions and is therefore able to conduct electricity.

Electromagnetic – energy transmitted as waves.

Electromagnetic waves – includes radio waves, visible light and gamma, all of which can travel through a vacuum at the speed of light.

Empirical formula – the simplest whole number ratio of each type of atom in a compound.

Enzyme – a protein molecule and biological catalyst found in living organisms that helps chemical reactions to take place.

Equilibrium – the state in which a chemical reaction proceeds at the same rate as its reverse reaction. (The quantities of reactants and products stay balanced.)

Excretion – the removal of waste products from the body.

Expiration – exhaling (breathing out) air.

Fermentation – the process by which microorganisms obtain energy and produce other substances through respiration; the process by which yeast converts sugars to alcohol and carbon dioxide through anaerobic respiration.

Fermenter – a controlled environment that maintains ideal conditions for microorganisms to carry out fermentation.

Fertilisation – the fusion of a male gamete with a female gamete.

Fertiliser – any substance used to make soil more fertile.

Focal length – a measure of how strongly an optical system focuses or diverges.

Focal point – the point at which all light rays parallel to the axis of the lens converge.

Force – a push or pull acting on an object; measured in newtons (N).

Fractional distillation – a method of separating a mixture of liquids each with a different boiling point.

Frequency – the number of waves produced (or that pass a particular point) in one second.

Flagellum – a 'whip-like' tail found on bacterial cells and used for movement.

FSH – (follicle-stimulating hormone) – hormone involved in the menstrual cycle.

Fuel cell – an electrochemical cell that converts chemical energy into electricity.

Full-wave rectification – the whole of an input current is converted to a constant polarity (positive or negative) at its output.

Fungi – single-celled microscopic organisms.

GDA (Guideline Daily Amount) – the recommended guidelines for daily amounts of nutrients.

Gene – a small section of DNA, in a chromosome, that determines a particular characteristic on its own or in combination with other genes.

Genetic engineering/modification – the alteration of the genetic make-up of an organism, e.g. by introducing new genes from another organism.

Gravitational force – a force of attraction between masses.

Gravity (gravitational force) – a force of attraction between masses.

Growth – an increase in mass, length or size.

Haemoglobin – the pigment that carries oxygen in the red blood cells.

Half-wave rectification – either the positive or negative half of an AC wave is allowed to pass through a diode, while the other half is blocked.

Hardness – the inability of water to make a lather with soap due to dissolved ions in the water.

Herbivore – animals that eat plants.

Hormone – a chemical messenger that travels around the body in the blood to affect target organs.

Humus – decayed remains of animals and plants which were in the soil.

Hydrophilic – water loving.

Hydrophobic – water hating.

Hypothesis – a scientific explanation that will be tested through experiments.

Indicator – a chemical that changes colour to show changes in pH.

Indicator species – a species that acts as an indicator of pollution.

Inspiration – inhaling (breathing in) air.

Insulin – a hormone, produced by the pancreas, which controls blood glucose concentrations.

Interference – when a signal is corrupted, e.g. hissing on the radio.

***In vitro* fertilisation (IVF)** – fertilisation that takes place outside the body, usually in a Petri dish.

Ion – a positively or negatively charged particle formed when an atom or group of atoms gains or loses one or more electron(s).

Glossary

Ion-exchange column – a piece of equipment used to swap ions that cause hardness for sodium or hydrogen ions. This softens the water.

Ionise – to make into ions.

Ionosphere – a layer of charged particles in the Earth's atmosphere.

LH – (luteinising hormone) – involved in the menstrual cycle, works with FSH.

Ligament – the tissue that connects a bone to a joint.

Limescale – insoluble calcium carbonate deposits; found on the heating element of a kettle.

Limiting reactant – the reactant that gets used up first in a reaction.

Longitudinal wave – a wave where the particles vibrate in the direction of energy transfer.

Magnification – enlarging the size of an image; measured as $\frac{\text{image size}}{\text{object size}}$.

Menstrual cycle – the monthly shedding of the uterus lining and unfertilised egg.

Microorganism – an organism that can only be seen with a microscope, e.g. bacteria.

Model – a representation of a system or idea, used to describe or explain the system or idea.

Mole – a measurement of the amount of substance. Contains 6×10^{23} particles.

Momentum – a measure of the state of motion of an object as a product of its mass and velocity.

Neutralisation – reaction between an acid and a base which forms a neutral solution.

Orbit – the path of an object around a larger object.

Orbital period – the time it takes an object to make one complete orbit.

Ovary – the female reproductive organ that produces eggs.

Oxygenated – with/containing oxygen.

Oxidation – a reaction involving the gain of oxygen, the loss of hydrogen or the loss of electrons.

Ozone – an allotrope of oxygen made from O_3 molecules.

Pacemaker – the group of cells that control the beating of the heart.

Parabolic – curved path taken by a projectile.

Pasteurisation – the heat treatment of liquids which prolong their shelf life by limiting bacterial growth.

Pathogen – a disease-causing microorganism.

Penicillin – an antibiotic/chemical that kills bacteria; used to treat infections.

pH – a measure of the acidity of a solution.

Photosynthesis – the chemical process that takes place in green plants where water combines with carbon dioxide to produce glucose using light energy.

Plankton – microscopic plants (phytoplankton) and animals (zooplankton) that float in water.

Polarisation – the blocking of light waves that oscillate in certain directions, for example, to cut out glare.

Pollution – the contamination of an environment by chemicals, waste or heat.

Precipitate – an insoluble solid formed during a reaction involving ionic solutions.

Producers – organisms that produce biomass when they photosynthesise, i.e. green plants; organisms that occupy the first trophic level of a food chain.

Projectile – an object that's projected forward, for example, fired into the air.

Rarefaction – area of low pressure in a medium caused by a wave, e.g. sound.

Real image – an image produced by rays of light meeting at a point; can be projected onto a screen.

Redox reaction – a reaction that involves both reduction and oxidation.

Reduction – a reaction involving the loss of oxygen, the gain of hydrogen or the gain of electrons.

Reflection – change in direction of a wave at a boundary between two media.

Refraction – change in direction of a light ray as it passes from one medium to another and changes speed.

Refractive index – a measure of a medium's ability to bend light due to slowing the light down.

Relative formula mass (M_r) – the sum of the atomic masses of all the atoms in a compound.

Relative speed – the speed of an object, relative to another object that is being treated to be at rest.

Residual air – the amount of gas remaining in the lung at the end of a maximal exhalation.

Respiration – a process that takes place in cells, which releases energy from glucose.

Respiratory system – where gas exchange occurs, e.g. the lungs in humans or gills in fish.

Reversible reaction – a reaction in which the products can react to reform the original reactants under the same conditions.

Rust – hydrated iron(III) oxide.

Glossary

Saponification – the process used to make soap by reacting vegetable oil with hot sodium hydroxide.

Satellite – an object that orbits a planet.

Scalar quantity – a quantity where there is only size.

Skeleton – the supporting framework of an animal's body.

Soluble – a property that means a substance can dissolve in a solvent.

Solute – the substance that gets dissolved.

Solution – the mixture formed when a solute dissolves in a solvent.

Solvent – a liquid that can dissolve another substance to produce a solution.

Speed – the rate at which an object moves.

Strong acid – an acid that fully ionises when added to water.

Surrogacy – carrying and delivering a baby to give to someone else. Usually the baby is not genetically linked to the surrogate.

Synovial joint – type of joint allowing movement in places such as elbow and knee.

Tidal air – the volume of air inhaled and exhaled at each breath.

Titration – a method used to find the concentration of an acid or an alkali.

Titre – the volume of acid needed to neutralise an alkali (or vice versa) in a titration.

Total internal reflection – complete reflection of a light or infrared ray back into a medium.

Toxin – a poison produced by a living organism.

Trachea – the windpipe (through which air gets to the lungs).

Trajectory – the path of a moving body.

Transgenic organism – an organism that has had new genes inserted into it.

Transpiration – the loss of water (by diffusion and evaporation) from plants, especially from their leaves.

Transverse wave – a wave in which the vibrations are at 90° to the direction of wave travel.

Variable – something that changes during the course of an experiment/investigation.

Vector quantity – a quantity where both size and direction are known.

Vein – a type of blood vessel that transports blood towards the heart.

Velocity – an object's rate of displacement or speed in a particular direction.

Ventilation – breathing.

Virus – a tiny microorganism with a very simple structure.

Vital capacity – the volume of air that can be exhaled from the lungs after the deepest possible breath has been taken.

Wavelength – the distance between corresponding points on two adjacent disturbances.

Weak acid – an acid that partially ionises when added to water.

HT **Active transport** – the movement of substances against a concentration gradient; requires energy.

Agglutinin – an agglutinin is a substance that causes particles to coagulate to form a thickened mass. Agglutinins can be antibodies that cause antigens to aggregate by binding to the antigen-binding sites of antibodies.

Anti-diuretic hormone (ADH) – a hormone that controls the amount of water reabsorbed by the kidneys and, therefore, the concentration of urine.

Chain reaction – a reaction, e.g. nuclear fission, that is self-sustaining.

Contractile vacuole – a tiny organelle found in some organisms that pumps fluid in a cyclical manner from within the cell to the outside; helps maintain water balance.

Emulsify – to break down fats into small droplets to form an emulsion.

Immunosuppressive drugs – drugs which dampen down the immune system.

Marine snow – a continuous shower of mostly organic detritus falling from the upper layers of the ocean.

Ossification – the replacement of cartilage with sodium and phosphorus salts to make bones hard during growth.

Ultrafiltration – the process that takes place in the kidneys in which water and molecules are squeezed out of the blood into the tubules.

Virtual image – an image produced by rays of light appearing to come from a point; can't be projected onto a screen.

Notes

Notes

Periodic Table

Key

relative atomic mass
atomic symbol
name
atomic (proton) number

1	2											3	4	5	6	7	0
					1 **H** hydrogen 1												4 **He** helium 2
7 **Li** lithium 3	9 **Be** beryllium 4											11 **B** boron 5	12 **C** carbon 6	14 **N** nitrogen 7	16 **O** oxygen 8	19 **F** fluorine 9	20 **Ne** neon 10
23 **Na** sodium 11	24 **Mg** magnesium 12											27 **Al** aluminium 13	28 **Si** silicon 14	31 **P** phosphorus 15	32 **S** sulfur 16	35.5 **Cl** chlorine 17	40 **Ar** argon 18
39 **K** potassium 19	40 **Ca** calcium 20	45 **Sc** scandium 21	48 **Ti** titanium 22	51 **V** vanadium 23	52 **Cr** chromium 24	55 **Mn** manganese 25	56 **Fe** iron 26	59 **Co** cobalt 27	59 **Ni** nickel 28	63.5 **Cu** copper 29	65 **Zn** zinc 30	70 **Ga** gallium 31	73 **Ge** germanium 32	75 **As** arsenic 33	79 **Se** selenium 34	80 **Br** bromine 35	84 **Kr** krypton 36
85 **Rb** rubidium 37	88 **Sr** strontium 38	89 **Y** yttrium 39	91 **Zr** zirconium 40	93 **Nb** niobium 41	96 **Mo** molybdenum 42	[98] **Tc** technetium 43	101 **Ru** ruthenium 44	103 **Rh** rhodium 45	106 **Pd** palladium 46	108 **Ag** silver 47	112 **Cd** cadmium 48	115 **In** indium 49	119 **Sn** tin 50	122 **Sb** antimony 51	128 **Te** tellurium 52	127 **I** iodine 53	131 **Xe** xenon 54
133 **Cs** caesium 55	137 **Ba** barium 56	139 **La*** lanthanum 57	178 **Hf** hafnium 72	181 **Ta** tantalum 73	184 **W** tungsten 74	186 **Re** rhenium 75	190 **Os** osmium 76	192 **Ir** iridium 77	195 **Pt** platinum 78	197 **Au** gold 79	201 **Hg** mercury 80	204 **Tl** thallium 81	207 **Pb** lead 82	209 **Bi** bismuth 83	[209] **Po** polonium 84	[210] **At** astatine 85	[222] **Rn** radon 86
[223] **Fr** francium 87	[226] **Ra** radium 88	[227] **Ac*** actinium 89	[261] **Rf** rutherfordium 104	[262] **Db** dubnium 105	[266] **Sg** seaborgium 106	[264] **Bh** bohrium 107	[277] **Hs** hassium 108	[268] **Mt** meitnerium 109	[271] **Ds** darmstadtium 110	[272] **Rg** roentgenium 111							

Elements with atomic numbers 112–116 have been reported but not fully authenticated

*The lanthanoids (atomic numbers 58–71) and the actinoids (atomic numbers 90–103) have been omitted.

Equations Sheet

energy = mass × specific heat capacity × temperature change	weight = mass × gravitational field strength
energy = mass × specific latent heat	work done = force × distance
efficiency = $\dfrac{\text{useful energy output (×100\%)}}{\text{total energy input}}$	power = $\dfrac{\text{work done}}{\text{time}}$
wave speed = frequency × wavelength	power = force × speed
power = voltage × current	KE = $\tfrac{1}{2}mv^2$
energy supplied = power × time	momentum = mass × velocity
average speed = $\dfrac{\text{distance}}{\text{time}}$	force = $\dfrac{\text{change in momentum}}{\text{time}}$
distance = average speed × time	GPE = mgh
$s = \dfrac{(u+v)}{2} \times t$	$mgh = \tfrac{1}{2}mv^2$
acceleration = $\dfrac{\text{change in speed}}{\text{time taken}}$	resistance = $\dfrac{\text{voltage}}{\text{current}}$
force = mass × acceleration	$v = u + at$
$v^2 = u^2 + 2as$	$s = ut + \tfrac{1}{2}at^2$
$m_1 u_1 + m_2 u_2 = (m_1 + m_2)v$	refractive index = $\dfrac{\text{speed of light in a vacuum}}{\text{speed of light in medium}}$
magnification = $\dfrac{\text{image size}}{\text{object size}}$	$I_e = I_b + I_c$
$\dfrac{\text{voltage across primary coil}}{\text{voltage across secondary coil}} = \dfrac{\text{number of primary turns}}{\text{number of secondary turns}}$	power loss = (current)² × resistance
$V_p I_p = V_s I_s$	

Index

A
acceleration 51
acids 35, 42
actions 51
active transport 77
aerobic respiration 17
agglutinins 16
alcohol 65, 69, 88-89
alternating current (AC) 108
alveoli 17-18
amino acids 21
anaerobic respiration 68-69
anodes 84-85
antagonistic muscles 11
antibiotics 67
anticoagulants 16
anti-diuretic hormone 22
antiseptics 67
arteries 15
asbestosis 19
aseptic techniques 65
asthma 19
atoms 6

B
bacteria 64, 68
balancing equations 8
bias 5
bioaccumulation 76
biodiversity 77
biofuels 70-71
biogas 70
biomass 70
blood 16, 22
bones 10
breathing 18
bronchi 17
bronchioles 17
budding 65

C
capacitors 113
cardiac cycle 13
carnivores 74
catalysts 40, 78, 84-85
centripetal force 46
chlorofluorocarbons 90
cholesterol 15
circuit symbols 98
circulatory systems 12
clone 80
closed systems 41
clots 16
collisions 51-52
comets 46
compounds 6, 9, 32
concentration 33-34, 36, 42
conservation of mass 30-31
conservation of momentum 52
Contact process 40-41
contractile vacuoles 77
convex lenses 61
covalence 6
critical angle 59
current 98

D
data 4-5
decomposers 74
deoxygenated blood 12-13
detergents 94-95
detritivores 74
diabetes 79
dialysis 22, 25
diffraction 54-55
diffusion 12, 17, 20
digestion 20
digestive system 20
dilution 33
diodes 112
direct current (DC) 107
disease 19, 27, 66-67
dispersion 60
displacement 49
displacement reactions 87
displayed formulae 7
distillation 69
DNA 64, 81
dynamo effect 108

E
earthworms 74
echocardiograms 14
egestion 21
electrocardiograms 14
electrolysis 42, 84-85
electrolytes 84
electromagnetic waves 56-57
elements 6, 32
empirical formula 32
emulsification 20
enzymes 20, 20, 78-81, 94
equilibrium 39, 41
esters 93
ethics 25
eutrophication 76
evaluation 5
excretion 21
expiration 18

A
fats 93
fermentation 68-69, 88-89
fermenters 64, 68, 81
fertilisation 24
fertiliser 70, 76
fertility 23-24
flagellum 64
Fleming's left-hand rule 106
focal length 61
focal point 61
foetal screening 24
follicle-stimulating hormone (FSH) 23
food webs 74-75
forces 49, 51, 106
formulae 7, 9
fractional distillation 88
fractures (bone) 10
frequencies 54
fuel cells 86
full-wave rectification 113
fungus 65

G
gas exchange 17-18
gas volumes 37
generators 108
genes 27
genetic engineering 80
graphs of reactions 38
gravitational force 46
gravity 46, 50
growth 26-27
guideline daily amounts (GDA) 34

H
haemoglobin 16
half-wave rectification 112
halides 43
hard water 91-92
heart beat 14
heart disease 15
herbivores 74
hormones 27
humus 72-73
hydration 89
hydrogen 86
hydrophilic 95
hydrophobic 95
hypotheses 4

I
immunosuppressive drugs 25
In vitro fertilisation 24
indicators 35, 77
induction 109
infertility 24
inspiration 18
insulin 79, 81
interference 56
ion-exchange column 92
ionic 6
ionosphere 54
ions 42-43, 84, 87, 90

J
joints 11

K
kidneys 21-22

L
lactose 79
life expectancy 27
ligaments 1
light 56-61
light dependent resistors (LDR) 101, 104
light emitting diodes (LED) 104
limescale 91
limiting reactant 37
logic gates 102-105
lungs 17-18
luteinising hormone (LH) 23

M
magnetic field 106-109
magnification 61
marine snow 75
mass 32, 37

Index

mechanical replacements 25
menstrual cycle 23
microorganisms 66
microwaves 43
models 4
molar mass 30
moles 30
momentum 51
motors 107

N
National grid 111
natural disasters 66
nephrons 22
neutralisation 35
neutrons 6
nuclei 6

O
Ohm's law 98
oils 93
optical fibres 60
optics 61
orbits 46-47
organ donation 25
ossification 10
ovaries 24
oxidation 87
oxygenated blood 12-13
ozone 90

P
pacemakers 14
parabolic trajectory 50
pasteurisation 69
pathogens 66, 68
peer review 5
penicillin 67
percentage composition 32
pH curves 36
photosynthesis 72, 75
plankton 75-76
polarisation 57
pollution 76
potential difference 100
potential dividers 100-101
precipitates 43
pressure 52-53
producers 74-75
products 7
projectile motion 50
protons 6
pulse rate 14

R
radial fields 107
radicals 90
radio waves 54
reactants 7
reacting ratios 31
reactions 51
real images 61
redox reactions 87
reduction 87

reflectors 60
refraction 56, 58
refractive index 58-59
relative formula mass 30
relative speed 48
relays 104
residual air 18
resistance 98-100, 104
respiratory systems 19-21
reversible reactions 39
rockets 52-53
rusting 87

S
saponification 93
satellites 46-47, 54-55
scalar quantities 48
sexual reproduction 23
skeletons 10
smoothing 113
soil 72-74
solubility 94
solutions 74
solvents 94
speed 48
strong acids 42
sulfuric acid 40
surrogacy 24
sweeteners 78
synovial joints 11

T
thermistors 101, 104
tidal air 18
titration 35
total internal reflection 59-60
toxins 66, 76
trachea 17
trajectories 50
transformers 110-111
transgenic organism 80
transistors 102
transpiration 72
transplants 15
transverse waves 57
truth tables 105

U
ultrafiltration 22
ultrasound 24

V
variables 4
vector quantities 48
vectors 49-50
veins 16
velocity 49
ventilation 18
virtual images 61
viruses 65
vital capacity 18
voltage 98-99, 109
voltage-current graphs 99
volume 33, 37-38

W
washing powder 78
waste products 21
water 75-77, 91-92
wavelength 54-55
waves 54-60
weak acids 42

Y
yeast 65
yoghurt 68